Five Comedies of Aristophanes

Aristophanes, the greatest of the Greek comic poets, and the only one whose plays have survived in complete versions, was born about 445 B.C. and died in 385 B.C. His life thus coincided with the flourishing years of Periclean Athens and the whole course of the Peloponnesian War, which brought defeat to Athens at the hands of Sparta in 404 B.C. His comedies, for all their exuberant farce and creative fantasy, are always seriously concerned with the major political and moral issues of those critical years.

Eleven of Aristophanes' forty comedies survive. His three earliest comedies were exhibited in the name of Callistratus; they are *The Banqueters* (427 B.C.), *The Babylonians* (426 B.C.), and *The Acharnians* (425 B.C.), of which only *The Acharnians* is extant. The remaining ten extant comedies are *The Knights* (424 B.C.), *The Clouds* (423 B.C.), *The Wasps* (422 B.C.), *The Peace* (421 B.C.), *The Birds* (414 B.C.), *Lysistrata* (411 B.C.), *The Thesmophoriazusae* (410 B.C.), *The Frogs* (405 B.C.), *The Ecclesiazusae* (392 B.C.), and *The Plutus* (388 B.C.).

The following are some basic studies of Aristophanes and Greek comedy:

F. M. Cornford: *The Origin of Attic Comedy.*

Maurice Croiset: *Aristophanes and the Political Parties at Athens.*

Werner Jaeger: "The Comic Poetry of Aristophanes" in *Paideia,* Volume 1.

Gilbert Murray: *Aristophanes, A Study.*

Gilbert Norwood: *Greek Comedy.*

Benjamin Bickley Rogers (1828–1919) published his translations of Aristophanes from 1902 to 1916.

Five Comedies of

ARISTOPHANES

Translated by Benjamin Bickley Rogers
Complete and Unabridged

With Rogers' Introductions and Notes
Edited by Andrew Chiappe

Doubleday Anchor Books

DOUBLEDAY & COMPANY, INC., GARDEN CITY, NEW YORK

Cover by Antonio Frasconi

Typography by Edward Gorey

LIBRARY OF CONGRESS CATALOG CARD NUMBER 55-9756

Editor's Note

B. B. Rogers' notes have been selected, edited, and abridged for this edition. Rogers' own words have been kept in nearly every case, though in a few cases his notes have been paraphrased. A few additional brief notes have been supplied by the editor.

A. J. C.

THE BIRDS

The Birds was exhibited at the Great Dionysia in the year 414 B.C. It was placed second of the three competitors; the prize was awarded to the *Revellers* of Ameipsias, a drama otherwise unknown.

At this time the Sicilian expedition was in the full tide of success and was apparently on the point of obtaining a triumphant issue. Athens was full of the wildest speculations and the most far-reaching ambitions. These feelings are mirrored in the present comedy. Two elderly Athenians leave the city and go to sojourn with the Birds, whom they persuade to claim the sovereignty of the world and to build up an enormous wall in the Mid-air, so that no sacrifices offered by men can henceforth reach the sky; and the Gods are presently starved into submission.

Thus did Aristophanes caricature the high schemes and ambitions which were then in the air; not as *encouraging* them, for his caricature is fantastic and ludicrous in the extreme; yet not as *discouraging* them, since even his fantastic adventure is crowned with a brilliant success.

Characters of the Drama

PEISTHETAERUS

EUELPIDES

THE PLOVER-PAGE or DUNLIN

THE HOOPOE

CHORUS OF BIRDS

PRIEST

POET

ORACLE-MONGER

METON

COMMISSIONER

STATUTE-SELLER

MESSENGER

GUARD

IRIS

HERALD

SIRE-STRIKER

CINESIAS

SYCOPHANT

PROMETHEUS

POSEIDON

HERACLES

TRIBALLIAN

SERVANT

THE BIRDS

*A desolate scene. In the background we see a solitary tree,
and a sheer rock rising like a wall. In front are two tired
old Athenians, each carrying a bird in his hand. The one
with a crow is* PEISTHETAERUS; *the other with a jackdaw,*
EUELPIDES. *The birds have guided them from Athens, but
now seem lost, pointing different ways, and sometimes
gaping up into the air. In truth, they have reached their
goal, but their masters do not know that; and the dialogue
is commenced by* EUELPIDES, *apostrophizing his jackdaw.*

EUELPIDES. Straight on do you bid me go, where the tree
    stands?

PEISTHETAERUS. O hang it all! mine's croaking back again.

EUELPIDES. Why are we wandering up and down, you rogue?
    This endless spin will make an end of *us.*

PEISTHETAERUS. To think that I, poor fool, at a crow's bidding,
    Should trudge about, an hundred miles and more!

EUELPIDES. To think that I, poor wretch, at a daw's bidding,
    Should wear the very nails from off my feet!

PEISTHETAERUS. Why, where we are, I've not the least idea.

EUELPIDES. Could you from hence find out your fatherland?

PEISTHETAERUS. No, that would pose even—Execestides![1]

EUELPIDES. O, here's a nuisance!

PEISTHETAERUS.   Go *you* there, then, friend.

EUELPIDES. I call Philocrates a regular cheat,
    The fool that sells the bird-trays in the market.
    He swore these two would lead us straight to Tereus,
    The hoopoe, made a bird in that same market.[2]
    So then this daw, this son of Tharreleides,[3]
    We bought for an obol, and that crow for three.

But what knew they? Nothing, but how to—bite!
Where are you gaping now? Do you want to lead us
Against the rocks? There's no road here, I tell you.

PEISTHETAERUS. No, nor yet here; not even the tiniest path.

EUELPIDES. Well, but what says your crow about the road?

PEISTHETAERUS. By Zeus, she croaks quite differently now.

EUELPIDES (*shouting*). *What does she say about the road?*

PEISTHETAERUS.   She says
She'll gnaw my fingers off: that's all she says.

EUELPIDES. Now isn't it a shame that when we are here
Ready and willing as two men can be
To go to the ravens, we can't find the way.[4]
For we are sick, spectators, with a sickness
Just the reverse of that which Sacas has.[5]
He, no true townsman, would perforce press in;
Whilst we, with rights of tribe and race unchallenged,
Townsmen mid townsmen, no man scaring us,
Spread both our—feet, and flew away from home.
Not that we hate our city, as not being
A prosperous mighty city, free for all
To spend their wealth in, paying fines and fees.
Aye, the cicalas chirp upon the boughs
One month, or two; but our Athenians chirp
Over their lawsuits all their whole life long,
That's why we are journeying on this journey now,
Trudging along with basket, pot, and myrtles,
To find some quiet easy-going spot,
Where we may settle down, and dwell in peace.
Tereus, the hoopoe, is our journey's aim,
To learn if he, in any place he has flown to,
Has seen the sort of city that we want.

PEISTHETAERUS. You there!

EUELPIDES.   What now?

PEISTHETAERUS.   My crow keeps croaking upwards
Ever so long.

EUELPIDES.   And here's my jackdaw gaping
Up in the air, as if to show me something.

There must be birds about, I am sure of that.
Let's make a noise and we shall soon find out.

PEISTHETAERUS. Then harkye; bang your leg against the rock.

EUELPIDES. And you, your head; and there'll be twice the
noise.

PEISTHETAERUS. Well, take a stone and knock.

EUELPIDES.   Yes, I'll do that.
Boy! Boy!

PEISTHETAERUS. Eh! What! do you call the hoopoe "Boy"?
You should call "Whoop-ho there," not "Boy" of course.

EUELPIDES. O, Whoop-ho there! What, must I knock again?
Whoop-ho!

(*A door suddenly opens in the rock, and an actor emerges,
wearing a head-dress or mask representing the head of a*
DUNLIN *or* PLOVER-PAGE *with a long and wide-gaping
beak.*)

PLOVER-PAGE.   Whoever are these? Who calls my master?

EUELPIDES. Apollo shield us, what a terrible gape!

PLOVER-PAGE. These be two bird-catchers. O dear, O dear!

EUELPIDES (*aside*). As nasty-speaking, as unpleasant-looking!

PLOVER-PAGE. Ye shall both die!

EUELPIDES.   O, we're not men.

PLOVER-PAGE.   What then?

EUELPIDES. Well, I'm the Panic-struck, a Libyan bird.

PLOVER-PAGE. Nonsense!

EUELPIDES.   No nonsense: look for yourself and see.

PLOVER-PAGE. And *he*—what bird is he? come, won't you
answer?

PEISTHETAERUS. I? I'm a pheasant, and a yellow-tailed one.

EUELPIDES. But O, by all the Gods, whatever are you?

PLOVER-PAGE. A serving-bird.

EUELPIDES.   What, vanquished by some gamecock
In fight?

PLOVER-PAGE. No, but my master, when he first
Became a hoopoe, prayed that I might turn
Into a bird, to be his servant still.

EUELPIDES. What, does a bird require a serving-bird?

PLOVER-PAGE. *He* does, as having been a man, I fancy.
So when he wants to taste Phaleric sardines,
I run for the sardines, catching up a dish.
Does he want soup? then where's the pot and ladle?
I run for the ladle.

EUELPIDES.   A regular running-page.
Now harkye, Plover-page, run in and call
Your master out.

PLOVER-PAGE.   Great Zeus! he has just been eating
Myrtles and midges, and is gone to roost.

EUELPIDES. But still, do wake him.

PLOVER-PAGE.   Well I know he won't
Like to be waked, still for your sake I'll do it.   (*Exit*)

PEISTHETAERUS. Confound the bird! he frightened me to death.

EUELPIDES. O dear! O dear! my heart went pit-a-pat,
My daw's gone too.

PEISTHETAERUS (*severely*). Gone! O you coward you,
You *let* him go!

EUELPIDES.   Well, didn't you fall down,
And let your crow go?

PEISTHETAERUS.   No, I didn't. No!

EUELPIDES. Where is she then?

PEISTHETAERUS.   She flew away herself.

EUELPIDES. You didn't let her go. You're a brave boy!

HOOPOE (*within*). Throw wide the wood, that I may issue
forth!

(*A turn of the eccyclema brings out the* HOOPOE, *together
with a portion of his dwelling, viz., a little copse.*)

EUELPIDES. O Heracles, why what in the world is this?
What feathering's here? What style of triple-cresting?

HOOPOE. Who be the folk that seek me?

EUELPIDES.   The Twelve Gods
   Would seem to have wrought your ruin.

HOOPOE.   What, do you jeer me,
   Seeing the way I'm feathered? Strangers, I
   Was once a man.

EUELPIDES.   It's not at you we're laughing.

HOOPOE. What is it then?

EUELPIDES.   Your beak looks rather funny.

HOOPOE. This is the way that Sophocles disfigures
   The manly form of Tereus in his Play.

EUELPIDES. What, are you Tereus? Are you bird or peacock?

HOOPOE. I am a bird.

EUELPIDES.   Then, where are all your feathers?

HOOPOE. They've fallen off!

EUELPIDES.   What! from disease, or why?

HOOPOE. No, but in winter-time all birds are wont
   To moult their feathers, and then fresh ones grow.
   But tell me what *ye* are.

EUELPIDES.   We? mortal men.

HOOPOE. And of what race?

EUELPIDES.   Whence the brave galleys come.

HOOPOE. Not dicasts, are ye?

EUELPIDES.   No, the other sort.
   We're anti-dicasts.

HOOPOE.   Grows that seedling there?

EUELPIDES. Aye in the country you can find a few,
   If you search closely.

HOOPOE.   But what brings you hither?

EUELPIDES. To talk with you a little.

HOOPOE.   What about?

EUELPIDES. You were a man at first, as we are now,
   And had your creditors, as we have now,
   And loved to shirk your debts, as we do now;
   And then you changed your nature, and became
   A bird, and flew round land and sea, and know
   All that men feel, and all that birds feel too.

That's why we are come as suppliants here, to ask
If you can tell us of some city, soft
As a thick rug, to lay us down within.

HOOPOE. Seek ye a mightier than the Cranaan town?

EUELPIDES. A mightier, no; a more commodious, yes.

HOOPOE. Aristocratic?

EUELPIDES.　　　　　Anything but that!
I loathe the very name of Scellias' son.[6]

HOOPOE. What sort of city would ye like?

EUELPIDES.　　　　　　　　Why, one
Where my worst trouble would be such as this;
A friend at daybreak coming to my door
And calling out *O by Olympian Zeus,*
Take your bath early: then come round to me,
You and your children, to the wedding banquet
I'm going to give. Now pray don't disappoint me,
Else, keep your distance, when my money's—gone.

HOOPOE. Upon my word, you are quite in love with troubles!
And *you?*

PEISTHETAERUS. I love the like.

HOOPOE.　　　　　　　But tell me what.

PEISTHETAERUS. To have the father of some handsome lad
Come up and chide me with complaints like these,
Fine things I hear of you, Stilbonides,
You met my son returning from the baths,
And never kissed, or hugged, or fondled him,
You, his paternal friend! You're a nice fellow.

HOOPOE. Poor Poppet, you are in love with ills indeed.
Well, there's the sort of city that ye want
By the Red Sea.

EUELPIDES.　　　　Not by the sea! Not where
The Salaminian, with a process-server[7]
On board, may heave in sight some early morn.
But can't you mention some Hellenic town?

HOOPOE. Why don't ye go and settle down in Elis,
At Lepreus?

EUELPIDES.   Leprous! I was never there,
But for Melanthius' sake I loathe the name.[8]

HOOPOE. Well then, the Opuntians up in Locris, there's
The place to dwell in!

EUELPIDES.   I become Opuntius!
No thank you, no, not for a talent of gold.
But this, this bird-life here, you know it well,
What is this like?

HOOPOE.   A pleasant life enough.
Foremost and first you don't require a purse.

EUELPIDES. There goes a grand corrupter of our life!

HOOPOE. Then in the gardens we enjoy the myrtles,
The cress, the poppy, the white sesame.

EUELPIDES. Why, then, ye live a bridegroom's jolly life.

PEISTHETAERUS. Oh! Oh!
O the grand scheme I see in the birds' reach,
And power to grasp it, if ye'd trust to me!

HOOPOE. Trust you in what?

PEISTHETAERUS.   What? First don't fly about
In all directions, with your mouths wide open.
That makes you quite despised. With *us*, for instance,
If you should ask the flighty people there,
Who is that fellow? Teleas would reply,
*The man's a bird, a flighty feckless bird,
Inconsequential, always on the move.*

HOOPOE. Well blamed, i' faith; but what we ought to do,
Tell us.

PEISTHETAERUS. Live all together: found one State.

HOOPOE. What sort of State are birds to found, I wonder.

PEISTHETAERUS. Aye, say you so? You who have made the most
Idiotic speech, look down.

HOOPOE.   I do.

PEISTHETAERUS.   Look up.

HOOPOE. I do.

PEISTHETAERUS. Twirl round your head.

HOOPOE.   Zeus! I shall be
  A marvellous gainer, if I twist my neck!

PEISTHETAERUS. What did you see?

HOOPOE.   I saw the clouds and sky.

PEISTHETAERUS. And is not that the Station of the Birds?

HOOPOE. Station?

PEISTHETAERUS.   As one should say, their habitation.
  Here while the heavens revolve, and yon great dome
  Is moving round, ye keep your Station still.
  Make this your city, fence it round with walls,
  And from your Station is evolved your State.
  So ye'll be lords of men, as now of locusts,
  And Melian famine shall destroy the Gods.

HOOPOE. Eh! how?

PEISTHETAERUS.   The Air's betwixt the Earth and Sky.
  And just as we, if we would go to Pytho,
  Must crave a grant of passage from Boeotia,
  Even so, when men slay victims to the Gods,
  Unless the Gods pay tribute, ye in turn
  Will grant no passage for the savoury steam
  To rise through Chaos, and a realm not theirs.

HOOPOE. Hurrah!
  O Earth! ods traps, and nets, and gins, and snares,
  This is the nattiest scheme that e'er I heard of!
  So with your aid I'm quite resolved to found
  The city, if the other birds concur.

PEISTHETAERUS. And who shall tell them of our plan?

HOOPOE.   Yourself.
  O they're not mere barbarians, as they were
  Before I came. I've taught them language now.

PEISTHETAERUS. But how to call them hither?

HOOPOE.   That's soon done.
  I've but to step within the coppice here,
  And wake my sleeping nightingale, and then
  We'll call them, both together. Bless the birds,
  When once they hear our voices, they'll come running.

PEISTHETAERUS. You darling bird, now don't delay one instant.
O I beseech you get at once within
Your little copse, and wake the nightingale!

The HOOPOE'S *Serenade*

HOOPOE. Awake, my mate!
Shake off thy slumbers, and clear and strong
Let loose the floods of thy glorious song,
The sacred dirge of thy mouth divine
For sore-wept Itys, thy child and mine;
Thy tender trillings his name prolong
With the liquid note of thy tawny throat;
Through the leafy curls of the woodbine sweet
The pure sound mounts to the heavenly seat,
And Phoebus, lord of the golden hair,
As he lists to thy wild plaint echoing there,
Draws answering strains from his ivoried lyre,
Till he stirs the dance of the heavenly choir,
And calls from the blessed lips on high
Of immortal Gods, a divine reply
To the tones of thy witching melody.

(*The sound of a flute is heard within, imitating the nightingale's song.*)

EUELPIDES. O Zeus and King, the little birdie's voice!
O how its sweetness honied all the copse!

PEISTHETAERUS. Hi!

EUELPIDES.   Well?

PEISTHETAERUS.   Keep quiet.

EUELPIDES.   Why?

PEISTHETAERUS.   The Hoopoe here
Is going to favour us with another song.

The Bird-call by the HOOPOE *and Nightingale conjointly; the Nightingale's song being imitated, as before, by the flute.*

HOOPOE. Whoop-ho! Whoop-ho! Whoop-hoop-hoop-hoop-hoop-ho!
Hoi! Hoi! Hoi! Come, come, come, come, come!

The land-birds

Come hither any bird with plumage like my own;
Come hither ye that batten on the acres newly sown,
   On the acres by the farmer neatly sown;
And the myriad tribes that feed on the barley and the seed,
The tribes that lightly fly, giving out a gentle cry;
And ye who round the clod, in the furrow-riven sod,
With voices sweet and low, twitter flitter to and fro,
   Singing, *tío, tio, tío, tiotinx;*
And ye who in the gardens a pleasant harvest glean,
Lurking in the branches of the ivy ever green;
And ye who top the mountains with gay and airy flight;
And ye who in the olive and the arbutus delight;
Come hither one and all, come flying to our call,
   Triotó, triotó, totobrinx.

The marsh-birds

Ye that snap up the gnats, shrilly voiced,
   Mid the deep water-glens of the fens,
Or on Marathon's expanse haunt the lea, fair to see,
   Or career o'er the swamps, dewy-moist.
And the bird with the gay mottled plumes, come away,
   Francolín! Francolín! come away!

The sea-birds

Ye with the halcyons flitting delightedly
Over the surge of the infinite Sea,
Come to the great Revolution awaiting us,
Hither, come hither, come hither to me.
Hither, to listen to wonderful words,
Hither we summon the taper-necked birds.

For hither has come a shrewd old file,
Such a deep old file, such a sharp old file,
His thoughts are new, new deeds he'll do,
Come here, and confer with this shrewd old file.
Come hither! Come hither! Come hither!
Toro-toro-toro-torotinx!
Kikkabau, Kikkabau!
Toro-toro-toro-toro-lililinx!

PEISTHETAERUS. See any bird?

EUELPIDES. By Apollo no, not I,
Though up I gaze with mouth and eyes wide open.

PEISTHETAERUS. Methinks the Hoopoe played the lapwing's trick,[9]
Went in the copse, and whooped, and whooped for nothing.

HOOPOE. Torotinx! Torotinx.

(*Four birds enter singly, pass before the audience, and disappear.*)

PEISTHETAERUS. Comrade here's a bird approaching, coming to receive our visit.

EUELPIDES. Aye by Zeus, what bird do you call it? Surely not a peacock, is it?

PEISTHETAERUS. That the Hoopoe here will teach us. Prithee, friend, what bird is he?

HOOPOE. That is not a common object, such as you can always see;
That's a marsh-bird.

EUELPIDES. Lovely creature! nice and red like flaming flame.

HOOPOE. So he should be, for Flamingo is the lovely creature's name.

EUELPIDES. Hi there!

PEISTHETAERUS. What? The row you're making!

EUELPIDES. Here's another, full in view.

PEISTHETAERUS. Aye by Zeus, another truly, with a foreign aspect too.
Who is he, the summit-ascending, Muse-prophetical, wondrous bird?

HOOPOE. He's a Median.

PEISTHETAERUS. He a Median! Heracles, the thing's absurd.
How on earth without a camel could a Median hither fly?

EUELPIDES. Here they're coming; here's another, with his crest erected high.

PEISTHETAERUS. Goodness gracious, that's a hoopoe; yes, by
  Zeus, another one!
  Are not *you* the only Hoopoe?

HOOPOE.   I'm his grandsire; he's the son[10]
  Of the Philocléan hoopoe: as with you a name will pass,
  Callias siring Hipponicus, Hipponicus Callias.[11]

PEISTHETAERUS. O then that is Callias is it? How his feathers
  moult away!

HOOPOE. Aye, the simple generous creature, he's to parasites
  a prey.
  And the females flock around him, plucking out his
  feathers too.

PEISTHETAERUS. O Poseidon, here's another; here's a bird of
  brilliant hue!
  What's the name of this, I wonder.

HOOPOE.   That's a Glutton styled by us.[12]

PEISTHETAERUS. Is there then another Glutton than our own
  Cleonymus?

EUELPIDES. Our Cleonymus, I fancy, would have thrown his
  crest away.

PEISTHETAERUS. But what means the crest-equipment of so
  many birds, I pray?
  Are they going to race in armour?

HOOPOE.   No, my worthy friend, they
  Make their dwellings, like the Carians, on the crests for
  safety's sake.

(*The twenty-four members of the* CHORUS *enter the orchestra.*)

PEISTHETAERUS. O Poseidon, what the mischief! see the birds
  are everywhere
  Fluttering onward.

EUELPIDES.   King Apollo, what a cloud! O! O! look there,
  Now we cannot see the entrance for the numbers crowd-
  ing in.

PEISTHETAERUS. Here you see a partridge coming, there by
  Zeus a francolin,

Here a widgeon onward hurries, there's a halcyon, sure as
fate.

EUELPIDES. Who's behind her?

PEISTHETAERUS. That's a clipper; he's the lady halcyon's mate.

EUELPIDES. Can a clipper be a bird then?

PEISTHETAERUS.   Sporgilus is surely so.[13]
Here's an owl.

EUELPIDES. And who to Athens brought an owl, I'd like to
know.

PEISTHETAERUS. Jay and turtle, lark and sedgebird, thyme-
finch, ring-dove first, and then
Rock-dove, stock-dove, cuckoo, falcon, fiery-crest, and
willow wren,
Lammergeyer, porphyrion, kestrel, waxwing, nuthatch,
water-hen.

EUELPIDES (singing). Ohó for the birds, Ohó! Ohó!
Ohó for the blackbirds, ho!
How they twitter, how they go, shrieking and screaming
to and fro.
Goodness! are they going to charge us? They are gazing
here, and see
All their beaks they open widely.

PEISTHETAERUS.   That is what occurs to me.

CHORUS. Wh-wh-wh-wh-wh-wh-wh-wh-where may he be that
was calling for me? In what locality pastureth he?

HOOPOE. I am ready, waiting here; never from my friends I
stir.

CHORUS. Te-te-te-te-te-te-te-te-teach me, I pray, in an amicable
way, what is the news you have gotten to say.

HOOPOE. News amazing! News auspicious! News delightful,
safe, and free!
Birds! Two men of subtlest genius hither have arrived to
me.

CHORUS. Who! What! When! say that again.

HOOPOE. Here, I say, have come two elders, travelling to the
birds from man,

And the stem they are bringing with them of a most
  stupendous plan.

CHORUS. You who have made the greatest error since my cal-
  low life began,
What you do say?

HOOPOE.   Now don't be nervous.

CHORUS.   What is the thing you have done to me?

HOOPOE. I've received two men, enamoured of your sweet
  society.

CHORUS. You have really dared to do it?

HOOPOE.   Gladly I the deed avow.

CHORUS. And the pair are now amongst us?

HOOPOE.   Aye, if I'm amongst you now.

CHORUS. O! O! Out upon you!
We are cheated and betrayed, we have suffered shame
  and wrong!
For our comrade and our friend who has fed with us so
  long,
He has broken every oath, and his holy plighted troth,
  And the old social customs of our clan.
He has led us unawares into wiles, and into snares,
He has given us a prey, all helpless and forlorn,
To those who were our foes from the time that they
  were born,
  To vile and abominable Man!

But for him, our bird-companion, comes a reckoning by
  and by;
As for these two old deceivers, they shall suffer instantly,
Bit by bit we'll tear and rend them.

PEISTHETAERUS.   Here's a very horrid mess.

EUELPIDES. Wretched man, 'twas you that caused it, you and
  all your cleverness!
Why you brought me I can't see.

PEISTHETAERUS.   Just that you might follow me.

EUELPIDES. Just that I might die of weeping.

PEISTHETAERUS. What a foolish thing to say!
Weeping will be quite beyond you, when your eyes are
    pecked away.

CHORUS. On! On! In upon them!
    Make a very bloody onset, spread your wings about
        your foes,
    Assail them and attack them, and surround them and
        enclose.
    Both, both of them shall die, and their bodies shall
        supply
    A rare dainty pasture for my beak.
    For never shall be found any distant spot of ground,
    Or shadowy mountain covert, or foamy Ocean wave,
    Or cloud in Ether floating, which these reprobates shall
        save
    From the doom that upon them I will wreak.

    On then, on, my flying squadrons, now is the time to tear
        and bite,
    Tarry ye not an instant longer. Brigadier, advance our
        right.

EUELPIDES. Here it comes! I'm off, confound them.

PEISTHETAERUS. Fool, why can't you remain with me?

EUELPIDES. What! that these may tear and rend me?

PEISTHETAERUS. How can you hope from birds to flee?

EUELPIDES. Truly, I haven't the least idea.

PEISTHETAERUS. Then it is I the affair must guide.
    Seize we a pot and, the charge awaiting, here we will
        combat side by side.

EUELPIDES. Pot! and how can a pot avail us?

PEISTHETAERUS. Never an owl will then come near.

EUELPIDES. What of these birds of prey with talons?

PEISTHETAERUS. Snatch up a spit, like a hoplite's spear,
    Planting it firmly there before you.

EUELPIDES. What shall I do about my eyes?

PEISTHETAERUS. Take a platter, or take a saucer, holding it
    over them buckler-wise.

EUELPIDES. What a skilful neat contrivance! O you clever fellow you,

In your military science Nicias you far outdo!

CHORUS. Eleleleu! advance! no loitering; level your beaks and
charge away.[14]

Shatter the pot at once to pieces; worry, and scratch, and
tear, and flay!

HOOPOE. O, whatever is your purpose? is your villainy so great,

You would slay two worthy persons, kinsmen, clansmen,
of my mate?[15]

Men who never sought to harm you, would you tear and
lacerate?

CHORUS. Why, I wonder, should we spare them, more than
ravening beasts of prey?

Shall we ever find, for vengeance, enemies more rank than
they?

HOOPOE. Enemies, I grant, by nature, very friends in heart and
will;

Here they come with kindly purpose, useful lessons to
instil.

CHORUS. What, they come with words of friendship? What,
you really then suppose

They will teach us useful lessons, they our fathers' fathers'
foes?

HOOPOE. Yet to clever folk a foeman very useful hints may
show;

Thus, that foresight brings us safety, from a friend we
ne'er should know,

But the truth is forced upon us, very quickly, by a foe.

Hence it is that all the Cities, taught by foe, and not by
friend,

Learn to build them ships of battle, and their lofty walls
extend;

So by this, a foeman's, teaching children, home, and wealth
defend.

CHORUS. Well, I really think 'tis better that their errand we
should know;

I admit that something useful may be taught us by a foe.

PEISTHETAERUS (*to* EUELPIDES). Now their anger grows more
    slack; now we had better just draw back.

HOOPOE (*to* CHORUS). This is right and friendly conduct, such
    as I deserve from you.

CHORUS. Well, I am sure that we have never gone against you
    hitherto.

PEISTHETAERUS. Now they are growing a deal more peaceful,
    now is the time the pot to ground,
    Now we may lower the platters twain.
    Nay, but the spit we had best retain,
    Walking within the encampment's bound,
    Letting our watchful glances skim
    Over the edge of the pot's top rim;
    Never a thought of flight must strike us.

EUELPIDES. Well, but tell me, suppose we die,
    Where in the world will our bodies lie?

PEISTHETAERUS. They shall be buried in Cerameicus,[16]
    That will be done at the public cost,
    For we will say that our lives we lost
    Gallantly fighting the public foe,
    (Yea, we will tell the commanders so.)
    Gallantly fighting at Orneae.[17]

CHORUS. Fall back, fall back to your ranks once more,
    And stand at ease as ye stood before,
    And lay your wrath on the ground, in line
    With your angry mood, as a warrior should;
    We'll ask the while who the men may be,
    And whence they come, and with what design.
    Hey, Hoopoe, hey! to you I speak.

HOOPOE. What is it that to learn you seek?

CHORUS. Whence are these visitors and who?

HOOPOE. From clever Hellas strangers two.

CHORUS. What 's their aim?   Canst thou tell
    Why they came   Here to dwell?

HOOPOE. Love of you,   Love of your
    Life and ways   Was the lure.
    Here they fain   Would remain
    Comrades true   All their days.

CHORUS. Hey, hey, what do you say?
    What is the tale they tell?

HOOPOE.   In brief,
    'Tis something more than past belief.

CHORUS. But wherefore is he come? What is it
    He seeks to compass by his visit?
    Think you he's got some cunning plan
    Whereby, allied with us, he can
    Assist a friend, or harm a foe?
    What brings him here, I'd like to know.

HOOPOE. Too great, too great, for thought or words,
    The bliss he promises the birds.
    All things are yours, he says, whate'er
    Exists in space, both here and there,
    And to and fro, and everywhere.

CHORUS. Mad a little, eh?

HOOPOE. More sane than words can say.

CHORUS. Wide awake?

HOOPOE.   Wide as day.
        The subtlest cunningest fox,
  All scheme, invention, craft; wit, wisdom, paradox.

CHORUS. His speech, his speech, bid him begin it.
    The things you show excite me so,
      I'm fit to fly this very minute.

HOOPOE. Now you and you, take back this panoply,[18]
    And hang it up, God bless it, out of sight
    Within the kitchen there, beside the Jack.
    But you (*to* PEISTHETAERUS) the things we summoned
        them to hear
    Expound, declare.

PEISTHETAERUS.   By Apollo no, not I,
    Unless they pledge me such a treaty-pledge
    As that small jackanapes who makes the swords
    Pledged with his wife, to wit that they'll not bite me
    Nor pull me about, nor scratch my—

CHORUS.   Fie, for shame!
    Not *this?* no, no!

PEISTHETAERUS.   *My eyes*, I was going to say.

CHORUS. I pledge it.

PEISTHETAERUS. Swear!

CHORUS.   I swear on these conditions;
    So may I win by every judge's vote,
    And the whole Theatre's.

PEISTHETAERUS.   *And so you shall.*

CHORUS. But if I'm false, then by one vote alone.

HOOPOE. O yes! O yes! Hoplites, take up your arms
    And march back homewards; there await the orders
    We're going to publish on the notice-boards.

CHORUS. Full of wiles, full of guiles, at all times, in all ways,
    Are the children of Men; still we'll hear what he says.
        Thou hast haply detected
    Something good for the Birds which we never suspected;
        Some power of achievement, too high
    For my own shallow wit by itself to descry.
        But if aught you espy,
    Tell it out; for whate'er of advantage shall fall
    To ourselves by your aid, shall be common to all.

    So expound us the plan you have brought us, my man, not
        doubting, it seems, of success
    And don't be afraid, for the treaty we made we won't be
        the first to transgress.

PEISTHETAERUS. I am hot to begin, and my spirit within is fer-
        menting the tale to declare.
    And my dough I will knead, for there's nought to impede.
        Boy, bring me a wreath for my hair,
    And a wash for my hands.

EUELPIDES.   Why, what mean these com-
        mands? Is a dinner in near contemplation?

PEISTHETAERUS. No dinner, I ween; 'tis a *speech* that I mean,
        a stalwart and brawny oration,
    Their spirit to batter, and shiver and shatter.
                                    (*To the Birds.*)
        So sorely I grieve for your lot
    Who once in the prime and beginning of time were
        Sovereigns—

CHORUS.   We Sovereigns! of what?

PEISTHETAERUS. Of all that you see; of him and of me; of
         Zeus up above on his throne;
     A lineage older and nobler by far than the Titans and
         Cronos ye own,
And than Earth.

CHORUS.   And than Earth!

PEISTHETAERUS.   By Apollo 'tis true.

CHORUS.   And I never had heard it before!

PEISTHETAERUS. Because you've a blind uninquisitive mind,
         unaccustomed on Aesop to pore.
The lark had her birth, so he says, before Earth; then her
         father fell sick and he died.
She laid out his body with dutiful care, but a grave she
         could nowhere provide;
For the Earth was not yet in existence; at last, by urgent
         necessity led,
When the fifth day arrived, the poor creature contrived to
         bury her sire in her head.

EUELPIDES. So the sire of the lark, give me leave to remark, on
         the crest of an headland lies dead.

PEISTHETAERUS. If therefore, by birth, ye are older than Earth,
         if before all the Gods ye existed,
By the right of the firstborn the sceptre is yours; your
         claim cannot well be resisted.

EUELPIDES. I advise you to nourish and strengthen your beak,
         and to keep it in trim for a stroke.
Zeus won't in a hurry the sceptre restore to the wood-
         pecker tapping the oak.

PEISTHETAERUS. In times prehistoric 'tis easily proved, by evi-
         dence weighty and ample,
That Birds, and not Gods, were the Rulers of men, and
         the Lords of the world; for example,
Time was that the Persians were ruled by the Cock, a
         King autocratic, alone;
The sceptre he wielded or ever the names "Megabazus,"
         "Darius" were known;

And the "Persian" he still by the people is called from the
Empire that once was his own.

EUELPIDES. And thus, to this hour, the symbol of power on his
head you can always detect:

Like the Sovereign of Persia, alone of the Birds, he stalks
with tiara erect.[19]

PEISTHETAERUS. So mighty and great was his former estate,
so ample he waxed and so strong,

That still the tradition is potent, and still, when he sings
in the morning his song,

At once from their sleep all mortals upleap, the cobblers,
the tanners, the bakers,

The potters, the bathmen, the smiths, and the shield-and-
the-musical-instrument-makers;

And some will at eve take their sandals and leave.

EUELPIDES.   I can answer for that, to my cost.
'Twas all through his crowing at eve that my cloak, the
softest of Phrygians, I lost.[20]

I was asked to the Tenth-day feast of a child; and I drank
ere the feast was begun;

Then I take my repose; and anon the cock crows; so thinking it daybreak I run

To return from the City to Halimus town; but scarce I
emerge from the wall,

When I get such a whack with a stick on my back from a
rascally thief, that I fall,

And he skims off my cloak from my shoulders or e'er for
assistance I'm able to bawl.

PEISTHETAERUS. Then a Kite was the Sovereign of Hellas of
old, and ruled with an absolute sway.

CHORUS. The Sovereign of Hellas!

PEISTHETAERUS. And, taught by his rule, we wallow on earth
to this day

When a Kite we espy.

EUELPIDES.   By Bacchus, 'twas I saw a Kite in
the air; so I wallow

Then raising my eyne from by posture supine, I give such
a gulp that I swallow

O what but an obol I've got in my mouth, and am forced
   to return empty-handed.

PEISTHETAERUS. And the whole of Phoenice and Egypt was
   erst by a masterful Cuckoo commanded.
When his loud cuckoo-cry was resounding on high, at
   once the Phoenicians would leap
All hands to the plain, rich-waving with grain, their wheat
   and their barley to reap.

EUELPIDES. So that's why we cry to the circumcised *Hi!
   Cuckoo! To the plain! Cuckoo!*[21]

PEISTHETAERUS. And whene'er in the cities of Hellas a chief
   to honour and dignity grew,
Menelaus or King Agamemnon perchance, your rule was
   so firm and decided
That a bird on his sceptre would perch, to partake of the
   gifts for his Lordship provided.

EUELPIDES. Now of that I declare I was never aware; and I
   oft have been filled with amaze,
When Priam so noble and stately appeared, with a bird,
   in the Tragedy-plays.
But the bird was no doubt for the gifts looking out, to
   Lysicrates brought on the sly.[22]

PEISTHETAERUS. But the strongest and clearest of proofs is that
   Zeus who at present is Lord of the sky
Stands wearing, as Royalty's emblem and badge, an Eagle
   erect on his head,
Our Lady an owl, and Apollo forsooth, as a lackey, a
   falcon instead.

EUELPIDES. By Demeter, 'tis true; that is just what they do;
   but tell me the reason, I pray.

PEISTHETAERUS. That the bird may be ready and able,
   whene'er the sacrificed inwards we lay,
As custom demands, in the deity's hands, to seize before
   Zeus on the fare.
And none by the Gods, but all by the Birds, were accus-
   tomed aforetime to swear:
And Lampon will vow by the Goose even now, whenever
   he's going to cheat you:[23]

So holy and mighty they deemed you of old, with so deep
    a respect did they treat you!
Now they treat you as knaves, and as fools, and as
    slaves;
    Yea they pelt you as though ye were mad.
No safety for you can the Temples ensure,
For the bird-catcher sets his nooses and nets,
And his traps, and his toils, and his bait, and his lure,
And his lime-covered rods in the shrine of the Gods!
Then he takes you, and sets you for sale in the lump;
And the customers, buying, come poking and prying
    And twitching and trying,
To feel if your bodies are tender and plump.
And if they decide on your flesh to sup
They don't just roast you and serve you up.
But over your bodies, as prone ye lie,
They grate their cheese and their silphium too,
    And oil and vinegar add,
Then a gravy, luscious and rich, they brew,
And pour it in soft warm streams o'er you,
As though ye were carrion noisome and dry.

CHORUS. O man, 'tis indeed a most pitiful tale
    Thou hast brought to our ears; and I can but bewail
        Our fathers' demerit,
Who born such an Empire as this to inherit
        Have lost it, have lost it, for me!
But now thou art come, by good Fortune's decree,
        Our Saviour to be,
And under thy charge, whatsoever befall,
I will place my own self, and my nestlings, and all.
Now therefore do you tell us what we must do; since life
    is not worth our retaining,
Unless we be Lords of the world as before, our ancient
    dominion regaining.

PEISTHETAERUS. Then first I propose that the Air ye enclose,
    and the space 'twixt the Earth and the sky,
Encircling it all with a brick-builded wall, like Babylon's,
    solid and high;
And there you must place the abode of your race, and
    make them one State, and one nation.

EUELPIDES. O Porphyrion! O Cebriones! how stupendous the
fortification!

PEISTHETAERUS. When the wall is complete, send a messenger
fleet, the empire from Zeus to reclaim.

And if he deny, or be slow to comply, nor retreat in con-
fusion and shame,

Proclaim ye against him a Holy War, and announce that
no longer below,

On their lawless amours through these regions of yours,
will the Gods be permitted to go.

No more through the air, (to their Alopes fair, their
Alcmenas, their Semeles wending)

May they post in hot love, as of old, from above, for if
ever you catch them descending,

You will clap on their dissolute persons a seal, their evil
designs to prevent!

And then let another ambassador-bird to men with this
message be sent,

That the Birds being Sovereigns, to them must be paid all
honour and worship divine,

And the Gods for the future to them be postponed. Now
therefore assort and combine

Each God with a bird, whichever will best with his nature
and attributes suit;

If to Queen Aphrodite a victim ye slay, first sacrifice grain
to the coot;

If a sheep to Poseidon ye slay, to the duck let wheat as a
victim be brought;

And a big honey-cake for the cormorant make, if ye offer
to Heracles aught.

Bring a ram for King Zeus! But ye first must produce for
our Kinglet, the gold-crested wren,

A masculine midge, full formed and entire, to be sacrificed
duly by men.

EUELPIDES. I am tickled and pleased with the sacrificed midge.
Now thunder away, great Zan![24]

CHORUS. But men, will they take us for Gods, and not daws,—
do ye really believe that they can—

If they see us on wings flying idly about?

PEISTHETAERUS. Don't say such ridiculous things!
Why Hermes, and lots of the deities too, go flying about
upon wings.
There is Victory, bold on her pinions of gold; and then,
by the Powers, there is Love;
And Iris, says Homer, shoots straight through the skies,
with the ease of a terrified dove.

EUELPIDES. And the thunderbolt flies upon wings, I surmise:
what if Zeus upon us let it fall?

PEISTHETAERUS. But suppose that mankind, being stupid and
blind, should account you as nothing at all,
And still in the Gods of Olympus believe—why then, like
a cloud, shall a swarm
Of sparrows and rooks settle down on their stooks, and
devour all the seed in the farm.
Demeter may fill them with grain, if she will, when hungry and pinched they entreat her.

EUELPIDES. O no, for by Zeus, she will make some excuse; that
is always the way with Demeter.

PEISTHETAERUS. And truly the ravens shall pluck out the eyes
of the oxen that work in the plough,
Of the flocks and the herds, as a proof that the Birds are
the Masters and Potentates now.
Apollo the leech, if his aid they beseech, may cure them;
but then they must pay!

EUELPIDES. Nay but hold, nay but hold, nor begin till I've sold
my two little oxen I pray.

PEISTHETAERUS. But when once to esteem you as God, and as
Life, and as Cronos and Earth they've begun,
And as noble Poseidon, what joys shall be theirs!

CHORUS. Will you kindly inform me of one?

PEISTHETAERUS. The delicate tendrils and bloom of the vine
no more shall the locusts molest,
One gallant brigade of the kestrels and owls shall rid them
at once of the pest.
No more shall the mite and the gall-making blight the
fruit of the fig-tree devour;
Of thrushes one troop on their armies shall swoop, and
clear them all off in an hour.

CHORUS. But how shall we furnish the people with wealth? It is wealth that they mostly desire.

PEISTHETAERUS. Choice blessings and rare ye shall give them whene'er they come to your shrine to inquire.

To the seer ye shall tell when 'tis lucky and well for a merchant to sail o'er the seas,

So that never a skipper again shall be lost.

CHORUS.   What, "never"? Explain if you please.

PEISTHETAERUS. Are they seeking to know when a voyage to go? The Birds shall give answers to guide them.

Now stick to the land, there's a tempest at hand! Now sail! and good luck shall betide them.

EUELPIDES. A galley for me; I am off to the sea! No longer with you will I stay.

PEISTHETAERUS. The treasures of silver long since in the earth by their forefathers hidden away

To men ye shall show, for the secret ye know. How often a man will declare,

There is no one who knows where my treasures repose, if it be not a bird of the air.

EUELPIDES. My galley may go; I will buy me a hoe, and dig for the crock and the casket.

CHORUS. But Health, I opine, is a blessing divine; can we give it to men if they ask it?

PEISTHETAERUS. If they've plenty of wealth, they'll have plenty of health; ye may rest quite assured that they will.

Did you ever hear tell of a man that was well, when faring remarkably ill?

CHORUS. Long life 'tis Olympus alone can bestow; so can men live as long as before?

Must they die in their youth?

PEISTHETAERUS.   Die? No! why in truth their lives by three hundred or more

New years ye will lengthen.

CHORUS.   Why, whence will they come?

PEISTHETAERUS.   From your own inexhaustible store.

What! dost thou not know that the noisy-tongued crow
    lives five generations of men?

EUELPIDES. O fie! it is plain they are fitter to reign than the
    Gods; let us have them again.

PEISTHETAERUS. Ay, fitter by far!
    No need for their sakes to erect and adorn
    Great temples of marble with portals of gold.
    Enough for the birds on the brake and the thorn
    And the evergreen oak their receptions to hold.
    Or if any are noble, and courtly, and fine,
    The tree of the olive will serve for their shrine.
    No need, when a blessing we seek, to repair
    To Delphi or Ammon, and sacrifice there;
    We will under an olive or arbutus stand
        With a present of barley and wheat,
    And piously lifting our heart and our hand
        The birds for a boon we'll entreat,
    And the boon shall be ours, and our suit we shall gain
    At the cost of a few little handfuls of grain.

CHORUS. I thought thee at first of my foemen the worst; and
    lo, I have found thee the wisest
  And best of my friends, and our nation intends to do
    whatsoe'er thou advisest.
    A spirit so lofty and rare
    Thy words have within me excited,
    That I lift up my soul, and I swear
    That if Thou wilt with Me be united
    In bonds that are holy and true
    And honest and just and sincere,
    If our hearts are attuned to one song,
    We will march on the Gods without fear;
    The sceptre—*my* sceptre, *my* due,—
    They shall not be handling it long!
So all that by muscle and strength can be done, we Birds
    will assuredly do;
But whatever by prudence and skill must be won, we
    leave altogether to you.

HOOPOE. Aye, and, by Zeus, the time is over now
    For drowsy nods and Nicias-hesitations.

We must be up and doing! And do you,
Or e'er we start, visit this nest of mine,
My bits of things, my little sticks and straws;
And tell me what your names are.

PEISTHETAERUS.   That's soon done.
My name is Peisthetaerus.

HOOPOE.   And your friend's?

PEISTHETAERUS. Euelpides of Crio.

HOOPOE.   Well ye are both
Heartily welcome.

PEISTHETAERUS.   Thank you.

HOOPOE.   Come ye in.

PEISTHETAERUS. Aye, come we in; you, please, precede us.

HOOPOE.   Come.

PEISTHETAERUS. But—dear! what was it? step you back a
      moment.
O yes,—but tell us, how can he and I
Consort with you, we wingless and you winged?

HOOPOE. Why, very well.

PEISTHETAERUS.   Nay but in Aesop's fables
There's something, mind you, told about the fox
How ill it fared, consorting with an eagle.

HOOPOE. O never fear; for there's a little root
Which when ye have eaten, ye will both be winged.

PEISTHETAERUS. That being so, we'll enter. Xanthias there.
And Manodorus, bring along the traps.

CHORUS. O stay, and O stay!

HOOPOE.   Why, what ails you to-day?

CHORUS.   Take the gentlemen
      in, and regale them, we say;
But O for the nightingale peerless in song, who chants in
      the choir of the Muses her lay;
Our sweetest and best, fetch her out of the nest, and leave
      her awhile with the Chorus to play.

PEISTHETAERUS. O do, by Zeus, grant them this one request;
Fetch out the little warbler from the reeds.

EUELPIDES. Yes, fetch her out by all the Gods, that so
    We too may gaze upon the nightingale.

HOOPOE. Well, if you wish it, so we'll have it. Procne,
    Come hither, dear, and let the strangers see you.

(*Enter the* NIGHTINGALE, *a flute-player dressed in a girl's
rich costume, wearing a nightingale's head and wings.*)

PEISTHETAERUS. Zeus, what a darling lovely little bird!
    How fair, and tender!

EUELPIDES.   O the little love,
    Wouldn't I like to be her mate this instant!

PEISTHETAERUS. And O the gold she is wearing, like a girl.

EUELPIDES. Upon my word, I've half a mind to kiss her!

PEISTHETAERUS. Kiss her, you fool! Her beak's a pair of spits.

EUELPIDES. But I would treat her like an egg, and strip
    The egg-shell from her poll, and kiss her so.

HOOPOE. Come, go we in.

PEISTHETAERUS.   Lead on, and luck go with us.

(*The* HOOPOE *and his two guests enter the Hoopoe's house,
and the rock is closed.*)

CHORUS. O darling! O tawny-throat!
        Love, whom I love the best,
        Dearer than all the rest,
        Playmate and partner in
            All my soft lays,
        Thou art come! Thou art come!
        Thou hast dawned on my gaze,
        I have heard thy sweet note,
        Nightingále! Nightingále!
Thou from thy flute   Softly-sounding canst bring
Music to suit   With our songs of the Spring:
        Begin then I pray
    Our own anapaestic address to essay.

Ye men who are dimly existing below, who perish and
        fade as the leaf,
Pale, woebegone, shadowlike, spiritless folk, life feeble
        and wingless and brief,

Frail castings in clay, who are gone in a day, like a dream
    full of sorrow and sighing,
Come listen with care to the Birds of the air, the ageless,
    the deathless, who flying
In the joy and the freshness of Ether, are wont to muse
    upon wisdom undying.
We will tell you of things transcendental; of Springs and
    of Rivers the mighty upheaval;
The nature of Birds; and the birth of the Gods: and of
    Chaos and Darkness primeval.
When this ye shall know, let old Prodicus go, and be
    hanged without hope of reprieval.
    There was Chaos at first, and Darkness, and Night, and
    Tartarus vasty and dismal;
But the Earth was not there, nor the Sky, nor the Air, till
    at length in the bosom abysmal
Of Darkness an egg, from the whirlwind conceived, was
    laid by the sable-plumed Night.
And out of that egg, as the Seasons revolved, sprang Love,
    the entrancing, the bright,
Love brilliant and bold with his pinions of gold, like a
    whirlwind, refulgent and sparkling!
Love hatched us, commingling in Tartarus wide, with
    Chaos, the murky, the darkling,
And brought us above, as the firstlings of love, and first to
    the light we ascended.
There was never a race of Immortals at all till Love had
    the universe blended;
Then all things commingling together in love, there arose
    the fair Earth, and the Sky,
And the limitless Sea; and the race of the Gods, the
    Blessed, who never shall die.
So we than the Blessed are older by far; and abundance of
    proof is existing
That we are the children of Love, for we fly, unfortunate
    lovers assisting.
And many a man who has found, to his cost, that his
    powers of persuasion have failed,
And his loves have abjured him for ever, again by the
    power of the Birds has prevailed;

For the gift of a quail, or a Porphyry rail, or a Persian, or
goose, will regain them.

And the chiefest of blessings ye mortals enjoy, by the help
of the Birds ye obtain them.

'Tis from us that the signs of the Seasons in turn, Spring,
Winter, and Autumn are known.

When to Libya the crane flies clanging again, it is time for
the seed to be sown,

And the skipper may hang up his rudder awhile, and
sleep after all his exertions,

And Orestes may weave him a wrap to be warm when he's
out on his thievish excursions.

Then cometh the kite, with its hovering flight, of the
advent of Spring to tell,

And the Spring sheep-shearing begins; and next, your
woollen attire you sell,

And buy you a lighter and daintier garb, when you note
the return of the swallow.

Thus your Ammon, Dodona, and Delphi are we; we are
also your Phoebus Apollo.

For whatever you do, if a trade you pursue, or goods in
the market are buying,

Or the wedding attend of a neighbour and friend, first
you look to the Birds and their flying.

And whene'er you of omen or augury speak, *'tis a bird*
you are always repeating;

A Rumour's a bird, and a sneeze is a bird, and so is a word
or a meeting,

A servant's a bird, and an ass is a bird. It must therefore
assuredly follow

That the birds are to you (I protest it is true) your prophetic divining Apollo.

Then take us for Gods, as is proper and fit,
And Muses Prophetic ye'll have at your call
Spring, winter, and summer, and autumn and all.
And we won't run away from your worship, and sit
Up above in the clouds, very stately and grand,
Like Zeus in his tempers: but always at hand
Health and wealth we'll bestow, as the formula runs,

On yourselves, and your sons, and the sons of your sons;
And happiness, plenty, and peace shall belong
To you all; and the revel, the dance, and the song,
And laughter, and youth, and the milk of the birds
    We'll supply, and we'll never forsake you.
Ye'll be quite overburdened with pleasures and joys,
    So happy and blest we will make you.

    O woodland Muse,
     tío, tio, tío, tiotinx,
    Of varied plume, with whose dear aid
    On the mountain top, and the sylvan glade,
     tío, tio, tío, tiotinx,
    I, sitting up aloft on a leafy ash, full oft,
     tío, tio, tío, tiotinx,
Pour forth a warbling note from my little tawny throat,
Pour festive choral dances to the mountain mother's
    praise,
And to Pan the holy music of his own immortal lays;
    totótotótotótotótotinx,
    Whence Phrynichus of old,
    Sipping the fruit of our ambrosial lay,
    Bore, like a bee, the honied store away,
     His own sweet songs to mould.
     tio, tío, tio, tío, tiotinx.

Is there any one amongst you, O spectators, who would
    lead
With the birds a life of pleasure, let him come to us with
    speed.
All that here is reckoned shameful, all that here the laws
    condemn,
With the birds is right and proper, you may do it all with
    them.
Is it here by law forbidden for a son to beat his sire?
That a chick should strike his father, strutting up with
    youthful ire,
Crowing *Raise your spur and fight me,* that is what the
    birds admire.
Come you runaway deserter, spotted o'er with marks of
    shame,

Spotted Francolin we'll call you, that, with us, shall be
your name.
You who style yourself a tribesman, Phrygian pure as
Spintharus,
Come and be a Phrygian linnet, of Philemon's breed, with
us.
Come along, you slave and Carian, Execestides to wit,
Breed with us your Cuckoo-rearers, they'll be guildsmen
apt and fit.
Son of Peisias, who to outlaws would the city gates betray,
Come to us, and be a partridge (*cockerel like the cock,
they say*),
We esteem it no dishonour knavish partridge-tricks to
play.
Even thus the Swans,
tío, tio, tío, tiotinx,
Their clamorous cry were erst up-raising,
With clatter of wings Apollo praising,
tío, tio, tío, tiotinx,
As they sat in serried ranks on the river Hebrus' banks.
tío, tio, tío, tiotinx,
Right upward went the cry through the cloud and through
the sky.
Quailed the wild-beast in his covert, and the bird within
her nest,
And the still and windless Ether lulled the ocean-waves
to rest.
totótotótotótotótotótotinx.
Loudly Olympus rang!
Amazement seized the kings; and every Grace
And every Muse within that heavenly place
Took up the strain, and sang.
tío, tio, tío, tiotinx.

Truly to be clad in feathers is the very best of things.
Only fancy, dear spectators, had you each a brace of
wings,
Never need you, tired and hungry, at a Tragic Chorus
stay,[25]

You would lightly, when it bored you, spread your wings
       and fly away,
Back returning, after luncheon, to enjoy our Comic Play.
Never need a Patrocleides, sitting here, his garment stain;
When the dire occasion seized him, he would off with
       might and main
Flying home, then flying hither, lightened and relieved,
       again.
If a gallant should the husband on the Council-bench
       behold
Of a gay and charming lady, one whom he had loved of
       old,
Off at once he'd fly to greet her, have a little converse
       sweet,
Then be back, or e'er ye missed him, calm and smiling in
       his seat.
Is not then a suit of feathers quite the very best of things?
Why, Diitrephes was chosen, though he had but wicker
       wings,[26]
First a Captain, then a Colonel, till from nothing he of late
Has become a tawny cock-horse, yea a pillar of the State!

(PEISTHETAERUS *and* EUELPIDES *re-enter. They have eaten
"the little root" and are now furnished with wings.*)

PEISTHETAERUS. Well, here we are. By Zeus, I never saw
In all my life a sight more laughable.

EUELPIDES. What are you laughing at?

PEISTHETAERUS.   At your flight-feathers.
I'll tell you what you're like, your wings and you,
Just like a gander, sketched by some cheap-Jack.

EUELPIDES. And you, a blackbird, with a bowl-cropped noddle.

PEISTHETAERUS. These shafts of ridicule are winged by nought
But our own plumes, as Aeschylus would say.

CHORUS. What's the next step?

PEISTHETAERUS.   First we must give the city
Some grand big name: and then we'll sacrifice
To the high Gods.

EUELPIDES.   That's my opinion also.

CHORUS. Then let's consider what the name shall be.

PEISTHETAERUS. What think you of that grand Laconian name,
Sparta?

EUELPIDES. What! Sparta for my city? No.
I wouldn't use esparto for my pallet,
Not if I'd cords; by Heracles, not I.

PEISTHETAERUS. How shall we name it then?

CHORUS. Invent some fine
Magniloquent name, drawn from these upper spaces
And clouds.

PEISTHETAERUS. What think you of Cloudcuckoobury?

CHORUS. Good! Good!
You have found a good big name, and no mistake.

EUELPIDES. Is this the great Cloudcuckoobury town
Where all the wealth of Aeschines lies hid,
And all Theagenes's?[27]

PEISTHETAERUS. Best of all,
This is the plain of Phlegra, where the Gods
Outshot the giants at the game of Brag.

EUELPIDES. A glistering sort of a city! Who shall be
Its guardian God? For whom shall we weave the Peplus?

PEISTHETAERUS. Why not retain Athene, City-keeper?

EUELPIDES. And how can that be a well-ordered State,
Where she, a woman born, a Goddess, stands
Full-armed, and Cleisthenes assumes a spindle?

PEISTHETAERUS. And who shall hold the citadel's Storkade?

CHORUS. A bird of ours, one of the Persian breed,
Everywhere noted as the War-god's own
Armipotent cockerel.

EUELPIDES. O, Prince Cockerel? Yes,
He's just the God to perch upon the rocks.

PEISTHETAERUS. Now, comrade, get you up into the air,
And lend a hand to those that build the wall.
Bring up the rubble; strip, and mix the mortar;
Run up the ladder with the hod; fall off;
Station the sentinels; conceal the fire;
Round with the alarum bell; go fast asleep;

And send two heralds, one to heaven above,
And one to earth below; and let them come
From thence, for me.

EUELPIDES.　　　　　And you, remaining here,
Be hanged—for me!

PEISTHETAERUS.　　　　　Go where I send you, comrade,
Without your help there nothing will be done.

(*Exit* EUELPIDES.)

But I, to sacrifice to these new Gods,
Must call the priest to regulate the show.
Boy! Boy! take up the basket and the laver.

CHORUS. I'm with you, you'll find me quite willing:
　　　　I highly approve of your killing
　　　A lambkin, to win us the favour divine,
　　　Mid holy processionals, stately and fine.
　　　Up high, up high, let the Pythian cry,
　　　The Pythian cry to the God be sent;
　　　Let Chaeris play the accompaniment.

(*Talk of Chaeris and he is sure to appear. An actor enters
with a raven's head and wings, but otherwise made up to
resemble that unwelcome piper. He is playing the pipe
with a mouth-band on.*)

PEISTHETAERUS. O stop that puffing! Heracles, what's this?
Faith, I've seen many a sight, but never yet
A mouth-band-wearing raven! Now then, priest,
To the new Gods commence the sacrifice.

PRIEST. I'll do your bidding. Where's the basket-bearer?
　　　　Let us pray
To the Hestia-bird of the household shrine,
And the Kite that watches her feasts divine,
And to all the Olympian birds and birdesses,

PEISTHETAERUS. O Sunium-hawking, King of the Sea—mew,
　　　　hail!

PRIEST. And to the holy Swan, the Pythian and Delian one,
And to thee too, Quail-guide Leto,
And to Artemis the Thistle-finch,

PEISTHETAERUS. Aye, Thistle-finch; no more Colaenis now!

PRIEST. And to Sabazius the Phrygian linnet; and then
    To Rhea the Great Mother of Gods and men;

PEISTHETAERUS. Aye, Ostrich-queen, Cleocritus's Mother!

PRIEST. That they may grant health and salvation
    To the whole Cloudcuckooburian nation,
        For themselves and the Chians,

PEISTHETAERUS. I like the Chians everywhere tacked on.

PRIEST. And to the hero-birds and sons of heroes,
    And to the Porphyrion rail;
    And to the pelican white, and pelican grey;
    And to the eagle, and to the capercaillie;
    And to the peacock, and to the sedgewarbler;
    And to the teal, and to the skua;
    And to the heron, and to the gannet;
    And to the blackcap, and to the titmouse;—

PEISTHETAERUS. Stop, stop your calling, hang you. O, look
        here.
    To what a victim, idiot, are you calling
    Ospreys and vultures? Don't you see that one,
    One single kite could carry off the whole?
    Get away hence, you and your garlands too!
    Myself alone will sacrifice this victim.

CHORUS. Once more as the laver they're bringing,
        Once more I my hymns must be singing,
        Hymns holy and pious, the Gods to invite—
        One alone, only one,—to our festival rite.
        Your feast for two, I am sure won't do.
        For what you are going to offer there
        Is nothing at all but horns and hair.

PEISTHETAERUS. Let us pray,
    Offering our victim to the feathery gods.

(*Just as he is commencing the sacrifice he is interrupted
by the entry of a needy Pindaric* POET.)

POET (*singing*). Cloudcuckoobury
        With praise and glory crown,
        Singing, O Muse,
        Of the new and happy town!

PEISTHETAERUS. Whatever's this? Why, who in the world are
you?

POET. O I'm a warbler, carolling sweet lays,
An eager meagre servant of the Muses,
As Homer says.

PEISTHETAERUS. What! you a slave and wear your hair so
long?

POET. No, but all we who teach sweet choral lays
Are eager meagre servants of the Muses,
As Homer says.

PEISTHETAERUS. That's why your cloak so meagre seems, no
doubt.
But, poet, what ill wind has blown you hither?

POET. O, I've been making, making lovely songs,
Simonideans, virgin songs, and sweet
Dithyrambic songs, on your Cloudcuckooburies.

PEISTHETAERUS. When did you first begin these lovely songs?

POET. Long, long ago, O yes! Long, long ago!

PEISTHETAERUS. Why, is not this the City's Tenth-day feast?
I've just this instant given the child its name.

POET. But fleet, as the merry many-twinkling horses' feet,
The airy fairy Rumour of the Muses.
Aetna's Founder, father mine,
Whose name is the same as the holy altar flame,[28]
Give to me what thy bounty chooses
To give me willingly of thine.

PEISTHETAERUS. He'll cause us trouble now, unless we give
him
Something, and so get off. Hallo, you priest,
Why, you've a jerkin and a tunic too;
Strip, give the jerkin to this clever poet.
Take it; upon my word you *do* seem cold.

POET. This little kindly gift the Muse
Accepts with willing condescension;
But let me to an apt remark
Of Pindar call my lord's attention.

PEISTHETAERUS. The fellow does not seem inclined to leave us.

POET. Out among the Scythians yonder
    See poor Straton wander, wander,
Poor poor Straton, not possessed of a whirly-woven vest.
All inglorious comes, I trow, leather jerkin, if below
    No soft tunic it can show.
    Conceive my drift, I pray.

PEISTHETAERUS. Aye, I conceive you want the tunic too.
Off with it, you. Needs must assist a Poet.
There, take it, and depart.

POET.   Yes, I'll depart,
And make to the city pretty songs like this;
    O Thou of the golden throne,
    Sing Her, the quivering, shivering;
    I came to the plains many-sown,
    I came to the snowy, the blowy.
          Alalae!   (*Exit.*)

PRIEST. Well, well, but now you surely have escaped
From all those shiverings, with that nice warm vest.
This is, by Zeus, a plague I never dreamed of
That he should find our city out so soon.
Boy, take the laver and walk round once more.
Now hush!

(*A second interruption. This time by an* ORACLE-MONGER.)

ORACLE-MONGER. Forbear! touch not the goat awhile.

PEISTHETAERUS. Eh? Who are you?

ORACLE-MONGER.   A soothsayer.

PEISTHETAERUS.   *You be hanged!*

ORACLE-MONGER. O think not lightly, friend, of things divine;
Know I've an oracle of Bakis, bearing
On your Cloudcuckooburies.

PEISTHETAERUS.   Eh? then why
Did you not soothsay that before I founded
My city here?

ORACLE-MONGER. The Power within forbade me.

PEISTHETAERUS. Well, well, there's nought like hearing what
    it says.

ORACLE-MONGER. *Nay but if once grey crows and wolves shall be banding together,*
 Out in the midway space, 'twixt Corinth and Sicyon, dwelling,—

PEISTHETAERUS. But what in the world have I to do with Corinth?

ORACLE-MONGER. Bakis is riddling: Bakis means the Air.
 First to Pandora offer a white-fleeced ram for a victim.
 Next, who first shall arrive my verses prophetic expounding,
 Give him a brand-new cloak and a pair of excellent sandals.

PEISTHETAERUS. Are sandals in it?

ORACLE-MONGER. Take the book and see.
 Give him moreover a cup, and fill his hands with the inwards.

PEISTHETAERUS. Are inwards in it?

ORACLE-MONGER. Take the book and see.
 Youth, divinely inspired, if thou dost as I bid, thou shalt surely
 Soar in the clouds as an Eagle; refuse, and thou ne'er shalt become an
 Eagle, or even a dove, or a wood-pecker tapping the oaktree.

PEISTHETAERUS. Is all that in it?

ORACLE-MONGER. Take the book and see.

PEISTHETAERUS. O how unlike your oracle to mine,
 Which from Apollo's words I copied out;
 But if a cheat, an impostor, presume to appear uninvited,
 Troubling the sacred rites, and lusting to taste of the inwards,
 Hit him betwixt the ribs with all your force and your fury.

ORACLE-MONGER. You're jesting surely.

PEISTHETAERUS. Take the book and see.
 See that ye spare not the rogue, though he soar in the clouds as an Eagle,
 Yea, be he Lampon himself or even the great Diopeithes.

ORACLE-MONGER. Is all that in it?

PEISTHETAERUS.   Take the book and see.
Get out! be off, confound you! (*Striking him.*)

ORACLE-MONGER.   O! O! O!   (*Exit.*)

PEISTHETAERUS. There, run away and soothsay somewhere
    else.

(*A third interruption. This time by* METON, *the celebrated
astronomer.*)

METON. I come amongst you—

PEISTHETAERUS.   Some new misery this!
    Come to do what? What's your scheme's form and outline?
    What's your design? What buskin's on your foot?

METON. I come to land-survey this Air of yours,
    And mete it out by acres.

PEISTHETAERUS.   Heaven and Earth!
    Whoever are you?

METON (*scandalized*). Whoever am I! I'm Meton.
    Known throughout Hellas and Colonus.[29]

PEISTHETAERUS.   Aye,
    And what are *these?*

METON.   They're rods for Air-surveying.
    I'll just explain. The Air's, in outline, like
    One vast extinguisher; so then, observe,
    Applying here my flexible rod, and fixing
    My compass there,—you understand?

PEISTHETAERUS.   I don't.

METON. With the straight rod I measure out, that so
    The circle may be squared; and in the centre
    A market-place; and streets be leading to it
    Straight to the very centre; just as from
    A star, though circular, straight rays flash out
    In all directions.

PEISTHETAERUS.   Why, the man's a Thales!
    Meton!

METON. Yes, what?

PEISTHETAERUS.   You know I love you, Meton,
    Take my advice, and slip away unnoticed.

METON. Why, what's the matter?

PEISTHETAERUS. As in Lacedaemon
There's stranger-hunting; and a great disturbance;
And blows in plenty.

METON. What, a Revolution?

PEISTHETAERUS. No, no, not that.

METON. What then?

PEISTHETAERUS. They've all resolved
With one consent to wallop every quack.

METON. I'd best be going.

PEISTHETAERUS. Faith, I'm not quite certain
If you're in time; see, see the blows are coming!
(*Striking him.*)

METON. O, murder! help!

PEISTHETAERUS. I told you how 'twould be.
Come, measure off your steps some other way.

(METON *disappears, but a fourth visitor immediately
makes his appearance. He is a smart and gorgeous official,
one of the Commissioners who were despatched from
Athens to superintend, organize, and report upon the
affairs of a colony or new acquisition.*)

COMMISSIONER. Ho! consuls, ho!

PEISTHETAERUS. Sardanapalus, surely!

COMMISSIONER. Lo, I to your Cloudcuckooburies come,
By lot Commissioner.

PEISTHETAERUS. Commissioner?
Who sent you hither?

COMMISSIONER. Lo, a paltry scroll
Of Teleas.

PEISTHETAERUS. Come now, will you take your pay
And get you gone in peace?

COMMISSIONER. By Heaven I will.
I ought to be at home on public business,
Some little jobs I've had with Pharnaces.[30]

PEISTHETAERUS. Then take your pay, and go: your pay's just—
this. (*Striking him.*)

COMMISSIONER. What's that?

PEISTHETAERUS. A motion about Pharnaces.

COMMISSIONER. Witness! he's striking a Commissioner.

PEISTHETAERUS. Shoo! shoo! begone; you and your verdict-
urns. (*The* COMMISSIONER *disappears.*)
The shame it is! They send Commissioners
Before we've finished our inaugural rites.

(*The last of these intruders is a* SELLER OF STATUTES.)

STATUTE-SELLER (*reading*). *But if the Cloudcuckooburian
wrong the Athenian—*

PEISTHETAERUS. Here's some more writing. What new misery's
this?

STATUTE-SELLER. I am a Statute-seller, and I'm come
Bringing new laws to sell you.

PEISTHETAERUS. Such as what?

STATUTE-SELLER. *Item, the Cloudcuckooburians are to use the
selfsame weights and measures, and the selfsame
coinage as the Olophyxians.*

PEISTHETAERUS. And you the selfsame as the Oh! Oh! -tyxians.
(*Striking him.*)

STATUTE-SELLER. Hi! what are you at?

PEISTHETAERUS. Take off those laws, you rascal.
Laws you won't like I'll give you in a minute.

COMMISSIONER (*reappearing*). I summon Peisthetaerus for
next Munychion on a charge of outrage.[31]

PEISTHETAERUS. O that's it, is it? What, are you there still?

STATUTE-SELLER (*reappearing*). *Item, if any man drive away
the magistrates, and do not receive them according
to the pillar—*

PEISTHETAERUS. O mercy upon us, and are *you* there still?

COMMISSIONER (*reappearing*). I'll ruin you! I claim ten thousand drachmas!

PEISTHETAERUS. I'll overturn your verdict-urn, I will.

STATUTE-SELLER (*reappearing*). Think of that evening when
you fouled the pillar.

PEISTHETAERUS. Ugh! seize him, somebody! Ha, you're off
there, are you?

Let's get away from this, and go within,
And there we'll sacrifice the goat in peace.

(*They all go out.*)

CHORUS. Unto me, the All-controlling,
        All-surveying,
    Now will men, at every altar,
        Prayers be praying;
    Me who watch the land, protecting
        Fruit and flower,
    Slay the myriad-swarming insects
    Who the tender buds devour
In the earth and on the branches with a never-satiate
        malice,
Nipping off the blossom as it widens from the chalice.
        And I slay the noisome creatures
            Which consume
    And pollute the garden's freshly scented bloom;
And every little biter, and every creeping thing
Perish in destruction at the onset of my wing.

Listen to the City's notice, specially proclaimed to-day;
Sirs, Diagoras the Melian whosoever of you slay,[32]
Shall receive, reward, one talent; and another we'll bestow
If you slay some ancient tyrant, dead and buried long ago.
We, the Birds, will give a notice, we proclaim with right
        good will,
Sirs, Philocrates, Sparrovian, whosoever of you kill,
Shall receive, reward, one talent, if alive you bring him,
        four;
Him who strings and sells the finches, seven an obol, at his
        store,
Blows the thrushes out and, rudely, to the public gaze ex-
        poses,
Shamefully entreats the blackbirds, thrusting feathers up
        their noses.
Pigeons too the rascal catches, keeps and mews them up
        with care,
Makes them labour as decoy-birds, tethered underneath a
        snare.
Such the notice we would give you. And we wish you all
        to know,

Who are keeping birds in cages, you had better let them
    go.
Else the Birds will surely catch you, and yourselves in
    turn employ,
Tied and tethered up securely, other rascals to decoy.
    O the happy clan of birds
        Clad in feather;
    Needing not a woollen vest in
        Wintry weather;
    Heeding not the warm far-flashing
        Summer ray,
    For within the leafy bosoms
    Of the flowery meads I stay,
When the Chirruper in ecstasy is shrilling forth his tune,
Maddened with the sunshine, and the rapture of the noon.
    And I winter in the cavern's
        Hollow spaces,
  With the happy Oreads playing; and in Spring
I crop the virgin flowers of the myrtles white and tender,
Dainties that are fashioned in the gardens of the Graces.

Now we wish to tell the Judges, in a friendly sort of way,
All the blessings we shall give them if we gain the prize
    to-day.
Ne'er were made to Alexander lovelier promises or
    grander.[33]
First, what every Judge amongst you most of all desires
    to win,
Little Lauriotic owlets shall be always flocking in.[34]
Ye shall find them all about you, as the dainty brood in-
    creases,
Building nests within your purses, hatching little silver
    pieces.
Then as if in stately Temples shall your happy lives be
    spent,
For the birds will top your mansions with the Eagle pedi-
    ment.
If you hold some petty office, if you wish to steal and pick,
In your hands we'll place a falcon, very keen and small
    and quick.

If a dinner is in question, crops we'll send you for diges-
tion.

But should you the prize deny us, you had better all prepare,

Like the statues in the open, little copper disks to wear;

Else whene'er abroad ye're walking, clad in raiment white
and new,

Angry birds will wreak their vengeance, spattering over
it and you.

(PEISTHETAERUS re-enters, having at last completed the
sacrifice.)

PEISTHETAERUS. Dear Birds, our sacrifice is most auspicious.
But strange it is, no messenger has come
From the great wall we are building, with the news.
Hah! here runs one with true Alpheian pantings.[35]

MESSENGER. Where, where,—O where, where, where,—O
where, where, where,
Where, where's our leader Peisthetaerus?

PEISTHETAERUS.   Here.

MESSENGER. Your building's built. The Wall's complete!

PEISTHETAERUS.   Well done.

MESSENGER. And a most grand, magnificent work it is.
So broad, that on its top the Braggadocian
Proxenides could pass Theagenes
Each driving in his chariot, drawn by horses
As bulky as the Trojan.

PEISTHETAERUS.   Heracles!

MESSENGER. And then its height, I measured that, is just
Six hundred feet.

PEISTHETAERUS.   Poseidon, what a height!
Who built it up to that enormous size?

MESSENGER. The birds, none other; no Egyptian, bearing
The bricks, no mason, carpenter was there;
Their own hands wrought it, marvellous to see.
From Libya came some thirty thousand cranes
With great foundation stones they had swallowed down;[36]
And these the corn-crakes fashioned with their beaks.

Ten thousand storks were carrying up the bricks;
And lapwings helped, and the other water-birds,
To bring the water up into the air.

PEISTHETAERUS. Who bare aloft the mortar for them?

MESSENGER. Herons
In hods.

PEISTHETAERUS. But how did they get the mortar in?

MESSENGER. O, that was most ingeniously contrived.
The geese struck down their feet, and slid them under,
Like shovels, and so heaved it on the hods.

PEISTHETAERUS. Then is there anything that *feet* can't do!

MESSENGER. And then the ducks, with girdles round their
waists,
Carried the bricks: and up the swallows flew,
Like serving-lads, carrying behind them, each
His trowel, and the mortar in their mouths.

PEISTHETAERUS. Then why should men hire hirelings any
more!
Well, well, go on; who was it finished off
The great wall's woodwork?

MESSENGER. Canny pelicans,
Excellent workmen, hewing with huge beaks
Gate-timber; and the uproar as they hewed
Was like an arsenal when ships are building.
Now every gateway has its gate, fast-barred,
And watched the whole way round; and birds are pacing
Their beats, and carrying bells, and everywhere
The guards are stationed, and the beacons blaze
On every tower. But I must hurry off
And wash myself. You, manage what remains.

CHORUS. O man, what ails you? Do you feel surprised
To hear the building has been built so soon?

PEISTHETAERUS. By all the Gods I do; and well I may.
In very truth it seems to me like—lies.
But see! a guard, a messenger from thence
Is running towards us with a war-dance look!

GUARD. Hallo! Hallo! Hallo! Hallo! Hallo!

PEISTHETAERUS. Why, what's up now?

GUARD. A terrible thing has happened.
One of the Gods, of Zeus's Gods, has just,
Giving our jackdaw sentinels the slip,
Shot through the gates and flown into the air.

PEISTHETAERUS. A dreadful deed! A wicked scandalous deed!
Which of the Gods?

GUARD. We know not. Wings he had,
So much we know.

PEISTHETAERUS. Ye should have sent at once
The civic guard in hot pursuit.

GUARD. We sent
The mounted archers, thirty thousand falcons,
All with their talons curved, in fighting trim,
Hawk, buzzard, vulture, eagle, eagle-owl.
Yea, Ether vibrates with the whizz and whirr
Of beating pinions, as they seek the God.
Ay, and he's near methinks; he's very near;
He's somewhere here.

PEISTHETAERUS. A sling, a sling, I say!
Arrows and bows! Fall in, my merrymen all!
Shoot, smite, be resolute. A sling! a sling!

CHORUS. War is begun, inexpressive war,
  War is begun twixt the Gods and me!
  Look out, look out, through the cloud-wrapt air
  Which erst the Darkness of Erebus bare,
  Lest a God slip by, and we fail to see.
  Glance eager-eyed on every side,
For close at hand the winged sound I hear
Of some Immortal hurtling through the Sky.

(*After all, the intruder who has caused such a commotion is only poor timorous* IRIS, *who now makes her appearance flying across the stage.*)

PEISTHETAERUS. Hoi! whither away there? whither away?
    Stop! stop!
Stop where you are! keep quiet! stay! remain!
Who, what, whence are you? where do you come from?
    Quick!

IRIS. Whence do I come? From the Olympian Gods.

PEISTHETAERUS. Your name! What is it? Sloop or Head-
dress?[37]

IRIS.   Iris
The fleet.

PEISTHETAERUS. The Paralus, or the Salaminian?[38]

IRIS. Why, what's all this?

PEISTHETAERUS.   Fly up, some buzzard there,
Fly up, and seize her.

IRIS.   Me! Seize *me*, do you say?
What the plague's this?

PEISTHETAERUS.   You'll find to your cost, directly.

IRIS. Well now, this passes!

PEISTHETAERUS.   Answer! By what gates
Got you within the city wall, Miss Minx?

IRIS. I' faith, I know not, fellow, by what gates.

PEISTHETAERUS. You hear the jade, how she prevaricates!
Saw you the daw-commanders? What, no answer?
Where's your stork-pass?

IRIS.   My patience, what do you mean?

PEISTHETAERUS. You never got one?

IRIS.   Have you lost your wits?

PEISTHETAERUS. Did no bird-captain stick a label on you?

IRIS. On *me*? None stuck a label, wretch, on *me*.

PEISTHETAERUS. So then you thought in this sly stealthy way
To fly through Chaos and a realm not yours.

IRIS. And by what route, then, ought the Gods to fly?

PEISTHETAERUS. I' faith, I know not. Only not by this.
This is a trespass! If you got your rights,
Of all the Irises that ever were
You'd be most justly seized and put to death.

IRIS. But I am deathless.

PEISTHETAERUS.   All the same for that
You should have died. A pretty thing, forsooth,
If, whilst all else obey us, you the Gods
Run riot, and forget that you in turn
Must learn to yield obedience to your betters.
But tell me, where do you navigate your wings?

IRIS. I? From the Father to mankind I'm flying,
    To bid them on their bullock-slaughtering hearths
    Slay sheep to the Olympian Gods, and steam
    The streets with savour.

PEISTHETAERUS.   What do you say? What Gods?

IRIS. What Gods? To us, the Gods in Heaven, of course.

PEISTHETAERUS (*with supreme contempt*). What, are *you*
    Gods?

IRIS.   What other Gods exist?

PEISTHETAERUS. Birds are now Gods to men; and men must
    slay
    Victims to them; and not, by Zeus, to Zeus.

IRIS. O fool, fool, fool! Stir not the mighty wrath[39]
    Of angry Gods, lest Justice, with the spade
    Of vengeful Zeus, demolish all thy race,
    And fiery vapour, with Licymnian strokes,
    Incinerate thy palace and thyself!

PEISTHETAERUS. Now listen, girl; have done with that bom-
    bast.
    (Don't move.) A Lydian or a Phrygian is it,[40]
    You think to terrify with words like those?
    Look here. If Zeus keep troubling me, I'll soon
    Incinerate his great Amphion's domes
    And halls of state with eagles carrying fire.
    And up against him, to high heaven, I'll send
    More than six hundred stout Porphyrion rails
    All clad in leopard-skins. Yet I remember
    When one Porphyrion gave him toil enough.
    And as for you, his waiting-maid, if you
    Keep troubling me with your outrageous ways,
    I'll outrage *you,* and you'll be quite surprised
    To find the strength of an old man like me.

IRIS. O shame upon you, wretch, your words and you.

PEISTHETAERUS. Now then begone: shoo, shoo! Eurax patax![41]

IRIS. My father won't stand this; I vow he won't.

PEISTHETAERUS. Now Zeus-a-mercy, maiden; fly you off,
    Incinerate some younger man than I.

    (IRIS *flies back the way she came.*)

CHORUS. Never again shall the Zeus-born Gods,
    Never again shall they pass this way!
    Never again through this realm of ours
    Shall men send up to the heavenly Powers
    The savour of beasts which on earth they slay!

PEISTHETAERUS. Well, but that herald whom we sent to men,
    'Tis strange if he should nevermore return.

(*The* HERALD *enters.*)

HERALD. O Peisthetaerus, O thou wisest, best,
    Thou wisest, deepest, happiest of mankind,
    Most glorious, most—O give the word!

PEISTHETAERUS.   What news?

HERALD. Accept this golden crown, wherewith all peoples
    Crown and revere thee for thy wisdom's sake!

PEISTHETAERUS. I do. What makes them all revere me so?

HERALD. O thou who hast built the ethereal glorious city,
    Dost thou not know how men revere thy name,
    And burn with ardour for this realm of thine?
    Why, till ye built this city in the air,
    All men had gone Laconian-mad; they went
    Long-haired, half-starved, unwashed, Socratified,
    With scytales in their hands; but O the change!
    They are all bird-mad now, and imitate
    The birds, and joy to do whate'er birds do.
    Soon as they rise from bed at early dawn,
    They settle down on laws, as ye on lawns,
    And then they brood upon their leaves and leaflets,
    And feed their fill upon a crop of statutes.
    So undisguised their madness, that full oft
    The names of birds are fastened on to men.
    One limping tradesman now is known as "Partridge";
    They dub Menippus "Swallow"; and Opuntius
    "Blind Raven"; Philocles is "Crested Lark,"
    Theagenes is nicknamed "Sheldrake" now;
    Lycurgus "Ibis"; Chaerephon the "Vampire";
    And Syracosius "Jay"; whilst Meidias there
    Is called the "Quail"; aye and he's like a quail
    Flipped on the head by some quail-filliper.

So fond they are of birds that all are singing
Songs where a swallow figures in the verse,
Or goose, or may-be widgeon, or ring-dove,
Or wings, or even the scantiest shred of feather.
So much from earth. And let me tell you this;
More than ten thousand men will soon be here,
All wanting wings and taloned modes of life.
Somehow or other you must find them wings.

PEISTHETAERUS. O then, by Zeus, no time for dallying now;
Quick, run you in; collect the crates and baskets,
And fill them all with wings; that done, let Manes
Bring me them out; whilst I, remaining here,
Receive the wingless travellers as they come.

(*The* HERALD *goes out.*)

CHORUS. Very soon "fully-manned" will this City be called,
    If men in such numbers invade us.

PEISTHETAERUS. So fortune continue to aid us.

CHORUS. O, the love of my City the world has enthralled!

PEISTHETAERUS (*to* MANES). Bring quicker the baskets they're
    packing.

CHORUS. For in what is it lacking
    That a man for his home can require?
Here is Wisdom, and Wit, and each exquisite Grace,
And here the unruffled, benevolent face
    Of Quiet, and loving Desire.

PEISTHETAERUS. Why, what a lazy loon are you! Come, move
    a little faster, do.
O see that he brings me a basket of wings.
    Rush out in a whirlwind of passion,
    And wallop him, after this fashion.
For the rogue is as slow as a donkey to go.

PEISTHETAERUS. No pluck has your Manes, 'tis true.

CHORUS. But now 'tis for *you*
    The wings in due order to set;
Both the musical wings, and the wings of the seers,
And the wings of the sea, that as each one appears,
    The wings that he wants you can get.

PEISTHETAERUS. O, by the kestrels, I can't keep my hands
From banging you, you lazy, crazy oaf.

(*One of the expected visitors is heard approaching, sing-*
ing some verses from the Oenomaus of Sophocles.)

SIRE-STRIKER (*singing*). O that I might as an eagle be,
Flying, flying, flying, flying
Over the surge of the untilled sea!

PEISTHETAERUS. Not false, methinks, the tale our envoy told
us.
For here comes one whose song is all of eagles.

SIRE-STRIKER. Fie on it!
There's nothing in this world so sweet as flying;
I've quite a passion for these same bird-laws.
In fact I'm gone bird-mad, and fly, and long
To dwell with you, and hunger for your laws.

PEISTHETAERUS. Which of our laws? for birds have many laws.

SIRE-STRIKER. All! All! but most of all that jolly law
Which lets a youngster throttle and beat his father.

PEISTHETAERUS. Aye if a cockerel beat his father here,
We do indeed account him quite a—Man.

SIRE-STRIKER. That's why I moved up hither and would fain
Throttle my father and get all he has.

PEISTHETAERUS. But there's an ancient law among the birds,
You'll find it in the tablets of the storks;
When the old stork has brought his storklings up,
And all are fully fledged for flight, then they
Must in their turn maintain the stork their father.

SIRE-STRIKER. A jolly lot of good I've gained by coming,
If now I've got to feed my father too!

PEISTHETAERUS. Nay, my poor boy, you came here well-dis-
posed,
And so I'll rig you like an orphan bird.[42]
And here's a new suggestion, not a bad one,
But what I learnt myself when I was young.
Don't beat your father, lad; but take his wing,[43]
And grasp this spur of battle in your hand,
And think this crest a game-cock's martial comb.

Now march, keep guard, live on your soldier's pay,
And let your father be. If you want fighting,
Fly off to Thraceward regions, and fight there.

SIRE-STRIKER. By Dionysus, I believe you're right.
I'll do it too.

PEISTHETAERUS.   You'll show your sense, by Zeus!

(*He goes out and* CINESIAS *the dithyrambic poet comes in.
His first line is from Anacreon.*)

CINESIAS (*singing*). On the lightest of wings I am soaring on
high,
    Lightly from measure to measure I fly.

PEISTHETAERUS. Bless me, this creature wants a pack of wings!

CINESIAS (*singing*). And ever the new I am flitting to find,
    With timorless body, and timorless mind.

PEISTHETAERUS. We clasp Cinesias, man of linden-wyth.[44]
Why in the world have you whirled your splay foot
hither?

CINESIAS (*singing*). To be a bird, a bird, I long,
    A nightingale of thrilling song.

PEISTHETAERUS. O stop that singing; prithee speak in prose.

CINESIAS. O give me wings, that I may soar on high,
And pluck poetic fancies from the clouds,
Wild as the whirling winds, and driving snows.

PEISTHETAERUS. What, do you pluck your fancies from the
clouds?

CINESIAS. Why our whole trade depends upon the clouds;
What are our noblest dithyrambs but things
Of air, and mist, and purple-gleaming depths,
And feathery whirlwings? You shall hear, and judge.

PEISTHETAERUS. No, no, I won't.

CINESIAS.   By Heracles you shall.
I'll go through all the air, dear friend, for you.
    (*Singing.*) Shadowy visions of
        Wing-spreading, air-treading,
          Taper-necked birds.

PEISTHETAERUS. Steady, there!

CINESIAS (*singing*). Bounding along on the path to the seas,
    Fain would I float on the stream of the breeze.

PEISTHETAERUS. O by the Powers, I'll stop your streams and
    breezes.

CINESIAS (*singing*). First do I stray on a southerly way;
    Then to the northward my body I bear,
    Cutting a harbourless furrow of air.

(PEISTHETAERUS, *while* CINESIAS *is singing, has been making an elaborate combination of wings with which he now
begins to flap the songster.*)

A nice trick that, a pleasant trick, old man.

PEISTHETAERUS. O, you don't like being feathery-whirl-winged,
    do you?

CINESIAS. That's how you treat the Cyclian-chorus-trainer
    For whose possession all the tribes compete!

PEISTHETAERUS. Well, will you stop and train a chorus here
    For Leotrophides, all flying birds,[45]
    Crake-oppidans?

CINESIAS.   You're jeering me, that's plain.
    But I won't stop, be sure of that, until
    I get me wings, and peragrate the air.

(CINESIAS *disappears and is immediately succeeded by a
Common Informer or* SYCOPHANT. *His first line is adapted
from Alcaeus.*)

SYCOPHANT (*singing*). Who be these on varied wing, birds
    who have not anything?
    O tell me, swallow, tell me, tell me true,
    O long-winged bird, O bird of varied hue!

PEISTHETAERUS. Come, it's no joke, this plague that's broken
    out;
    Here comes another, warbling like the rest.

SYCOPHANT (*singing*). Again I ask thee, tell me, tell me true,
    O long-winged bird, O bird of varied hue!

PEISTHETAERUS. At his own cloak his catch appears to point;
    More than one swallow *that* requires, I'm thinking.

SYCOPHANT. Which is the man that wings the visitors?

PEISTHETAERUS. He stands before you. What do you please to want?

SYCOPHANT. Wings, wings I want. You need not ask me twice.

PEISTHETAERUS. Is it Pellene that you're going to fly to?[46]

SYCOPHANT. No, no: but I'm a sompnour for the Isles, Informer,—

PEISTHETAERUS. O the jolly trade you've got!

SYCOPHANT. And law-suit-hatcher; so I want the wings
To scare the cities, serving writs all round.

PEISTHETAERUS. You'll summon them more cleverly, I suppose,
To the tune of wings?

SYCOPHANT.   No, but to dodge the pirates,
I'll then come flying homeward with the cranes,
First swallowing down a lot of suits for ballast.

PEISTHETAERUS. Is this your business? you, a sturdy youngster,
Live by informing on the stranger-folk?

SYCOPHANT. What can I do? I never learnt to dig.

PEISTHETAERUS. O but, by Zeus, there's many an honest calling
Whence men like you can earn a livelihood,
By means more suitable than hatching suits.

SYCOPHANT. Come, come, no preaching; wing me, wing me, please.

PEISTHETAERUS. I wing you now by talking.

SYCOPHANT.   What, by talk
Can you wing men?

PEISTHETAERUS.   Undoubtedly. By talk
All men are winged.

SYCOPHANT.   All!

PEISTHETAERUS.   Have you never heard
The way the fathers in the barbers' shops
Talk to the children, saying things like these,
*"Diitrephes has winged my youngster so
By specious talk, he's all for chariot-driving."*
"Aye," says another, *"and that boy of mine
Flutters his wings at every Tragic Play."*

SYCOPHANT. So then by talk they are winged.

PEISTHETAERUS.   Exactly so.
Through talk the mind flutters and soars aloft,
And all the man takes wing. And so even now
I wish to turn you, winging you by talk,
To some more honest trade.

SYCOPHANT.   But I *don't* wish.

PEISTHETAERUS. How then?

SYCOPHANT.   I'll not disgrace my bringing up.
I'll ply the trade my father's fathers plied.
So wing me, please, with light quick-darting wings,
Falcon's or kestrel's, so I'll serve my writs
Abroad on strangers; then accuse them here;
Then dart back there again.

PEISTHETAERUS.   I understand.
So when they come, they'll find the suit decided,
And payment ordered.

SYCOPHANT.   Right! you understand.

PEISTHETAERUS. And while they're sailing hither you'll fly
          there,
And seize their goods for payment.

SYCOPHANT.   That's the trick!
Round like a top I'll whizz.

PEISTHETAERUS.   I understand.
A whipping-top; and here by Zeus I've got
Fine Corcyraean wings to set you whizzing.[47]

SYCOPHANT. O, it's a whip!

PEISTHETAERUS.   Nay, friend, a pair of wings,
To set you spinning round and round to-day.
                                        (*Striking him.*)

SYCOPHANT. O! O! O! O!

PEISTHETAERUS.   Come, wing yourself from hence.
Wobble away, you most confounded rascal!
I'll make you spin! I'll law-perverting-trick you!
Now let us gather up the wings and go.

(*They all leave the stage. And the* CHORUS *commence an
account of the wonders they have seen while flying about
the world. The first stanza is a satire on the bulky and
cowardly Cleonymus.*)

CHORUS. We've been flying, we've been flying
    Over sea and land, espying
       Many a wonder strange and new.
    First, a tree of monstrous girth,
    Tall and stout, yet nothing worth,
       For 'tis rotten through and through;
    It has got no heart, and we
    Heard it called "Cleonymus-tree."
    In the spring it blooms gigantic,
    Fig-traducing, sycophantic,
    Yet in falling leaf-time yields
    Nothing but a fall of shields.

    Next a spot by darkness skirted,[48]
    Spot, by every light deserted,
       Lone and gloomy, we descried.
    There the human and divine,
    Men with heroes, mix and dine
       Freely, save at even-tide.
    'Tis not safe for mortal men
    To encounter heroes then.
    Then the great Orestes, looming
    Vast and awful through the glooming,
    On their right a stroke delivering,
    Leaves them palsied, stript, and shivering.

(PEISTHETAERUS *returns just as a suspicious-looking stranger—with his face and head muffled up in such voluminous wrappers that no eye can penetrate his disguise and no voice reach his ears with sufficient distinctness to be clearly understood—enters the stage. He is really* PROMETHEUS.)

PROMETHEUS. O dear! O dear! Pray Heaven that Zeus won't see me!
    Where's Peisthetaerus?

PEISTHETAERUS.   Why, whatever is here?
    What's this enwrapment?

PROMETHEUS.   See you any God
    Following behind me there?

PEISTHETAERUS. Not I, by Zeus.
But who are you?

PROMETHEUS. And what's the time of day?

PEISTHETAERUS. The time of day? A little after noon.
(*Shouting.*) *But who are you?*

PROMETHEUS. Ox-loosing time, or later?[49]

PEISTHETAERUS. Disgusting idiot!

PROMETHEUS. What's Zeus doing now?
The clouds collecting or the clouds dispersing?

PEISTHETAERUS. Out on you, stupid!

PROMETHEUS. Now then, I'll unwrap.

PEISTHETAERUS. My dear Prometheus!

PROMETHEUS. Hush! don't shout like that.

PEISTHETAERUS. Why, what's up now?

PROMETHEUS. Don't speak my name
so loudly.
'Twould be my ruin, if Zeus see me here.
But now I'll tell you all that's going on
Up in the sky, if you'll just take the umbrella,
And hold it over, that no God may see me.

PEISTHETAERUS. Ha! Ha!
The crafty thought! Prometheus-like all over.
Get under then; make haste: and speak out freely.

PROMETHEUS. Then listen.

PEISTHETAERUS. Speak: I'm listening, never fear.

PROMETHEUS. All's up with Zeus!

PEISTHETAERUS. Good gracious me! since when?

PROMETHEUS. Since first you built your city in the air.
For never from that hour does mortal bring
Burnt-offerings to the Gods, or savoury steam
Ascend to heaven from flesh of victims slain.
So now we fast a Thesmophorian fast,
No altars burning; and the Barbarous Gods
Half-starved, and gibbering like Illyrians, vow
That they'll come marching down on Zeus, unless
He gets the marts reopened, and the bits
Of savoury inwards introduced once more.

PEISTHETAERUS. What, are there really other Gods, Barbarians,
Up above you?

PROMETHEUS.   Barbarians? Yes; thence comes
The ancestral God of Execestides.

PEISTHETAERUS. And what's the name of these Barbarian
Gods?

PROMETHEUS. The name? Triballians.

PEISTHETAERUS.   Aye, I understand.
'Tis from that quarter Tribulation comes.

PROMETHEUS. Exactly so. And now I tell you this;
Envoys will soon be here to treat for peace,
Sent down by Zeus and those Triballians there.
But make no peace, mind that, unless king Zeus
Restores the sceptre to the Birds again,
And gives yourself Miss Sovereignty to wife.

PEISTHETAERUS. And who's Miss Sovereignty?

PROMETHEUS.   The loveliest girl.
'Tis she who keeps the thunderbolts of Zeus,
And all his stores,—good counsels, happy laws,
Sound common sense, dockyards, abusive speech,
All his three-obols, and the man who pays them.

PEISTHETAERUS. Then she keeps *everything!*

PROMETHEUS.   Of course she does.
Win her from Zeus, and *you'll* have *everything.*
I hastened here that I might tell you this,
You know I am always well-disposed to men.

PEISTHETAERUS. Aye, but for you we could not fry our fish.

PROMETHEUS. And I hate every God, you know that, don't
you?

PEISTHETAERUS. Yes, hatred of the Gods; you always felt it.

PROMETHEUS. A regular Timon! but 'tis time to go;
Let's have the umbrella; then, if Zeus perceives me,
He'll think I'm following the Basket-bearer.[50]

PEISTHETAERUS. Here, take the chair, and act the Chair-girl
too.

CHORUS. Next time we saw a sight appalling,[51]
          Socrates, unwashed, was calling
          Spirits from the lake below,

> ('Twas on that enchanted ground
> Where the Shadow-feet are found).
> There Peisander came to know
> If the spirit cowards lack
> Socrates could conjure back;
> Then a camel-lamb he slew,[52]
> Like Odysseus, but withdrew,
> Whilst the camel's blood upon
> Pounced the Vampire, Chaerephon.

(The divine envoys, whose approaching visit had been indicated by PROMETHEUS, *now make their appearance. They are three in number,* POSEIDON, HERACLES, *and the uncivilized* TRIBALLIAN.*)*

POSEIDON. There, fellow envoys, full in sight, the town
Whereto we are bound, Cloudcuckoobury, stands!
(*To the* TRIBALLIAN.) You, what are you at, wearing your
cloak left-sided?
Shift it round rightly; so. My goodness, you're
A born Laispodias! O Democracy,[53]
What will you bring us to at last, I wonder,
If voting Gods elect a clown like this!

TRIBALLIAN. Hands off there, will yer?

POSEIDON.   Hang you, you're by far
The uncouthest God I ever came across.
Now, Heracles, what's to be done?

HERACLES.   You have heard
What I propose; I'd throttle the man off-hand,
Whoever he is, that dares blockade the Gods.

POSEIDON. My dear good fellow, you forget we are sent
To treat for peace.

HERACLES.   I'd throttle him all the more.

PEISTHETAERUS (*to Servants*). Hand me the grater; bring the
silphium, you;
Now then, the cheese; blow up the fire a little.

POSEIDON. We three, immortal Gods, with words of greeting
Salute the Man!

PEISTHETAERUS.   I'm grating silphium now.

HERACLES. What's this the flesh of?

PEISTHETAERUS.   Birds! Birds tried and sentenced
For rising up against the popular party
Amongst the birds.

HERACLES.   Then you grate silphium, do you,
Over them first.

PEISTHETAERUS.   O welcome, Heracles!
What brings you hither?

POSEIDON.   We are envoys, sent
Down by the Gods to settle terms of peace.

SERVANT. There's no more oil remaining in the flask.

HERACLES. O dear! and birds-flesh should be rich and glister-
         ing.

POSEIDON. We Gods gain nothing by the war; and you,
Think what ye'll get by being friends with us;
Rain-water in pools, and halcyon days
Shall be your perquisites the whole year through.
We've ample powers to settle on these terms.

PEISTHETAERUS. It was not we who ever wished for war,
And now, if even now ye come prepared
With fair proposals, ye will find us ready
To treat for peace. What I call fair is this;
Let Zeus restore the sceptre to the birds,
And all make friends. If ye accept this offer,
I ask the envoys in to share our banquet.

HERACLES. I'm altogether satisfied, and vote—

POSEIDON (*interrupting*). What, wretch? A fool and glutton,
                 that's what *you* are!
What! would you rob your father of his kingdom?

PEISTHETAERUS. Aye, say you so? Why, ye'll be mightier far,
Ye Gods above, if Birds bear rule below.
Now men go skulking underneath the clouds,
And swear false oaths, and call the Gods to witness.
But when ye've got the Birds for your allies,
If a man swear by the Raven and by Zeus,
The Raven will come by, and unawares
Fly up, and swoop, and peck the perjurer's eye out.

POSEIDON. Now by Poseidon there's some sense in that.

HERACLES. And so say I.

PEISTHETAERUS (*to* TRIBALLIAN). And you?

TRIBALLIAN.   Persuasitree.

PEISTHETAERUS. You see? he quite assents. And now I'll give
  you
  Another instance of the good ye'll gain.
  If a man vow a victim to a God,
  And then would shuffle off with cunning words,
  Saying, in greedy lust, *The Gods wait long*,
  This too we'll make him pay you.

POSEIDON.   Tell me how?

PEISTHETAERUS. Why, when that man is counting out his
  money,
  Or sitting in his bath, a kite shall pounce
  Down unawares, and carry off the price
  Of two fat lambs, and bear it to the God.

HERACLES. I say again, I vote we give the sceptre
  Back to the Birds.

POSEIDON.   Ask the Triballian next.

HERACLES. You there, do you want a drubbing?

TRIBALLIAN.   Hideythine
  I'se stickybeatums.

HERACLES.   There! he's all for me.

POSEIDON. Well then, if so you wish it, so we'll have it.

HERACLES (*to* PEISTHETAERUS). Hi! we accept your terms
  about the sceptre.

PEISTHETAERUS. By Zeus, there's one thing more I've just
  remembered.
  Zeus may retain his Hera, if he will,
  But the young girl, Miss Sovereignty, he must
  Give me to wife.

POSEIDON.   This looks not like a treaty.
  Let us be journeying homewards.

PEISTHETAERUS.   As you will.
  Now, cook, be sure you make the gravy rich.

HERACLES. Why, man alive, Poseidon, where are you off to?
  What, are we going to fight about one woman?

POSEIDON. What shall we do?

HERACLES.   Do? Come to terms at once.

POSEIDON. You oaf, he's gulling you, and you can't see it.
Well, it's yourself you are ruining. If Zeus
Restore the kingdom to the Birds, and die,
You'll be a pauper. You are the one to get
Whatever money Zeus may leave behind him.

PEISTHETAERUS. O! O! the way he's trying to cozen you!
Hist, step aside, I want to whisper something.
Your uncle's fooling you, poor dupe. By law
No shred of all your father's money falls
To you. Why, you're a bastard, you're not heir.

HERACLES. Eh! What? A bastard? I?

PEISTHETAERUS.   Of course you are.
Your mother was an alien. Bless the fool,
How did you think Athene could be "Heiress,"
(Being a girl), if she had lawful brethren?

HERACLES. Well, but suppose my father leaves me all
As bastard's heritage?

PEISTHETAERUS.   The law won't let him.
Poseidon here, who now excites you on,
Will be the first to claim the money then,
As lawful brother, and your father's heir.
Why here, I'll read you Solon's law about it.
   "A bastard is to have no right of inheritance, if there
      be lawful children. And if there be no lawful chil-
      dren, the goods are to fall to the next of kin."

HERACLES. What! none of all my father's goods to fall
To me?

PEISTHETAERUS. No, not one farthing! tell me this,
Has he enrolled you ever in the guild?

HERACLES. He never has. I've often wondered why.

PEISTHETAERUS. Come, don't look up assault-and-battery-wise.
Join *us*, my boy; I'll make you autocrat,
And feed you all your days on pigeon's milk.

HERACLES. I'm quite convinced you're right about the girl;
I said Restore her; and I say so now.

PEISTHETAERUS (*to* POSEIDON). And what say you?

POSEIDON.   I vote the other way.

PEISTHETAERUS. All rests with this Triballian. What say you?

TRIBALLIAN. Me gulna charmi grati Sovranau
    Birdito stori.

HERACLES.   There! he said Restore her.

POSEIDON. O no by Zeus, he never said Restore her;
    He said to migrate as the swallows do.

HERACLES. O then he said Restore her to the swallows.

POSEIDON. You two conclude, and settle terms of peace,
    Since you both vote it, I will say no more.

HERACLES (*to* PEISTHETAERUS). We're quite prepared to give
    you all you ask.
So come along, come up to heaven yourself,
And take Miss Sovereignty and all that's there.

PEISTHETAERUS. So then these birds were slaughtered just in
    time
To grace our wedding banquet.

HERACLES.   Would you like me
    To stay, and roast the meat, while you three go?

POSEIDON. To *roast* the meat! To *taste* the meat, you mean.
Come along, do.

HERACLES.   I'd have enjoyed it though.

PEISTHETAERUS. Ho there within! bring out a wedding robe.

(*They all leave the stage.*)

CHORUS. In the fields of Litigation,[54]
        Near the Water-clock, a nation
          With its tongue its belly fills;
        With its tongue it sows and reaps,
        Gathers grapes and figs in heaps,
          With its tongue the soil it tills.
        For a Barbarous tribe it passes,
        Philips all and Gorgiases.
        And from this tongue-bellying band
        Everywhere on Attic land,
        People who a victim slay
        Always cut the tongue away.

(A MESSENGER *comes from the sky to announce the return of* PEISTHETAERUS *and* MISS SOVEREIGNTY.*)*

MESSENGER. O all-successful, more than tongue can tell!
O ye, thrice blessed wingèd race of birds,
Welcome your King returning to his halls!
He comes; no Star has ever gleamed so fair,
Sparkling refulgent in its gold-rayed home.
The full far-flashing splendour of the Sun
Ne'er shone so gloriously as he, who comes
Bringing a bride too beautiful for words,
Wielding the wingèd thunderbolt of Zeus.
Up to Heaven's highest vault, sweet sight, ascends
Fragrance ineffable; while gentlest airs
The fume of incense scatter far and wide.
He comes; he is here! Now let the heavenly Muse
Open her lips with pure auspicious strains.

(The bride and bridegroom enter.)

CHORUS. Back with you! out with you! off with you! up with
          you!
                    Flying around
Welcome the Blessèd with blessedness crowned.
     O! O! for the youth and the beauty, O!
Well hast thou wed for the town of the Birds.

Great are the blessings, and mighty, and wonderful,
     Which through his favour our nation possesses.
Welcome them back, both himself and Miss Sovereignty,
     Welcome with nuptial and bridal addresses.

          Mid just such a song hymenaean
          Aforetime the Destinies led
          The King of the thrones empyréan,
          The Ruler of Gods, to the bed
          Of Hera his beautiful bride.
          Hymen, O Hymenaeus!
          And Love, with his pinions of gold,
          Came driving, all blooming and spruce,
          As groomsman and squire to behold[55]

The wedding of Hera and Zeus,
Of Zeus and his beautiful bride.
Hymen, O Hymenaeus!
Hymen, O Hymenaeus!

PEISTHETAERUS. I delight in your hymns, I delight in your
　　　　songs;
　　　　Your words I admire.

CHORUS. Now sing of the trophies he brings us from Heaven,
The earth-crashing thunders, deadly and dire,
And the lightning's angry flashes of fire,
And the dread white bolt of the levin.

Blaze of the lightning, so terribly beautiful,
　　　　　　　　　Golden and Grand!
Fire-flashing javelin, glittering ever in
　　　　　　　　　Zeus's right hand!
Earth-crashing thunder, the hoarsely resounding, the
　　　　　　　　　Bringer of showers!
He is your Master, 'tis he that is shaking the
　　　　　　　　　Earth with your powers!

All that was Zeus's of old
Now is our hero's alone;
Sovereignty, fair to behold,
Partner of Zeus on his throne,
Now is for ever his own.
Hymen, O Hymenaeus!

PEISTHETAERUS. Now follow on, dear feathered tribes,
To see us wed, to see us wed;
Mount up to Zeus's golden floor,
And nuptial bed, and nuptial bed.
And O, my darling, reach thine hand,
And take my wing and dance with me,
And I will lightly bear thee up,
And carry thee, and carry thee.

CHORUS. Raise the joyous Paean-cry,
Raise the song of Victory.
Io Paean, alalalae,
Mightiest of the Powers, to thee!

1. *Even Execestides.* A man so clever in finding a fatherland that, though a Carian slave, he managed to find one in Athens itself, and passed himself off as a genuine Athenian citizen.

2. *In that same market.* The actor, as in the comedies of Aristophanes so frequently happens, is speaking in his own person, and not in the character he represents in the drama. The hoopoe, whom the adventurers are seeking, is really another actor, and how then has he become a bird? By means of plumage which, like the jackdaw and the crow themselves, was obtained from the bird market. Those two birds might not unreasonably be expected to find out the person disguised in feathers which had come from the same small stall as themselves.

3. *Son of Tharreleides.* This is undoubtedly a skit on some person of diminutive stature, whether that person was Tharreleides himself, or his son Asopodorus.

4. *To the Ravens.* The way to go to the ravens (in the sense of our English expression "to go to the dogs") was far too easily found out by many a young Athenian; whilst these two elderly and highly respectable citizens, however much they may desire to go to the ravens (that is, to the realm of the birds), are quite unable to find out the way.

5. *Sacas.* This was Acestor, the tragic poet, who was nicknamed Sacas from the strain of Scythian blood he was supposed to have in his veins; for the Persians, says Herodotus, vii, 64, call all the Scythians by this name of Sacas.

6. *Scellias' son.* I.e., Aristocrates. He did in fact afterwards become one of the most prominent leaders of the aristocratical party. He took part in the oligarchic Revolution

of the Four Hundred, was an influential member of that body, but ultimately seceded from it with Theramenes.

7. *The Salaminian*. The galley dispatched in the autumn of 415 B.C. (some five or six months before the exhibition of *The Birds*) to bring back Alcibiades, just as he was approaching the Sicilian coast at the head of the great Athenian armament. And the observation of Euelpides was doubtless intended to remind the spectators of that dramatic and most momentous event.

8. *Melanthius*. The obnoxious tragic poet was said to be afflicted with leprosy. *Opuntius* was a one-eyed common informer.

9. *The lapwing's trick*. The Bird-call has met with no response, and Peisthetaerus suggests that just as the plover, to divert attention from her nest, flies to some distant spot and calls as if to her young, where her young are not; so the Hoopoe has gone into the copse and whooped for birds where no birds are. It is in the absence of response, and not in its tone, that the Bird-call is said to resemble the cry of the lapwing.

10. *Grandsire*. We must imagine three generations of hoopoes: (1) the speaker, who considers himself the Tereus of Sophocles; (2) the Tereus or hoopoe of Philocles; (3) the dilapidated creature now before them. The object of this little fictitious pedigree is to show that the grandfather and grandson both bore the same name, and so to afford an opportunity for a fling at Callias. The intermediate name, the name of the *father*, is for this purpose unimportant.

11. *Callias*. The profligate and prodigal Callias was a familiar figure in Athenian literature. In his house Plato laid the scene of his *Protagoras*, and Xenophon the scene of his *Symposium*.

12. *A Glutton*. This is a fictitious bird, invented to throw ridicule upon Cleonymus. Here two charges are combined: his voracity and his cowardice.

13. *Sporgilus*. A barber, and doubtless also a "bird" within the definition of Teleas above. To bring an owl to Athens

where owls were so numerous was proverbial in the sense of "carrying coals to Newcastle."

14. *Eleleleu!* This was the regular war cry with which Hellenic troops were accustomed to charge the enemy.

15. *Clansmen of my mate.* For these were Athenians, and Procne, the Hoopoe's wife, was a daughter of Pandion King of Athens.

16. *Cerameicus.* For *there* were buried, at the public cost, all those who had fallen in battle for Athens. All, with one notable exception. The men who fell at Marathon were for their pre-eminent valour, buried on the battlefield which they had made forever memorable.

17. *Orneae.* A town in Argolis. It is selected here because its name is similar to the Greek word for "bird" (*ornis*).

18. *You and you.* Matters having thus taken a pacific turn, the Hoopoe calls two of the theatrical attendants and directs them to carry back the spit, the platters, and the pot into the kitchen from which they had originally been taken.

19. *Tiara.* The tiara was the ordinary Persian head-dress, but only the king might wear it erect.

20. *The softest of Phrygians.* Euelpides had naturally donned his smartest attire for the Tenth-day feast. Phrygian fleeces were famous not merely for their superior quality, but for the brilliant colouring imparted to them by the dyers of Asia Minor. And the Tenth-day feast, the feast for the naming of the child, was a specially festive occasion.

21. *Cuckoo! To the plain! Cuckoo!* The tale about the influence which the advent of the cuckoo is supposed to exercise upon the circumcised peoples of Phoenicia and Egypt is merely intended to lead up to this vulgar phrase with which Euelpides immediately caps it. The phrase was no doubt in vogue among the rustics of Attica, not referring to the rite of circumcision at all, but calling on the lusty youths, when the voice of the cuckoo was heard in the land, to give over their pleasures and be off to their work in the fields.

22. *Lysicrates,* the Scholiast tells us, was a dishonest rogue always open to bribes. His name is introduced here as a surprise.

23. *Lampon.* A famous soothsayer of the day.

24. *Zan.* This is the Doric name for Zeus.

25. *At a Tragic Chorus.* The dramatic contests extended over three consecutive days, one tragic trilogy being performed in the forenoon, and one Comedy in the afternoon, of each day.

26. *Diitrephes.* An Athenian general, who had made his fortune by the manufacture of wicker flasks, the handles of which were called wings.

27. *Theagenes and Aeschines.* Two needy braggarts, perpetually boasting of their wealth, which, not being apparent, might therefore perhaps be found in this city of clouds and cuckoos.

28. *Whose name is the same.* This is a quotation from Pindar, who played thus on Hiero's name.

29. *Colonus.* Not the village about a mile to the northwest of Athens, but an eminence in the Athenian Agora, where Meton had recently erected a horologe worked by water.

30. *Pharnaces.* The satrap of the northwest provinces of Asia Minor, during the earlier period of the Peloponnesian War.

31. *For next Munychion.* That is, for the sittings of the law courts next April or May.

32. *Diagoras.* It was in the year in which this comedy was exhibited that Diagoras the Melian, being accused of impiety, fled from Athens, and a resolution was passed setting a price upon his head.

33. *To Alexander.* The gifts offered will be nobler far than those offered to Paris, or Alexander, by the three goddesses, Hera, Athene, and Aphrodite.

34. *Lauriotic owlets.* Athenian coins were stamped on the front with the head of Athene, and on the reverse with the figure of an owl and the letters ΑΘΗ or ΑΘΕ. And as the silver of which they were made came from the mines of Laureium, Aristophanes calls the coins themselves Lauriotic owls.

35. *With true Alpheian panting.* Panting like a runner in the Olympian races on the banks of the river Alpheius.

36. *They had swallowed.* He is alluding here to the popular belief that cranes swallowed pebbles to serve as ballast and keep them steady in their migrations over the Mediterranean Sea.

37. *Sloop or Head-dress.* Owing to her rapid movement through the air, her long robes, probably brilliant with all the colors of the rainbow, float back like a schooner's sails, and with her wings outspread and her hair, with the ribbons and fillets, streaming behind her like pennons from a masthead, she looks like a stately ship sailing onward with all haste, or a gay bedizened head-dress.

38. *Iris the fleet.* "Fleet" was a sort of technical name, as applied to a ship. To Peisthetaerus, therefore, the name "Iris the fleet" sounds, or he pretends that it sounds, like an affirmative answer to the question "Is she a sloop?" and he further puzzles the bewildered damsel by demanding whether she is one of those specially fleet vessels, the Paralus or the Salaminian.

39. *O fool, fool, fool!* At this audacious pronouncement of Peisthetaerus, Iris starts off in a vein of high tragedy. Her language is partly borrowed from the ancient tragedians, partly composed in imitation of their style. For a thunderbolt Iris substitutes "Licymnian strokes." The allusion here is to the "Licymnius" of Euripides, in which somebody, or something, was destroyed by lightning.

40. *Don't move.* Iris, for all her brave words, is evidently quaking at the menacing tone and gesture of Peisthetaerus, and is timorously spreading her wings to fly out of his reach, when he thus bids her to keep still.

41. *Eurax patax.* An exclamation intended to imitate, and accompany, the clapping of hands.

42. *Like an orphan bird.* Aristophanes is referring to a very remarkable and imposing ceremony which the audience had been witnessing, in the theatre itself, at the opening of these very performances. For it was at the Great Dionysia, "when the tragedies were about to commence," as Aeschines says, "that a herald came forward with a band of youths clad in shining armour, and made a proclamation than which none could be nobler, none a greater

incentive to patriotic virtue, saying: These are the orphans of brave men who fell in battle, valiantly fighting in their country's cause. Wherefore the City of Athens has maintained them during their boyhood, and now having armed them in full panoply dismisses them with her blessing to their homes, and invites them to a front seat in the theatre" (*Against Ctesiphon,* 154). Doubtless they would retain their front seat in the theatre during the dramatic contest, so that these very orphans, accoutred as they were, would be sitting in full view of actors and audience at the very moment when Peisthetaerus was arming in full panoply (to use the words of Aeschines) the youthful Athenian before him.

43. *Wing.* The wing is a shield, the spur a sword, and the cock's comb a soldier's helmet.

44. *Linden-wyth.* An allusion to the extreme thinness of Cinesias.

45. *Leotrophides.* An Athenian of extremely light and birdlike make, often mentioned by the comic poets. *Crakeoppidans,* in the following line, is a play on "Cecropids," a well-known Athenian tribe.

46. *Pellene* was famous for its soft woolen robes. The Sycophant, it is suggested, must be anxious to exchange his torn and tattered cloak for some warmer garment.

47. *Corcyraean wings.* He produces a double-thonged Corcyraean scourge.

48. The second stanza deals with the noted highway-robber Orestes; and the humour of it consists in speaking of the nightly thief as if he were the hero whose name he bore. The Chorus describe a rendezvous of thieves situated in some region of darkness (really of course in some obscure part of Athens), where in the daytime you might with impunity meet Orestes, or, as they word it, consort with heroes. When it grew dark, however, it would be safer to keep out of his way. There was a superstition that if after nightfall you met the ghost of a departed hero, such as was Orestes, the son of Agamemnon, you might find your right side smitten with paralysis; and the Chorus observe that if after nightfall you were to meet Orestes the

Athenian robber, you might find not only your right side smitten, but your cloak gone as well.

49. *Ox-loosing time*. That is, eventide. Prometheus does not hear a word that Peisthetaerus says, so that the conversation is a series of cross-questions and crooked answers.

50. *The Basket-bearer*. He means the noble Athenian maiden who, for her grace and loveliness, no less than for her rank and virtue, was selected to bear the Sacred Basket in a religious procession. She was followed by a girl carrying her chair, and by another maiden carrying an umbrella to protect her from the sun.

51. The third stanza is a satire on the cowardice of Peisander. Socrates is described as calling up spirits, in the sense of dead men's ghosts. Peisander has lost his spirit, in the sense of courage, and comes to know if Socrates can call it back again. In order to see his lost spirit again, Peisander has to go through the process through which Odysseus went, in the Eleventh Odyssey, when he summoned up the souls (spirits) of the dead, in order to see Teiresias. He goes through the task well enough till the test of his courage begins; but he dared not remain, like Odysseus, to keep the ghosts from the blood till his own spirit came into sight; he turned and fled, leaving the road open to the dried-up, ghost-like Chaerephon.

52. A *camel-lamb*. I.e., a huge lamb, with an allusion to the size of Peisander himself.

53. *Laispodias*. An Athenian general who, having a stiff or withered leg, wore his cloak awry to conceal the defect.

54. The fourth and last stanza is concerned with a strange tribe of barbarians who settle down in Phanae (which here means "Informer's land") near the Water-clock (which timed the speeches of the pleaders in the law courts) and sow and reap with their tongues. They are connected with the famous sophist Gorgias, and Philip, his son or disciple.

55. *Groomsman*. The groomsman was the bridegroom's "best man," who drove with him to fetch the bride from her home.

THE FROGS

The Frogs was produced during the Lenaean festival at the commencement of the year 405 B.C. It at once took its position, which has never since been challenged amongst the masterpieces of the Athenian drama. It carried off the prize at the Lenaean contest, and the victorious poet was crowned in the full theatre with the usual wreath of Bacchic ivy. But it achieved a far higher success than this. It enjoyed the apparently unique distinction of being acted a second time, as we should say, by *request;* and at this second representation the poet was again crowned, not now with mere leaves of ivy, but with a wreath made from Athene's sacred olive, an honour reserved for citizens who were deemed to have rendered important services to Athene's city.

It was not for its wit and humour that these exceptional honours were accorded to the play; nor yet for what to modern readers constitutes its pre-eminent attraction, the literary contest between Aeschylus and Euripides. It was for the lofty strain of patriotism which breathed through all its political allusions, and was especially felt in the advice tendered, obviously with some misgiving as to the spirit in which the audience would receive it, by the Chorus. The poet appeals to the Athenian people to forget all party animosities, to forget and forgive all political offences, to place the state on a broader basis, to leave no Athenian disenfranchised. More particularly, he pleads for those who, having been implicated in the establishment of the Council of Four Hundred in 411 B.C., had ever since been deprived of all civic rights.

The play was acted out about six months after the great naval victory of Arginusae; about four months after the death of Euripides; and about two months after the death of Sophocles.

The poetical contest between Aeschylus and Euripides has always formed a most important, and to modern readers probably the most interesting, section of *The Frogs*. It consists of four distinct trials of strength, divided from each other by choral songs, the rivals discussing (1) their general merits and demerits, (2) their prologues, (3) their choral metres, and (4) the weight of their iambic verses.

Characters of the Drama

XANTHIAS, slave of Dionysus

DIONYSUS

HERACLES

A CORPSE

CHARON

CHORUS OF FROGS

MYSTIC CHORUS OF INITIATES

AEACUS

A MAID SERVANT of Persephone

HOSTESS of a cook-shop

PLATHANE

EURIPIDES

AESCHYLUS

PLUTO

THE FROGS

A house in the background is the residence of HERACLES.
*Two travellers are seen entering on the stage, one riding
on a donkey, the other walking by his side. The pedestrian
is* DIONYSUS, *the patron deity of theatrical performances,
who, in addition to the yellow robe and buskins which
formed part of his ordinary attire, has assumed for the
nonce the formidable club and lion's skin of* HERACLES.
The rider is his slave XANTHIAS, *who is carrying on a pole
over his shoulder a traveller's ordinary luggage.*

XANTHIAS. Shall I crack any of those old jokes, master,
At which the audience never fail to laugh?

DIONYSUS. Aye, what you will, except *I'm getting crushed:*
Fight shy of that: I'm sick of that already.

XANTHIAS. Nothing else smart?

DIONYSUS.   Aye, save *my shoulder's aching.*

XANTHIAS. Come now, that comical joke?[1]

DIONYSUS.   With all my heart.
Only be careful not to shift your pole,
And—

XANTHIAS. What?

DIONYSUS.   And vow that you've a belly-ache.

XANTHIAS. May I not say I'm overburdened so
That if none ease me, I must ease myself?

DIONYSUS. For mercy's sake, not till I'm going to vomit.

XANTHIAS. What! must I bear these burdens, and not make
One of the jokes Ameipsias and Lycis
And Phrynichus, in every play they write,[2]
Put in the mouths of all their burden-bearers?

DIONYSUS. Don't make them; no! I tell you when I see
    Their plays, and hear those jokes, I come away
    More than a twelvemonth older than I went.

XANTHIAS. O thrice unlucky neck of mine, which now
    Is *getting crushed,* yet must not crack its joke!

DIONYSUS. Now is not this fine pampered insolence
    When I myself, Dionysus, son of—Pipkin,[3]
    Toil on afoot, and let this fellow ride,
    Taking no trouble, and no burden bearing?

XANTHIAS. What, don't I bear?

DIONYSUS.   How can you when you're riding?

XANTHIAS. Why, I bear these.

DIONYSUS.   How?

XANTHIAS.   Most unwillingly.

DIONYSUS. Does not the donkey bear the load you're bearing?

XANTHIAS. Not what I bear myself: by Zeus, not he.

DIONYSUS. How can you bear, when you are borne yourself?

XANTHIAS. Don't know: but anyhow *my shoulder's aching.*

DIONYSUS. Then since you say the donkey helps you not,
    You lift him up and carry him in turn.

XANTHIAS. O hang it all! why didn't I fight at sea?[4]
    You should have smarted bitterly for this.

DIONYSUS. Get down, you rascal (XANTHIAS *dismounts.*); I've
    been trudging on
    Till now I've reached the portal, where I'm going
    First to turn in. Boy! Boy! I say there, Boy!

    (*Enter* HERACLES.)

HERACLES. Who banged the door? How like a prancing Cen-
    taur
    He drove against it! Mercy o' me, what's this?

DIONYSUS. Boy.

XANTHIAS.   Yes.

DIONYSUS.   Did you observe?

XANTHIAS.   What?

DIONYSUS.   How alarmed
    He is.

XANTHIAS. Aye truly, lest you've lost your wits.

HERACLES. O by Demeter, I can't choose but laugh.
  Biting my lips won't stop me. Ha! ha! ha!

DIONYSUS. Pray you, come hither, I have need of you.

HERACLES. I vow I can't help laughing, I can't help it.
  A lion's hide upon a yellow silk,
  A club and buskin! What's it all about?
  Where were you going?

DIONYSUS.   I was serving lately
  Aboard the—Cleisthenes.[5]

HERACLES.   And fought?

DIONYSUS.   And sank
  More than a dozen of the enemy's ships.

HERACLES. You two?

DIONYSUS.   We two.

HERACLES.   And then I awoke, and lo!

DIONYSUS. There as, on deck, I'm reading to myself
  The Andromeda, a sudden pang of longing[6]
  Shoots through my heart, you can't conceive how keenly.

HERACLES. How big a pang?

DIONYSUS.   A small one, Molon's size.[7]

HERACLES. Caused by a woman?

DIONYSUS.   No.

HERACLES.   A boy?

DIONYSUS.   No, no.

HERACLES. A man?

DIONYSUS.   Ah! ah!

HERACLES.   Was it for Cleisthenes?

DIONYSUS. Don't mock me, brother: on my life I am
  In a bad way: such fierce desire consumes me.

HERACLES. Aye, little brother? how?

DIONYSUS.   I can't describe it.
  But yet I'll tell you in a riddling way.
  Have you e'er felt a sudden lust for soup?

HERACLES. Soup! Zeus-a-mercy, yes, ten thousand times.

DIONYSUS. Is the thing clear, or must I speak again?

HERACLES. Not of the soup: I'm clear about the soup.

DIONYSUS. Well, just that sort of pang devours my heart
 For lost Euripides.

HERACLES.   A dead man too!

DIONYSUS. And no one shall persuade me not to go
 After the man.

HERACLES.   Do you mean below, to Hades?

DIONYSUS. And lower still, if there's a lower still.

HERACLES. What on earth for?

DIONYSUS.   I want a genuine poet,
 "For some are not, and those that are, are bad."[8]

HERACLES. What! does not Iophon live?[9]

DIONYSUS.   Well, he's the sole
 Good thing remaining, if even he is good.
 For even of that I'm not exactly certain.

HERACLES. If go you must, there's Sophocles—he comes
 Before Euripides—why not take *him*?

DIONYSUS. Not till I've tried if Iophon's coin rings true
 When he's alone, apart from Sophocles.
 Besides, Euripides, the crafty rogue,
 Will find a thousand shifts to get away,

HERACLES. But *he* was easy here, is easy there.
 But Agathon, where is he?[10]

DIONYSUS.   He has gone and left us.
 A genial poet, by his friends much missed.

HERACLES. Gone where?

DIONYSUS.   To join the blessed in their banquets.

HERACLES. But what of Xenocles?

DIONYSUS.   O he be hanged!

HERACLES. Pythangelus?

XANTHIAS.   But never a word of me,
 Not though my shoulder's chafed so terribly.

HERACLES. But have you not a shoal of little songsters,
 Tragedians by the myriad, who can chatter
 A furlong faster than Euripides?

DIONYSUS. Those be mere vintage-leavings, jabberers, choirs
    Of swallow-broods, degraders of their art,
    Who get one chorus, and are seen no more,[11]
    The Muses' love once gained. But O, my friend,
    Search where you will, you'll never find a true
    Creative genius, uttering startling things.

HERACLES. Creative? how do you mean?

DIONYSUS.   I mean a man
    Who'll dare some novel venturesome conceit,
    Air, Zeus's chamber, or *Time's foot,* or this,[12]
    'Twas not my mind that swore: my tongue committed
    A little perjury on its own account.

HERACLES. You like that style?

DIONYSUS.   Like it? I dote upon it.

HERACLES. I vow it's ribald nonsense, and you know it.

DIONYSUS. "Rule not my mind": you've got a house to mind.

HERACLES. Really and truly though 'tis paltry stuff.

DIONYSUS. Teach me to dine!

XANTHIAS.   But never a word of me.

DIONYSUS. But tell me truly—'twas for this I came
    Dressed up to mimic you—what friends received
    And entertained you when you went below
    To bring back Cerberus, in case I need them.
    And tell me too the havens, fountains, shops,
    Roads, resting-places, stews, refreshment rooms,
    Towns, lodgings, hostesses, with whom were found
    The fewest bugs.

XANTHIAS.   But never a word of me.

HERACLES. You are really game to go?

DIONYSUS.   O drop that, can't you?
    And tell me this: of all the roads you know
    Which is the quickest way to get to Hades?
    I want one not too warm, nor yet too cold.

HERACLES. Which shall I tell you first? which shall it be?
    There's one rope and bench: you launch away
    And—hang yourself.

DIONYSUS.   No thank you: that's too stifling.

HERACLES. Then there's a track, a short and beaten cut,
  By pestle and mortar.

DIONYSUS.   Hemlock, do you mean?

HERACLES. Just so.

DIONYSUS.   No, that's too deathly cold a way;
  You have hardly started ere your shins get numbed.

HERACLES. Well, would you like a steep and swift descent?

DIONYSUS. Aye, that's the style: my walking powers are small.

HERACLES. Go down to the Cerameicus.[13]

DIONYSUS.   And do what?

HERACLES. Climb to the tower's top pinnacle—

DIONYSUS.   And then?

HERACLES. Observe the torch-race started, and when all
  The multitude is shouting *Let them go,*
  Let yourself go.

DIONYSUS.   Go! whither?

HERACLES.   To the ground.

DIONYSUS. And lose, forsooth, two envelopes of brain.
  I'll not try that.

HERACLES.   Which *will* you try?

DIONYSUS.   The way
  You went yourself.

HERACLES.   A parlous voyage that,
  For first you'll come to an enormous lake[14]
  Of fathomless depth.

DIONYSUS.   And how am I to cross?

HERACLES. An ancient mariner will row you over[15]
  In a wee boat, *so* big. The fare's two obols.

DIONYSUS. Fie! The power two obols have, the whole world
              through!
  How came they thither!

HERACLES.   Theseus took them down.
  And next you'll see great snakes and savage monsters
  In tens of thousands.

DIONYSUS.   You needn't try to scare me,
  I'm going to go.

HERACLES.   Then weltering seas of filth
    And ever-rippling dung: and plunged therein,
    Whoso has wronged the stranger here on earth,
    Or robbed his boylove of the promised pay,
    Or swinged his mother, or profanely smitten
    His father's cheek, or sworn an oath forsworn,
    Or copied out a speech of Morsimus.[16]

DIONYSUS. There too, perdie, should *he* be plunged, whoe'er
    Has danced the sword-dance of Cinesias.[17]

HERACLES. And next the breath of flutes will float around you,
    And glorious sunshine, such as ours, you'll see,
    And myrtle groves, and happy bands who clap
    Their hands in triumph, men and women too.

DIONYSUS. And who are they?

HERACLES.   The happy mystic bands,

XANTHIAS. And I'm the donkey in the mystery show.
    But I'll not stand it, not one instant longer.

HERACLES. Who'll tell you everything you want to know.
    You'll find them dwelling close beside the road
    You are going to travel, just at Pluto's gate.
    And fare thee well, my brother.   (*Exit* HERACLES.)

DIONYSUS.   And to you
    Good cheer. (*To* XANTHIAS.) Now sirrah, pick you up the
        traps.

XANTHIAS. Before I've put them down?

DIONYSUS.   And quickly too.

XANTHIAS. No, prithee, no: but hire a body, one
    They're carrying out, on purpose for the trip.

DIONYSUS. If I can't find one?

XANTHIAS.   Then I'll take them.

DIONYSUS.   Good.

(*A* CORPSE, *wrapped in its grave-clothes, and lying on a
bier, is carried across the stage.*)

And see! they are carrying out a body now.
Hallo! you there, you deadman, are you willing
To carry down our little traps to Hades?

CORPSE. What are they?

DIONYSUS.   These.

CORPSE.   Two drachmas for the job.

DIONYSUS. Nay, that's too much.

CORPSE.   Out of the pathway, you!

DIONYSUS. Beshrew thee, stop: may-be we'll strike a bargain.

CORPSE. Pay me two drachmas, or it's no use talking.

DIONYSUS. One and a half.

CORPSE.   I'd liefer live again!

(*The* CORPSE *is carried off.*)

XANTHIAS. How absolute the knave is! He be hanged!
    I'll go myself.

DIONYSUS.   You're the right sort, my man.
    Now to the ferry.

(CHARON *is heard behind the scenes. In another moment
the scene is changed; a landscape, representing the
Acherusian Lake, being unrolled from the revolving pillar
on one side of the stage till it reaches the revolving pillar
on the other, so as to cover the entire background; whilst
* CHARON *with his ferryboat is visible in front.*)

CHARON.   Yoh, up! lay her to.

XANTHIAS. Whatever's that?

DIONYSUS.   Why, that's the lake, by Zeus,
    Whereof he spake, and yon's the ferry-boat.

XANTHIAS. Poseidon, yes, and that old fellow's Charon.

DIONYSUS. Charon! O welcome, Charon! welcome, Charon.

CHARON. Who's for the Rest from every pain and ill?[18]
    Who's for the Lethe's plain? the Donkey-shearings?
    Who's for Cerberia? Taenarum? or the Ravens?

DIONYSUS. I.

CHARON.   Hurry in.

DIONYSUS.   But where are you going really?
    In truth to the Ravens?

CHARON.   Aye, for your behoof.
    Step in.

DIONYSUS (*to* XANTHIAS). Now, lad.

CHARON. A slave? I take no slave,
Unless he has fought for his bodyrights at sea.

XANTHIAS. I couldn't go. I'd got the eye-disease.

CHARON. Then fetch a circuit round about the lake.

XANTHIAS. Where must I wait?

CHARON. Beside the Withering stone,
Hard by the Rest.

DIONYSUS. You understand?

XANTHIAS. Too well.
O, what ill omen crost me as I started!

(*Exit* XANTHIAS.)

CHARON (*to* DIONYSUS). Sit to the oar. (*Calling.*) Who else for
the boat? Be quick.
(*To* DIONYSUS). Hi! what are you doing?

DIONYSUS. What am I doing? Sitting
On to the oar. You told me to, yourself.

CHARON. Now sit you there, you little Potgut.

DIONYSUS. So?

CHARON. Now stretch your arms full length before you.

DIONYSUS. So?

CHARON. Come, don't keep fooling; plant your feet, and now
Pull with a will.

DIONYSUS. Why, how am *I* to pull?
I'm not an oarsman, seaman, Salaminian.[19]
I can't!

CHARON. You can. Just dip your oar in once,
You'll hear the loveliest timing songs.

DIONYSUS. What from?

CHARON. Frog-swans, most wonderful.

DIONYSUS. Then give the word.

CHARON. Heave ahoy! heave ahoy!

(*The* CHORUS OF FROGS *is heard singing behind the scenes.*)

FROGS. Brekekekex, ko-ax, ko-ax,
Brekekekex, ko-ax, ko-ax!

We children of the fountain and the lake
    Let us wake
Our full choir-shout, as the flutes are ringing out,
    Our symphony of clear-voiced song.
The song we used to love in the Marshland up above,
    In praise of Dionysus to produce,
    Of Nysaean Dionysus, son of Zeus,[20]
When the revel-tipsy throng, all crapulous and gay,
To our precinct reeled along on the holy Pitcher day,
    Brekekekex, ko-ax, ko-ax.

DIONYSUS. O, dear! O, dear! now I declare
    I've got a bump upon my rump,

FROGS. Brekekekex, ko-ax, ko-ax.

DIONYSUS. But you, perchance, don't care.

FROGS. Brekekekex, ko-ax, ko-ax.

DIONYSUS. Hang you, and your ko-axing too!
    There's nothing but ko-ax with you.

FROGS. That is right, Mr. Busybody, right!
    For the Muses of the lyre love us well;
And hornfoot Pan who plays on the pipe his jocund lays;
And Apollo, Harper bright, in our Chorus takes delight;
For the strong reed's sake which I grow within my lake
    To be girdled in his lyre's deep shell.
    Brekekekex, ko-ax, ko-ax.

DIONYSUS. My hands are blistered very sore;
    My stern below is sweltering so,
    'Twill soon, I know, upturn and roar
    Brekekekex, ko-ax, ko-ax.
    O tuneful race, O pray give o'er,
    O sing no more.

FROGS.   Ah, no! ah, no!
    Loud and louder our chant must flow.
    Sing if ever ye sang of yore,
    When in sunny and glorious days
    Through the rushes and marsh-flags springing
    On we swept, in the joy of singing
    Myriad-diving roundelays.
    Or when fleeing the storm, we went

> Down to the depths, and our choral song
> Wildly raised to a loud and long
> Bubble-bursting accompaniment.

FROGS and DIONYSUS. Brekekekex, ko-ax, ko-ax.

DIONYSUS. This timing song I take from you.

FROGS. That's a dreadful thing to do.

DIONYSUS. Much more dreadful, if I row
> Till I burst myself, I trow.

FROGS and DIONYSUS. Brekekekex, ko-ax, ko-ax.

DIONYSUS. Go, hang yourselves; for what care I?

FROGS. All the same we'll shout and cry,
> Stretching all our throats with song,
> Shouting, crying, all day long,

FROGS and DIONYSUS. Brekekekex, ko-ax, ko-ax.

DIONYSUS. In this you'll never, never win.

FROGS. This you shall not beat us in.

DIONYSUS. No, nor ye prevail o'er me.
> Never! never! I'll my song
> Shout, if need be, all day long,
> Until I've learned to master your ko-ax.
> Brekekekex, ko-ax, ko-ax.
> I thought I'd put a stop to your ko-ax.

(*They have now crossed the water, and are in Hades it-self.*)

CHARON. Stop! Easy! Take the oar and push her to.
Now pay your fare and go.

DIONYSUS.   Here 'tis: two obols.

(*Exit* CHARON.)

Xanthias! where's Xanthias? Is it Xanthias there?

(*Enter* XANTHIAS.)

XANTHIAS. Hoi, hoi!

DIONYSUS.   Come hither.

XANTHIAS.   Glad to meet you, master.

DIONYSUS. What have you there?

XANTHIAS.   Nothing but filth and darkness.

DIONYSUS. But tell me, did you see the parricides
    And perjured folk he mentioned?

XANTHIAS.   Didn't you?

DIONYSUS. Poseidon, yes. Why look! (*Pointing to the audience*)
            I see them now.
    What's the next step?

XANTHIAS.   We'd best be moving on.
    This is the spot where Heracles declared
    Those savage monsters dwell.

DIONYSUS.   O hang the fellow.
    That's all his bluff: he thought to scare me off,
    The jealous dog, knowing my plucky ways.
    There's no such swaggerer lives as Heracles.
    Why, I'd like nothing better than to achieve
    Some bold adventure, worthy of our trip.

XANTHIAS. I know you would. Hallo! I hear a noise.

DIONYSUS. Where? what?

XANTHIAS.   Behind us, there.

DIONYSUS.   Get you behind.

XANTHIAS. No, it's in front.

DIONYSUS.   Get you in front directly.

XANTHIAS. And now I see the most ferocious monster.

DIONYSUS. O, what's it like?

XANTHIAS.   Like everything by turns.
    Now it's a bull: now it's a mule: and now
    The loveliest girl.

DIONYSUS.   O, where? I'll go and meet her.

XANTHIAS. It's ceased to be a girl: it's a dog now.

DIONYSUS. It is Empusa![21]

XANTHIAS.   Well, its face is all
    Ablaze with fire.

DIONYSUS.   Has it a copper leg?

XANTHIAS. A copper leg? yes, one; and one of cow dung.

DIONYSUS. O, whither shall I flee?

XANTHIAS.   O, whither I?

DIONYSUS. My priest, protect me, and we'll sup together.[22]

XANTHIAS. King Heracles, we're done for.

DIONYSUS.   O, forbear,
Good fellow, call me anything but that.

XANTHIAS. Well then, Dionysus.

DIONYSUS.   O, that's worse again.

XANTHIAS (to the Spectre). Aye, go thy way. O master, here,
        come here.

DIONYSUS. O, what's up now?

XANTHIAS.   Take courage; all's serene.
And, like Hegelochus, we now may say
"Out of the storm there comes a new fine wether."[23]
Empusa's gone.

DIONYSUS.   Swear it.

XANTHIAS.   By Zeus she is.

DIONYSUS. Swear it again.

XANTHIAS.   By Zeus.

DIONYSUS.   Again.

XANTHIAS.   By Zeus.
O dear, O dear, how pale I grew to see her,
But *he*, from fright has yellowed me all over.

DIONYSUS. Ah me, whence fall these evils on my head?
Who is the god to blame for my destruction?
Air, Zeus's chamber, or the Foot of Time?

(*A flute is played behind the scenes.*)

DIONYSUS. Hist!

XANTHIAS.   What's the matter?

DIONYSUS.   Didn't you hear it?

XANTHIAS.   What?

DIONYSUS. The breath of flutes.

XANTHIAS   Aye, and a whiff of torches
Breathed o'er me too; a very mystic whiff.

DIONYSUS. Then crouch we down, and mark what's going on.

CHORUS (in the distance).   O Iacchus![24]
                         O Iacchus! O Iacchus!

XANTHIAS. I have it, master: 'tis those blessed Mystics,

Of whom he told us, sporting hereabouts.
They sing the Iacchus which Diagoras made.[25]

DIONYSUS. I think so too: we had better both keep quiet
And so find out exactly what it is.

(*The* MYSTIC CHORUS *enters, clothed in their robes of initiation into the Eleusinian Mysteries, and carrying lighted torches in their hands.*)

(*The calling forth of Iacchus.*)[26]

CHORUS. O Iacchus! power excelling, here in stately temples
                    dwelling,
           O Iacchus! O Iacchus!
           Come to tread this verdant level,
           Come to dance in mystic revel,
           Come whilst round thy forehead hurtles
           Many a wreath of fruitful myrtles,
           Come with wild and saucy paces
           Mingling in our joyous dance,
     Pure and holy, which embraces all the charms of all the
                    Graces,
           When the mystic choirs advance.

XANTHIAS. Holy and sacred queen, Demeter's daughter,
           O, what a jolly whiff of pork breathed o'er me![27]

DIONYSUS. Hist! and perchance you'll get some tripe yourself.

(*The welcome to Iacchus.*)

CHORUS. Come, arise, from sleep awaking, come the fiery
                    torches shaking,
           O Iacchus! O Iacchus!
           Morning Star that shinest nightly.
           Lo, the mead is blazing brightly,
           Age forgets its years and sadness,
           Agèd knees curvet for gladness,
           Lift thy flashing torches o'er us,
           Marshal all thy blameless train,
     Lead, O lead the way before us; lead the lovely youthful
                    Chorus
           To the marshy flowery plain.

(*The warning-off of the profane.*)

All evil thoughts and profane be still: far hence, far hence
    from our choirs depart,
Who knows not well what the Mystics tell, or is not holy
    and pure of heart;
Who ne'er has the noble revelry learned, or danced the
    dance of the Muses high;
Or shared in the Bacchic rites which old bull-eating
    Cratinus's words supply;[28]
Who vulgar coarse buffoonery loves, though all untimely
    the jests they make;
Or lives not easy and kind with all, or kindling faction for-
    bears to slake,
But fans the fire, from a base desire some pitiful gain for
    himself to reap;
Or takes, in office, his gifts and bribes, while the city is
    tossed on the stormy deep;
Who fort or fleet to the foe betrays; or, a vile Thorycion,
    ships away[29]
Forbidden stores from Aegina's shores, to Epidaurus across
    the Bay
Transmitting oarpads and sails and tar, that curst collector
    of five per cents;
The knave who tries to procure supplies for the use of the
    enemy's armaments;
The Cyclian singer who dares befoul the Lady Hecate's
    wayside shrine;[30]
The public speaker who once lampooned in our Bacchic
    feasts would, with heart malign,
Keep nibbling away the Comedians' pay;—to these I utter
    my warning cry,
I charge them once, I charge them twice, I charge them
    thrice, that they draw not nigh
To the sacred dance of the Mystic choir. But *ye*, my com-
    rades, awake the song,
The night-long revels of joy and mirth which ever of right
    to our feast belong.

(*The start of the procession.*)

    Advance, true hearts, advance!
    On to the gladsome bowers,

On to the sward, with flowers
  Embosomed bright!
March on with jest, and jeer, and dance,
  Full well ye've supped to-night.

(*The processional hymn to Persephone.*)[31]

March, chanting loud your lays,
Your hearts and voices raising,
The Saviour goddess praising
  Who vows she'll still
Our city save to endless days,
  Whate'er Thorycion's will.

Break off the measure, and change the time; and now with
    chanting and hymns adorn
Demeter, goddess mighty and high, the harvest-queen,
    the giver of corn.

(*The processional hymn to Demeter.*)

O Lady, over our rites presiding,
Preserve and succour thy choral throng,
And grant us all, in thy help confiding,
To dance and revel the whole day long;
And much in earnest, and much in jest,
Worthy thy feast, may we speak therein.
And when we have bantered and laughed our best,
The victor's wreath be it ours to win.

Call we now the youthful god, call him hither without
    delay,
Him who travels amongst his chorus, dancing along on
    the Sacred Way.

(*The processional hymn to Iacchus.*)

O, come with the joy of thy festival song,
O, come to the goddess, O, mix with our throng
Untired, though the journey be never so long.
  O Lord of the frolic and dance,
  Iacchus, beside me advance!
For fun, and for cheapness, our dress thou hast rent,

Through thee we may dance to the top of our bent,
Reviling, and jeering, and none will resent.
 O Lord of the frolic and dance,
 Iacchus, beside me advance!
A sweet pretty girl I observed in the show,
Her robe had been torn in the scuffle, and lo,
There peeped through the tatters a bosom of snow.
 O Lord of the frolic and dance,
 Iacchus, beside me advance!

DIONYSUS. Wouldn't I like to follow on, and try
 A little sport and dancing?

XANTHIAS.   Wouldn't I?

 (*The banter at the bridge of Cephisus.*)[32]

CHORUS. Shall we all a merry joke
 At Archedemus poke,[33]
Who has not cut his guildsmen yet, though seven years
 old;
 Yet up among the dead
 He is demagogue and head,
And contrives the topmost place of the rascaldom to hold?
 And Cleisthenes, they say,
 Is among the tombs all day,
Bewailing for his lover with a lamentable whine.
 And Callias, I'm told,
 Has become a sailor bold,
And casts a lion's hide o'er his members feminine.

DIONYSUS. Can any of you tell
 Where Pluto here may dwell,
For we, sirs, are two strangers who were never here be-
 fore?

CHORUS. O, then no further stray,
 Nor again enquire the way,
For know that ye have journeyed to his very entrance-
 door.

DIONYSUS. Take up the wraps, my lad.

XANTHIAS. Now is not this too bad?
 Like "Zeus's Corinth," he "the wraps" keeps saying o'er
 and o'er.[34]

CHORUS. Now wheel your sacred dances through the glade
        with flowers bedight,
  All ye who are partakers of the holy festal rite;
  And I will with the women and the holy maidens go
  Where they keep the nightly vigil, an auspicious light to
      show.

(The departure for the Thriasian Plain.)

      Now haste we to the roses,
      And the meadows full of posies,
      Now haste we to the meadows
        In our own old way,
      In choral dances blending,
      In dances never ending,
      Which only for the holy
        The Destinies array.
      O, happy mystic chorus,
      The blessed sunshine o'er us
      On us alone is smiling,
        In its soft sweet light:
      On us who strove for ever
      With holy, pure endeavour,
      Alike by friend and stranger
        To guide our steps aright.

DIONYSUS. What's the right way to knock? I wonder how
  The natives here are wont to knock at doors.

XANTHIAS. No dawdling: taste the door. You've got, remember,
  The lion-hide and pride of Heracles.

DIONYSUS. Boy! boy!

(Enter AEACUS.) [35]

AEACUS.   Who's there?

DIONYSUS.   I, Heracles the strong!

AEACUS. O, you most shameless desperate ruffian, you!
  O, villain, villain, arrant vilest villain!
  Who seized our Cerberus by the throat, and fled,
  And ran, and rushed, and bolted, haling off
  The dog, my charge! But now I've got thee fast.
  So close the Styx's inky-hearted rock,

The blood-bedabbled peak of Acheron
Shall hem thee in: the hell-hounds of Cocytus
Prowl round thee; whilst the hundred-headed Asp
Shall rive thy heart-strings: the Tartesian Lamprey[36]
Prey on thy lungs: and those Tithrasian Gorgons
Mangle and tear thy kidneys, mauling them,
Entrails and all, into one bloody mash.
I'll speed a running foot to fetch them hither.

(*Exit* AEACUS.)

XANTHIAS. Hallo! what now?

DIONYSUS.   I've done it: called the god.

XANTHIAS. Get up, you laughing-stock; get up directly,
    Before you're seen.

DIONYSUS.   What, *I* get up? I'm fainting.
    Please dab a sponge of water on my heart.

XANTHIAS. Here!

DIONYSUS.   Dab it, you.

XANTHIAS.   Where? O, ye golden gods,
    Lies your heart *there*?

DIONYSUS.   It got so terrified
    It fluttered down into my stomach's pit.

XANTHIAS. Cowardliest of gods and men!

DIONYSUS.   The cowardliest? I?
    What I, who asked you for a sponge, a thing
    A coward never would have done!

XANTHIAS.   What then?

DIONYSUS. A coward would have lain there wallowing;
    But I stood up, and wiped myself withal.

XANTHIAS. Poseidon! quite heroic.

DIONYSUS.   'Deed I think so.
    But weren't *you* frightened at those dreadful threats
    And shoutings?

XANTHIAS.   Frightened? Not a bit. I cared not.

DIONYSUS. Come then, if you're so *very* brave a man,
    Will you be I, and take the hero's club

And lion's skin, since you're so monstrous plucky?
And I'll be now the slave, and bear the luggage.

XANTHIAS. Hand them across. I cannot choose but take them.
And now observe the Xanthio-heracles
If I'm a coward and a sneak like you.

DIONYSUS. Nay, you're the rogue from Melite's own self.[37]
And I'll pick up and carry on the traps.

(*Enter* MAID-SERVANT *of Persephone.*)

MAID-SERVANT. O welcome, Heracles! come in, sweetheart.
My Lady, when they told her, set to work,
Baked mighty loaves, boiled two or three tureens
Of lentil soup, roasted a prime ox whole,
Made rolls and honey-cakes. So come along.

XANTHIAS (*declining*). You are too kind.

MAID-SERVANT.   I will not let you go.
I will not *let* you! Why, she's stewing slices
Of juicy bird's-flesh, and she's making comfits,
And tempering down her richest wine. Come, dear,
Come along in.

XANTHIAS. (*still declining*). Pray thank her.

MAID-SERVANT.   O you're jesting,
I shall not let you off: there's such a lovely
Flute-girl all ready, and we've two or three
Dancing-girls also.

XANTHIAS.   Eh! what! Dancing girls?

MAID-SERVANT. Young budding virgins, freshly tired and
          trimmed.
Come, dear, come in. The cook was dishing up
The cutlets, and they are bringing in the tables.

XANTHIAS. Then go you in, and tell those dancing-girls
Of whom you spake, I'm coming in Myself.

(*Exit* MAID-SERVANT.)

Pick up the traps, my lad, and follow me.

DIONYSUS. Hi! stop! you're not in earnest, just because
I dressed you up, in fun, as Heracles?
Come, don't keep fooling, Xanthias, but lift
And carry in the traps yourself.

XANTHIAS. Why! what!
  You are never going to strip me of these togs
  You gave me!

DIONYSUS. Going to? No, I'm doing it now.
  Off with that lion-skin.

XANTHIAS. Bear witness all,
  The gods shall judge between us.

DIONYSUS. Gods, indeed!
  Why, how could *you* (the vain and foolish thought!)
  A slave, a mortal, act Alcmena's son?

XANTHIAS. All right then, take them; maybe, if God will,
  You'll soon require my services again.

CHORUS. This is the part of a dexterous clever
  Man with his wits about him ever,
  One who has travelled the world to see;
  Always to shift, and to keep through all
  Close to the sunny side of the wall;
  Not like a pictured block to be,
  Standing always in one position;
  Nay but to veer, with expedition,
  And ever to catch the favouring breeze,
  This is the part of a shrewd tactician,
  This is to be a—THERAMENES![38]

DIONYSUS. Truly an exquisite joke 'twould be,
  Him with a dancing girl to see,
  Lolling at ease on Milesian rugs;
  Me, like a slave, beside him standing,
  Aught that he wants to his lordship handing;
  Then as the damsel fair he hugs,
  Seeing me all on fire to embrace her,
  He would perchance (for there's no man baser),
  Turning him round like a lazy lout,
  Straight on my mouth deliver a facer,
  Knocking my ivory choirmen out.

  (*Enter the* HOSTESS *of a cook-shop, and* PLATHANE, *her
  associate.*)

HOSTESS. O Plathane! Plathane! Here's that naughty man,
  That's he who got into our tavern once,
  And ate up sixteen loaves.

PLATHANE.   O, so he is!
   The very man.

XANTHIAS.   Bad luck for somebody!

HOSTESS. O and, besides, those twenty bits of stew,
   Half-obol pieces.

XANTHIAS.   Somebody's going to catch it!

HOSTESS. That garlic too.

DIONYSUS.   Woman, you're talking nonsense.
   You don't know what you're saying.

HOSTESS.   O, you thought
   I shouldn't know you with your buskins on!
   Ah, and I've not yet mentioned all that fish,
   No, nor the new-made cheese: he gulped it down,
   Baskets and all, unlucky that we were.[39]
   And when I just alluded to the price,
   He looked so fierce, and bellowed like a bull.

XANTHIAS. Yes, that's his way: that's what he always does.

HOSTESS. O, and he drew his sword, and seemed quite mad.

PLATHANE. O, that he did.

HOSTESS.   And terrified us so
   We sprang up to the cockloft, she and I.
   Then out he hurled, decamping with the rugs.

XANTHIAS. That's his way too; but something must be done.

HOSTESS. Quick, run and call my patron Cleon here!

PLATHANE. O, if you meet him, call Hyperbolus![40]
   We'll pay you out to-day.

HOSTESS.   O filthy throat,
   O how I'd like to take a stone, and hack
   Those grinders out with which you chawed my wares.

PLATHANE. I'd like to pitch you in the deadman's pit.[41]

HOSTESS. I'd like to get a reaping-hook and scoop
   That gullet out with which you gorged my tripe.
   But I'll to Cleon: he'll soon serve his writs;
   He'll twist it out of you to-day, he will.

   (*Exeunt* HOSTESS *and* PLATHANE.)

DIONYSUS. Perdition seize me, if I don't love Xanthias.

XANTHIAS. Aye, aye, I know your drift: stop, stop that talking.
I won't be Heracles.

DIONYSUS.   O, don't say so,
Dear, darling Xanthias.

XANTHIAS.   Why, how can I,
A slave, a mortal, act Alcmena's son!

DIONYSUS. Aye, aye, I know you are vexed, and I deserve it,
And if you pummel me, I won't complain.
But if I strip you of these togs again,
Perdition seize myself, my wife, my children,
And, most of all, that blear-eyed Archedemus.

XANTHIAS. That oath contents me: on those terms I take them.

CHORUS. Now that at last you appear once more,
Wearing the garb that at first you wore,
Wielding the club and the tawny skin,
Now it is yours to be up and doing,
Glaring like mad, and your youth renewing,
Mindful of him whose guise you are in.
If, when caught in a bit of a scrape, you
Suffer a word of alarm to escape you,
Showing yourself but a feckless knave,
Then will your master at once undrape you,
Then you'll again be the toiling slave.

XANTHIAS. There, I admit, you have given to me a
Capital hint, and the like idea,
Friends, had occurred to myself before.
Truly if anything good befell
He would be wanting, I know full well,
Wanting to take to the togs once more.
Nevertheless, while in these I'm vested,
Ne'er shall you find me craven-crested,
No, for a dittany look I'll wear,
Aye and methinks it will soon be tested,
Hark! how the portals are rustling there.

(*Enter* AEACUS *accompanied by his underlings.*)

AEACUS. Seize the dog-stealer, bind him, pinion him,
Drag him to justice!

DIONYSUS.   Somebody's going to catch it.

XANTHIAS (*striking out*). Hands off! get away! stand back!

AEACUS.   Eh? You're for fighting
Ho! Ditylas, Sceblyas, and Pardocas,
Come hither, quick; fight me this sturdy knave.

DIONYSUS. Now isn't it a shame the man should strike
And he a thief besides?

AEACUS.   A monstrous shame!

DIONYSUS. A regular burning shame!

XANTHIAS.   By the Lord Zeus,
If ever I was here before, if ever
I stole one hair's-worth from you, let me die!
And now I'll make you a right noble offer,
Arrest my lad: torture him as you will,
And if you find I'm guilty, take and kill me.

AEACUS. Torture him, how?

XANTHIAS.   In any mode you please.
Pile bricks upon him: stuff his nose with acid:
Flay, rack him, hoist him; flog him with a scourge
Of prickly bristles: only not with this,
A soft-leaved onion, or a tender leek.

AEACUS. A fair proposal. If I strike too hard
And maim the boy, I'll make you compensation.

XANTHIAS. I shan't require it. Take him out and flog him.

AEACUS. Nay, but I'll do it here before your eyes.
Now then, put down the traps, and mind you speak
The truth, young fellow.

DIONYSUS (*in agony*).   Man! don't torture *me*!
I am a god. You'll blame yourself hereafter
If you touch *me*.

AEACUS.   Hillo! What's that you are saying?

DIONYSUS. I say I'm Bacchus, son of Zeus, a god,
And *he's* the slave.

AEACUS.   You hear him?

XANTHIAS.   Hear him? Yes.
All the more reason you should flog him well.
For if he is a god, he won't perceive it.

DIONYSUS. Well, but you say that you're a god yourself.
  So why not *you* be flogged as well as I?

XANTHIAS. A fair proposal. And be this the test,
  Whichever of us two you first behold
  Flinching or crying out—he's not the god.

AEACUS. Upon my word you're quite the gentleman,
  You're all for right and justice. Strip then, both.

XANTHIAS. How can you test us fairly?

AEACUS.   Easily,
  I'll give you blow for blow.

XANTHIAS.   A good idea.
  We're ready! Now! (*Aeacus strikes him.*) see if you catch
      me flinching.

AEACUS. I struck you.

XANTHIAS (*incredulously*). No!

AEACUS.   Well, it seems "no," indeed.
  Now then I'll strike the other (*strikes Dionysus*).

DIONYSUS.   Tell me when?

AEACUS. I struck you.

DIONYSUS.   Struck me? Then why didn't I sneeze?

AEACUS. Don't know, I'm sure. I'll try the other again.

XANTHIAS. And quickly too. Good gracious!

AEACUS.   Why "good gracious"?
  Not hurt you, did I?

XANTHIAS.   No, I merely thought of
  The Diomeian feast of Heracles.[42]

AEACUS. A holy man! 'Tis now the other's turn.

DIONYSUS. Hi! Hi!

AEACUS.   Hallo!

DIONYSUS.   Look at those horsemen, look!

AEACUS. But why these tears?

DIONYSUS.   There's such a smell of onions.

AEACUS. Then you don't mind it?

DIONYSUS (*cheerfully*).   Mind it? Not a bit.

AEACUS. Well, I must go to the other one again.

XANTHIAS. O! O!

AEACUS.   Hallo!

XANTHIAS.   Do pray pull out this thorn.

AEACUS. What does it mean? 'Tis this one's turn again.

DIONYSUS (*shrieking*). Apollo! Lord! (*calmly*) of Delos and of
    Pytho.

XANTHIAS. He flinched! You heard him?

DIONYSUS.   Not at all; a jolly
    Verse of Hipponax flashed across my mind.[43]

XANTHIAS. You don't half do it: cut his flanks to pieces.

AEACUS. By Zeus, well thought on. Turn your belly here.

DIONYSUS (*screaming*). Poseidon!

XANTHIAS.   There! he's flinching.

DIONYSUS (*singing*).   who dost reign
      Amongst the Aegean peaks and creeks
      And o'er the deep blue main.

AEACUS. No, by Demeter, still I can't find out
    Which is the god, but come ye both indoors;
    My lord himself and Persephassa there,
    Being gods themselves, will soon find out the truth.

DIONYSUS. Right! right! I only wish you had thought of that
    Before you gave me those tremendous whacks.

(*The actors retire from the stage.*)

CHORUS. Come, Muse, to our Mystical Chorus, O come to the
      joy of my song,
    O see on the benches before us that countless and wonder-
      ful throng,
    Where wits by the thousand abide, with more than a
      Cleophon's pride—[44]
    On the lips of that foreigner base, of Athens the bane and
      disgrace,
      There is shrieking, his kinsman by race,
      The garrulous swallow of Thrace;
      From that perch of exotic descent,
      Rejoicing her sorrow to vent,
    She pours to her spirit's content, a nightingale's woeful
      lament,

That e'en though the voting be equal, his ruin will soon
    be the sequel.

Well it suits the holy Chorus evermore with counsel wise
To exhort and teach the city: this we therefore now ad-
    vise—
End the townsmen's apprehension; equalize the rights of
    all;
If by Phrynichus's wrestlings some perchance sustained a
    fall,[45]
Yet to these 'tis surely open, having put away their sin,
For their slips and vacillations pardon at your hands to
    win.
Give your brethren back their franchise. Sin and shame it
    were that slaves,
Who have once with stern devotion fought your battle on
    the waves
Should be straightway lords and masters, yea Plataeans
    fully blown—[46]
Not that this city, in her anguish, policy and wisdom
    shown—
Nay but these, of old accustomed on our ships to fight and
    win,
(They, their fathers too before them), these our very kith
    and kin,
You should likewise, when they ask you, pardon for their
    single sin.
O by nature best and wisest, O relax your jealous ire,
Let us all the world as kinsfolk and as citizens acquire,
All who on our ships will battle well and bravely by our
    side.
If we cocker up our city, narrowing her with senseless
    pride,
Now when she is rocked and reeling in the cradles of the
    sea,
Here again will after ages deem we acted brainlessly.

And O if I'm able to scan the habits and life of a man
Who shall rue his iniquities soon! not long shall that little
    baboon,

That Cleigenes shifty and small, the wickedest bathman
of all[47]
Who are lords of the earth—which is brought from the isle
of Cimolus, and wrought
With nitre and lye into soap—
Not long shall he vex us, I hope.
And this the unlucky one knows,
Yet ventures a peace to oppose,
And being addicted to blows he carries a stick as he goes,
Lest while he is tipsy and reeling, some robber his cloak
should be stealing.

Often has it crossed my fancy, that the city loves to deal
With the very best and noblest members of her common-
weal,
Just as with our ancient coinage, and the newly-minted
gold.
Yea for these, our sterling pieces, all of pure Athenian
mould,
All of perfect die and metal, all the fairest of the fair,
All of workmanship unequalled, proved and valued every-
where
Both amongst our own Hellenes and Barbarians far away,
These we use not: but the worthless pinchbeck coins of
yesterday,
Vilest die and basest metal, now we always use instead.
Even so, our sterling townsmen, nobly born and nobly
bred,
Men of worth and rank and mettle, men of honourable
fame,
Trained in every liberal science, choral dance and manly
game,
These we treat with scorn and insult, but the strangers
newliest come,
Worthless sons of worthless fathers, pinchbeck townsmen,
yellowy scum,
Whom in earlier days the city hardly would have stooped
to use
Even for her scapegoat victims, these for every task we
choose.

O unwise and foolish people, yet to mend your ways be-
    gin;
Use again the good and useful: so hereafter, if ye win
'Twill be due to this your wisdom: if ye fall, at least 'twill
    be
Not a fall that brings dishonour, falling from a worthy tree.

(*Enter* AEACUS *and* XANTHIAS.)

AEACUS. By Zeus the Saviour, quite the gentleman
    Your master is.

XANTHIAS.   Gentleman? I believe you.
    He's all for wine and women, is my master.

AEACUS. But not to have flogged you, when the truth came
    out
    That you, the slave, were passing off as master!

XANTHIAS. He'd get the worst of that.

AEACUS.   Bravo! that's spoken
    Like a true slave: that's what I love myself.

XANTHIAS. You love it, do you?

AEACUS.   Love it? I'm entranced
    When I can curse my lord behind his back.

XANTHIAS. How about grumbling, when you have felt the
    stick,
    And scurry out of doors?

AEACUS.   That's jolly too.

XANTHIAS. How about prying?

AEACUS.   That beats everything!

XANTHIAS. Great Kin-god Zeus! And what of overhearing[48]
    Your master's secrets?

AEACUS.   What? I'm mad with joy.

XANTHIAS. And blabbing them abroad?

AEACUS.   O heaven and earth!
    When I do that, I can't contain myself.

XANTHIAS. Phoebus Apollo! clap your hand in mine,
    Kiss and be kissed: and prithee tell me this,
    Tell me by Zeus, our rascaldom's own god,

What's all that noise within? What means this hubbub
And row?

AEACUS.　　　　That's Aeschylus and Euripides.

XANTHIAS. Eh?

AEACUS.　　　　Wonderful, wonderful things are going on.
　　The dead are rioting, taking different sides.

XANTHIAS. Why, what's the matter?

AEACUS.　　　　　　　　　There's a custom here
　　With all the crafts, the good and noble crafts,
　　That the chief master of his art in each
　　Shall have his dinner in the assembly hall,
　　And sit by Pluto's side,

XANTHIAS.　　　　　　I understand.

AEACUS. Until another comes, more wise than he
　　In the same art: then must the first give way.

XANTHIAS. And how has this disturbed our Aeschylus?

AEACUS. 'Twas he that occupied the tragic chair,
　　As, in his craft, the noblest.

XANTHIAS.　　　　　　　Who does now?

AEACUS. But when Euripides came down, he kept
　　Flourishing off before the highwaymen,
　　Thieves, burglars, parricides—these form our mob
　　In Hades—till with listening to his twists
　　And turns, and pleas and counterpleas, they went
　　Mad on the man, and hailed him first and wisest:
　　Elate with this, he claimed the tragic chair
　　Where Aeschylus was seated.

XANTHIAS. Wasn't he pelted?

AEACUS. Not he; the populace clamoured out to try
　　Which of the twain was wiser in his art.

XANTHIAS. You mean the rascals?

AEACUS.　　　　　　　　　Aye, as high as heaven!

XANTHIAS. But were there none to side with Aeschylus?

AEACUS. Scanty and sparse the good, (*regards the audience*)
　　the same as here.

XANTHIAS. And what does Pluto now propose to do?

AEACUS. He means to hold a tournament, and bring
    Their tragedies to the proof.

XANTHIAS.   But Sophocles,
    How came not he to claim the tragic chair?

AEACUS. Claim it? No he! When *he* came down, he kissed
    With reverence Aeschylus, and clasped his hand,
    And yielded willingly the chair to him.
    But now he's going, says Cleidemides,[49]
    To sit third-man; and then if Aeschylus win,
    He'll stay content; if not, for his art's sake,
    He'll fight to the death against Euripides.

XANTHIAS. Will it come off?

AEACUS.   O yes, by Zeus, directly.
    And then, I hear, will wonderful things be done,
    The art poetic will be weighed in scales.

XANTHIAS. What! weigh out tragedy, like butcher's meat?

AEACUS. Levels they'll bring, and measuring-tapes for words,
    And moulded oblongs.

XANTHIAS.   Is it bricks they are making?

AEACUS. Wedges and compasses: for Euripides
    Vows that he'll test the dramas, word by word.

XANTHIAS. Aeschylus chafes at this, I fancy.

AEACUS.   Well,
    He lowered his brows, upglaring like a bull.

XANTHIAS. And who's to be the judge?

AEACUS.   There came the rub.
    Skilled men were hard to find: for with the Athenians
    Aeschylus, somehow, did not hit it off,

XANTHIAS. Too many burglars, I expect, he thought.

AEACUS. And all the rest, he said, were trash and nonsense
    To judge poetic wits. So then at last
    They chose your lord, an expert in the art.
    But go we in: for when our lords are bent
    On urgent business, that means blows for us.

    (*Exeunt* AEACUS *and* XANTHIAS.)

CHORUS. O surely with terrible wrath will the thunder-voiced
        monarch be filled,

When he sees his opponent beside him, the tonguester, the
  artifice-skilled,
Stand, whetting his tusks for the fight! O surely, his eyes
  rolling-fell
  Will with terrible madness be fraught!
O then will be charging of plume-waving words with their
  wild-floating mane,
And then will be whirling of splinters, and phrases
  smoothed down with the plane,
When the man would the grand-stepping maxims, the
  language gigantic, repel
  Of the hero-creator of thought.
There will his shaggy-born crest upbristle for anger and
  woe,
Horribly frowning and growling, his fury will launch at
  the foe
Huge-clamped masses of words, with exertion Titanic up-
  tearing
  Great ship-timber planks for the fray.
But here will the tongue be at work, uncoiling, word-test-
  ing, refining,
Sophist-creator of phrases, dissecting, detracting, malign-
  ing,
Shaking the envious bits, and with subtle analysis paring
  The lung's large labour away.

(*There is a complete change of scene. We are introduced
into the Hall of Pluto, with* PLUTO *himself sitting on his
throne, and* DIONYSUS, AESCHYLUS *and* EURIPIDES *in the
foreground.*)

EURIPIDES. Don't talk to me; I won't give up the chair,
  I say I am better in the art than he.

DIONYSUS. You hear him, Aeschylus; why don't you speak?

EURIPIDES. He'll do the grand at first, the juggling trick
  He used to play in all his tragedies.

DIONYSUS. Come, my fine fellow, pray don't talk too big.

EURIPIDES. I know the man, I've scanned him through and
  through,
  A savage-creating stubborn-pulling fellow,

Uncurbed, unfettered, uncontrolled of speech,
Unperiphrastic, bombastiloquent.

AESCHYLUS. Hah! sayest thou so, child of the garden quean![50]
And this to *me*, thou chattery-babble-collector,
Thou pauper-creating rags-and-patches-stitcher?
Thou shalt abye it dearly!

DIONYSUS.   Pray, be still;
Nor heat thy soul to fury, Aeschylus.

AESCHYLUS. Not till I've made you see the sort of man
This cripple-maker is who crows so loudly.

DIONYSUS. Bring out a ewe, a black-fleeced ewe, my boys:[51]
Here's a typhoon about to burst upon us.

AESCHYLUS. Thou picker-up of Cretan monodies,
Foisting thy tales of incest on the stage—[52]

DIONYSUS. Forbear, forbear, most honoured Aeschylus;
And you, my poor Euripides, begone
If you are wise, out of this pitiless hail,
Lest with some heady word he crack your skull
And batter out your brain—less Telephus.[53]
And not with passion, Aeschylus, but calmly
Test and be tested. 'Tis not meet for poets
To scold each other, like two baking-girls.
But you go roaring like an oak on fire.

EURIPIDES. I'm ready, I! I don't draw back one bit.
I'll lash or, if he will, let him lash first
The talk, the lays, the sinews of a play:
Aye and my Peleus, aye and Aeolus,
And Meleager, aye and Telephus.

DIONYSUS. And what do *you* propose? Speak, Aeschylus.

AESCHYLUS. I could have wished to meet him otherwhere.
We fight not here on equal terms.

DIONYSUS.   Why not?

AESCHYLUS. My poetry survived me: his died with him:
He's got it here, all handy to recite.
Howbeit, if so you wish it, so we'll have it.

DIONYSUS. O bring me fire, and bring me frankincense.
I'll pray, or e'er the clash of wits begin,

To judge the strife with high poetic skill.
Meanwhile (*to the* CHORUS) invoke the Muses with a song.

CHORUS. O Muses, the daughters divine of Zeus, the immacu-
    late Nine,
Who gaze from your mansions serene on intellects subtle
    and keen,
When down to the tournament lists, in bright-polished wit
    they descend,
With wrestling and turnings and twists in the battle of
    words to contend,
O come and behold what the two antagonist poets can do,
Whose mouths are the swiftest to teach grand language
    and filings of speech:
For now of their wits is the sternest encounter commenc-
    ing in earnest.

DIONYSUS. Ye two, put up your prayers before ye start.

AESCHYLUS. Demeter, mistress, nourisher of my soul,
    O make me worthy of thy mystic rites!

DIONYSUS (*to* EURIPIDES). Now put on incense, you.

EURIPIDES.   Excuse me, no;
    My vows are paid to other gods than these.

DIONYSUS. What, a new coinage of your own?

EURIPIDES.   Precisely.

DIONYSUS. Pray then to them, those private gods of yours.

EURIPIDES. Ether, my pasture, volubly-rolling tongue,
    Intelligent wit and critic nostrils keen,
    O well and neatly may I trounce his plays!

CHORUS. We also are yearning from these to be learning
    Some stately measure, some majestic grand
    Movement telling of conflicts nigh.
    Now for battle arrayed they stand,
    Tongues embittered, and anger high.
    Each has got a venturesome will,
    Each an eager and nimble mind;
    One will wield, with artistic skill,
    Clearcut phrases, and wit refined;
    Then the other, with words defiant,
    Stern and strong, like an angry giant

Laying on with uprooted trees,
Soon will scatter a world of these
Superscholastic subtleties.

DIONYSUS. Now then, commence your arguments, and mind
you both display
True wit, not metaphors, nor things which any fool could
say.

EURIPIDES. As for myself, good people all, I'll tell you by-
and-by
My own poetic worth and claims; but first of all I'll try
To show how this portentous quack beguiled the silly fools
Whose tastes were nurtured, ere he came, in Phrynichus's
schools.[54]
He'd bring some single mourner on, seated and veiled,
'twould be
Achilles, say, or Niobe—the face you could not see—[55]
An empty show of tragic woe, who uttered not one thing.

DIONYSUS. 'Tis true.

EURIPIDES.   Then in the Chorus came, and rattled off
a string
Of four continuous lyric odes: the mourner never stirred.

DIONYSUS. I liked it too. I sometimes think that I those mutes
preferred
To all your chatterers now-a-days.

EURIPIDES.   Because, if you must know,
You were an ass.

DIONYSUS.   An ass, no doubt: what made him do it though?

EURIPIDES. That was his quackery, don't you see, to set the
audience guessing
When Niobe would speak; meanwhile, the drama was
progressing.

DIONYSUS. The rascal, how he took me in! 'Twas shameful,
was it not?
(*To* AESCHYLUS.) What makes you stamp and fidget so?

EURIPIDES.   He's catching it so hot.
So when he had humbugged thus awhile, and now his
wretched play

Was halfway through, a dozen words, great wild-bull
    words, he'd say,
Fierce Bugaboos, with bristling crests, and shaggy eye-
    brows too,
Which not a soul could understand.

AESCHYLUS.   O heavens!

DIONYSUS.   Be quiet, do.

EURIPIDES. But not one single word was clear,

DIONYSUS.   St! don't your teeth be gnashing.

EURIPIDES. 'Twas all Scamanders, moated camps, and griffin-
    eagles flashing
In burnished copper on the shields, chivalric-precipice-
    high
Expressions, hard to comprehend.

DIONYSUS.   Aye, by the Powers, and I
Full many a sleepless night have spent in anxious thought,
    because
I'd find the tawny cock-horse out, what sort of bird it
    was![56]

AESCHYLUS. It was a sign, you stupid dolt, engraved the ships
    upon.

DIONYSUS. Eryxis I supposed it was, Philoxenus's son.[57]

EURIPIDES. Now really should a cock be brought into a tragic
    play?

AESCHYLUS. You enemy of gods and men, what was *your* prac-
    tice, pray?

EURIPIDES. No cock-horse in *my* plays, by Zeus, no goat-stag
    there you'll see,
Such figures as are blazoned forth in Median tapestry.
When first I took the art from you, bloated and swoln,
    poor thing,
With turgid gasconading words and heavy dieting,
First I reduced and toned her down, and made her slim
    and neat
With wordlets and with exercise and poultices of beet,
And next a dose of chatterjuice, distilled from books, I
    gave her,

And monodies she took, with sharp Cephisophon for
    flavour.[58]
I never used haphazard words, or plunged abruptly in;
Who entered first explained at large the drama's origin
And source.

DIONYSUS. Its source, I really trust, was better than your own.

EURIPIDES. Then from the very opening lines no idleness was
    shown;
The mistress talked with all her might, the servant talked
    as much,
The master talked, the maiden talked, the beldame talked.

AESCHYLUS.   For such
An outrage was not death your due?

EURIPIDES.   No, by Apollo, no:
That was my democratic way.

DIONYSUS.   Ah, let that topic go.
Your record is not there, my friend, particularly good.[59]

EURIPIDES. Then next I taught all these to speak.

AESCHYLUS.   You did so, and I would
That ere such mischief you had wrought, your very lungs
    had split.

EURIPIDES. Canons of verse I introduced, and neatly chiselled
    wit;
To look, to scan: to plot, to plan: to twist, to turn, to woo:
On all to spy; in all to pry.

AESCHYLUS.   You did: I say so too.

EURIPIDES. I showed them scenes of common life, the things
    we know and see,
Where any blunder would at once by all detected be.
I never blustered on, or took their breath and wits away
By Cycnuses or Memnons clad in terrible array,[60]
With bells upon their horses' heads, the audience to dis-
    may.
Look at *his* pupils, look at mine: and there the contrast
    view.
Uncouth Megaenetus is his, and rough Phormisius too;[61]
Great long-beard-lance-and-trumpet-men, flesh-tearers
    with the pine:
But natty smart Theramenes, and Cleitophon are mine.[62]

DIONYSUS. Theramenes? a clever man and wonderfully sly:
　　Immerse him in a flood of ills, he'll soon be high and dry,
　　"A Kian with a kappa, sir, not Chian with a chi."[63]

EURIPIDES. I taught them all these knowing ways
　　　　By chopping logic in my plays,
　　　　And making all my speakers try
　　　　To reason out the How and Why.
　　　　So now the people trace the springs,
　　　　The sources and the roots of things,
　　　　And manage all their households too
　　　　Far better than they used to do,
　　　　Scanning and searching *What's amiss?*
　　　　And, *Why was that?* And, *How is this?*

DIONYSUS. Ay, truly, never now a man
　　　　Comes home, but he begins to scan;
　　　　And to his household loudly cries,
　　　　Why, where's my pitcher? What's the matter?
　　　　'Tis dead and gone my last year's platter.
　　　　Who gnawed these olives? Bless the sprat,
　　　　Who nibbled off the head of that?
　　　　And where's the garlic vanished, pray,
　　　　I purchased only yesterday?
　　　　—Whereas, of old, our stupid youths
　　　　Would sit, with open mouths and eyes,
　　　　Like any dull-brained Mammacouths.[64]

CHORUS. "All this thou beholdest, Achilles our boldest."[65]
　　　　And what wilt thou reply? Draw tight the rein
　　　　Lest that fiery soul of thine
　　　　Whirl thee out of the listed plain,
　　　　Past the olives, and o'er the line.
　　　　Dire and grievous the charge he brings.
　　　　See thou answer him, noble heart,
　　　　Not with passionate bickerings.
　　　　Shape thy course with a sailor's art,
　　　　Reef the canvas, shorten the sails,
　　　　Shift them edgewise to shun the gales.
　　　　When the breezes are soft and low,
　　　　Then, well under control, you'll go
　　　　Quick and quicker to strike the foe.

O first of all the Hellenic bards high loftily-towering verse
    to rear,
And tragic phrase from the dust to raise, pour forth thy
    fountain with right good cheer.

AESCHYLUS. My wrath is hot at this vile mischance, and my
    spirit revolts at the thought that I
Must bandy words with a fellow like *him:* but lest he
    should vaunt that I can't reply—
Come, tell me what are the points for which a noble poet
    our praise obtains.

EURIPIDES. For his ready wit, and his counsels sage, and be-
    cause the citizen folk he trains
To be better townsmen and worthier men.

AESCHYLUS.   If then you have done the very reverse,
Found noble-hearted and virtuous men, and altered them,
    each and all, for the worse,
Pray what is the meed you deserve to get?

DIONYSUS.   Nay, ask not *him.* He deserves to die.

AESCHYLUS. For just consider what style of men he received
    from me, great six-foot-high
Heroical souls, who never would blench from a towns-
    man's duties in peace or war;
Not idle loafers, or low buffoons, or rascally scamps such
    as now they are.
But men who were breathing spears and helms, and the
    snow-white plume in its crested pride
The greave, and the dart, and the warrior's heart in its
    sevenfold casing of tough bull-hide.

DIONYSUS. He'll stun me, I know, with his armoury-work; this
    business is going from bad to worse.

EURIPIDES. And how did you manage to make them so grand,
    exalted, and brave with your wonderful verse?

DIONYSUS. Come, Aeschylus, answer, and don't stand mute in
    your self-willed pride and arrogant spleen.

AESCHYLUS. A drama I wrote with the War-god filled.

DIONYSUS.   Its name?

AESCHYLUS. 'Tis the "Seven against Thebes" that I mean.
Which whoso beheld, with eagerness swelled to rush to
    the battlefield there and then.

DIONYSUS. O that was a scandalous thing you did! You have
made the Thebans mightier men,
More eager by far for the business of war. Now, therefore,
receive this punch on the head.

AESCHYLUS. Ah, *ye* might have practised the same yourselves,
but ye turned to other pursuits instead.
Then next the "Persians" I wrote, in praise of the noblest
deed that the world can show,
And each man longed for the victor's wreath, to fight and
to vanquish his country's foe.

DIONYSUS. I was pleased, I own, when I heard their moan for
old Darius, their great king, dead;
When they smote together their hands, like this, and *Evir
alake* the Chorus said.

AESCHYLUS. Aye, such are the poet's appropriate works: and
just consider how all along
From the very first they have wrought you good, the noble
bards, the masters of song.
First, Orpheus taught you religious rites, and from bloody
murder to stay your hands:
Musaeus healing and oracle lore; and Hesiod all the cul-
ture of lands,
The time to gather, the time to plough. And gat not
Homer his glory divine
By singing of valour, and honour, and right, and the sheen
of the battle-extended line,
The ranging of troops and the arming of men?

DIONYSUS.   O ay, but he didn't teach *that,* I opine,
To Pantacles; when he was leading the show I couldn't
imagine what he was at,
He had fastened his helm on the top of his head, he was
trying to fasten his plume upon that.

AESCHYLUS. But others, many and brave, he taught, of whom
was Lamachus, hero true;[66]
And thence my spirit the impress took, and many a lion-
heart chief I drew,
Patrocluses, Teucers, illustrious names; for I fain the citi-
zen-folk would spur
To stretch themselves to *their* measure and height, whenever the trumpet of war they hear.

But Phaedras and Stheneboeas? No! no harlotry business
    deformed my plays.[67]
And none can say that ever I drew a love-sick woman in
    all my days.

EURIPIDES. For *you* no lot or portion had got in Queen Aphro-
    dite.

AESCHYLUS.   Thank Heaven for that.
But ever on you and yours, my friend, the mighty goddess
    mightily sat;
Yourself she cast to the ground at last.[68]

DIONYSUS.   O ay, that came uncommonly pat.
You showed how cuckolds are made, and lo, you were
    struck yourself by the very same fate.

EURIPIDES. But say, you cross-grained censor of mine, how *my*
    Stheneboeas could harm the state.

AESCHYLUS. Full many a noble dame, the wife of a noble citi-
    zen, hemlock took,
And died, unable the shame and sin of your Bellerophon-
    scenes to brook.

EURIPIDES. Was then, I wonder, the tale I told of Phaedra's
    passionate love untrue?

AESCHYLUS. Not so: but tales of incestuous vice the sacred
    poet should hide from view,
Nor ever exhibit and blazon forth on the public stage to
    the public ken.
For boys a teacher at school is found, but we, the poets,
    are teachers of men.
We are *bound* things honest and pure to speak.

EURIPIDES.   And to speak great Lycabettuses, pray,[69]
And massive blocks of Parnassian rocks, is *that* things
    honest and pure to say?
In human fashion we ought to speak.

AESCHYLUS.   Alas, poor witling, and can't you see
That for mighty thoughts and heroic aims, the words
    themselves must appropriate be?
And grander belike on the ear should strike the speech of
    heroes and godlike powers,
Since even the robes that invest their limbs are statelier,
    grander robes than ours.

Such was *my* plan: but when *you* began, you spoilt and
　　degraded it all.

EURIPIDES.　　　　　　　　How so?

AESCHYLUS. Your kings in tatters and rags you dressed, and
　　brought them on, a beggarly show,
To move, forsooth, our pity and ruth.

EURIPIDES.　　And what was the harm, I should like to know?

AESCHYLUS. No more will a wealthy citizen now equip for the
　　state a galley of war.
He wraps his limbs in tatters and rags, and whines *he is
　　poor, too poor by far*.

DIONYSUS. But under his rags he is wearing a vest, as woolly
　　and soft as a man could wish.
Let him gull the state, and he's off to the mart; an eager
　　extravagant buyer of fish.

AESCHYLUS. Moreover to prate, to harangue, to debate, is now
　　the ambition of all in the state.
Each exercise-ground is in consequence found deserted
　　and empty: to evil repute
Your lessons have brought our youngsters, and taught our
　　sailors to challenge, discuss, and refute
The orders they get from their captains and yet, when *I*
　　was alive, I protest that the knaves
Knew nothing at all, save for rations to call, and to sing
　　"Rhyppapae" as they pulled through the waves.[70]

DIONYSUS. And bedad to let fly from their sterns in the eye of
　　the fellow who tugged at the undermost oar,
And a jolly young messmate with filth to besmirch, and to
　　land for a filching adventure ashore;
But now they harangue, and dispute, and won't row,
And idly and aimlessly float to and fro.

AESCHYLUS. Of what ills is he *not* the creator and cause?
Consider the scandalous scenes that he draws,
His bawds, and his panders, his women who give
　　Give birth in the sacredest shrine,
Whilst others with brothers are wedded and bedded,
　　And others opine
That "not to be living" is truly "to live."
And therefore our city is swarming to-day

With clerks and with demagogue-monkeys, who play
Their jackanape tricks at all times, in all places,
Deluding the people of Athens; but none
Has training enough in athletics to run
    With the torch in his hand at the races.[71]

DIONYSUS. By the Powers, you are right! At the Panathenaea
I laughed till I felt like a potsherd to see a
Pale, paunchy young gentleman pounding along,
With his head butting forward, the last of the throng,
In the direst of straits; and behold at the gates,
The Ceramites flapped him, and smacked him, and
    slapped him,
In the ribs, and the loin, and the flank, and the groin,
And still, as they spanked him, he puffed and he panted,
Till at one mighty cuff, he discharged such a puff
    That he blew out his torch and levanted.

CHORUS. Dread the battle, and stout the combat, mighty and
    manifold looms the war.
    Hard to decide in the fight they're waging,
    One like a stormy tempest raging,
One alert in the rally and skirmish, clever to parry and
    foin and spar.
    Nay but don't be content to sit
Always in one position only: many the fields for your
    keen-edged wit.
    On then, wrangle in every way,
    Argue, battle, be flayed and flay,
    Old and new from your stores display,
Yea, and strive with venturesome daring something subtle
    and neat to say.

Fear ye this, that to-day's spectators lack the grace of
    artistic lore,
    Lack the knowledge they need for taking
    All the points ye will soon be making?
Fear it not: the alarm is groundless: that, be sure, is the
    case no more.
    All have fought the campaign ere this:
Each a book of the words is holding; never a single point
    they'll miss.

Bright their natures, and now, I ween,
Newly whetted, and sharp, and keen.
Dread not any defect of wit,
Battle away without misgiving, sure that the audience, a
least, are fit.

EURIPIDES. Well then I'll turn me to your prologues now,
Beginning first to test the first beginning
Of this fine poet's plays. Why he's obscure
Even in the enunciation of the facts.

DIONYSUS. Which of them will you test?

EURIPIDES.   Many: but first
Give us that famous one from the Oresteia.

DIONYSUS. St! Silence all! Now, Aeschylus, begin.

AESCHYLUS. *Grave Hermes, witnessing a father's power,*
Be thou my saviour and mine aid to-day,
For here I come and hither I return.

DIONYSUS. Any fault there?

EURIPIDES.   A dozen faults and more.

DIONYSUS. Eh! why the lines are only three in all.

EURIPIDES. But every one contains a score of faults.

DIONYSUS. Now Aeschylus, keep silent; if you don't
You won't get off with three iambic lines.

AESCHYLUS. Silent for *him!*

DIONYSUS.   If *my* advice you'll take.

EURIPIDES. Why, at first starting here's a fault skyhigh.

AESCHYLUS (*to* DIONYSUS). You see your folly?

DIONYSUS.   Have your way; I care not.

AESCHYLUS (*to* EURIPIDES). What is my fault?

EURIPIDES.   Begin the lines again.

AESCHYLUS. *Grave Hermes, witnessing a father's power—*

EURIPIDES. And this beside his murdered father's grave
Orestes speaks?

AESCHYLUS.   I say not otherwise.

EURIPIDES. Then does he mean that when his father fell
By craft and violence at a woman's hand,
The god of craft was witnessing the deed?

AESCHYLUS. It was not he: it was the Helper Hermes
    He called the grave: and this he showed by adding
    It was his sire's prerogative he held.

EURIPIDES. Why this is worse than all. If from his father
    He held this office grave, why then—

DIONYSUS.   He was
    A graveyard rifler on his father's side.

AESCHYLUS. Bacchus, the wine you drink is stale and fusty.

DIONYSUS. Give him another: (*to* EURIPIDES) you, look out for
    faults.

AESCHYLUS. *Be thou my saviour and mine aid to-day,*
    For here I come, and hither I return.

EURIPIDES. The same thing twice says clever Aeschylus.

DIONYSUS. How twice?

EURIPIDES.   Why, just consider: I'll explain.
    "I come," says he; and "I return," says he:
    It's the same thing, to "come" and to "return."

DIONYSUS. Aye, just as if you said, "Good fellow, lend me
    A kneading trough: likewise, a trough to knead in."

AESCHYLUS. It is not so, you everlasting talker,
    They're not the same, the words are right enough.

DIONYSUS. How so? inform me how you use the words.

AESCHYLUS. A man, not banished from his home, may "come"
    To any land, with no especial chance.
    A home-bound exile both "returns" and "comes."

DIONYSUS. O good, by Apollo!
    What do you say, Euripides, to that?

EURIPIDES. I say Orestes never did "return."
    He came in secret: nobody recalled him.

DIONYSUS. O good, by Hermes!
    (*Aside.*) I've not the least suspicion what he means.

EURIPIDES. Repeat another line.

DIONYSUS.   Ay, Aeschylus,
    Repeat one instantly: *you*, mark what's wrong.

AESCHYLUS. *Now on this funeral mound I call my father*
    To hear, to hearken.

EURIPIDES.   There he is again.
To "hear," to "hearken"; the same thing, exactly.

DIONYSUS. Aye, but he's speaking to the dead, you knave,
Who cannot hear us though we call them thrice.

AESCHYLUS. And how do you make *your* prologues?

EURIPIDES.   You shall hear;
And if you find one single thing said twice,
Or any useless padding, spit upon me.

DIONYSUS. Well, fire away: I'm all agog to hear
Your very accurate and faultless prologues.

EURIPIDES. *A happy man was Oedipus at first—*[72]

AESCHYLUS. Not so, by Zeus; a most unhappy man.
Who, not yet born nor yet conceived, Apollo
Foretold would be his father's murderer.
How could *he* be a happy man at first?

EURIPIDES. *Then he became the wretchedest of men.*

AESCHYLUS. Not so, by Zeus; he never ceased to be.
No sooner born, than they exposed the babe,
(And that in winter), in an earthen crock,
Lest he should grow a man, and slay his father.
Then with both ankles pierced and swoln, he limped
Away to Polybus: still young, he married
An ancient crone, and her his mother too.
Then scratched out both his eyes.

DIONYSUS.   Happy indeed
Had he been Erasinides's colleague![73]

EURIPIDES.   Nonsense; I say my prologues are first rate.

AESCHYLUS. Nay then, by Zeus, no longer line by line
I'll maul your phrases: but with heaven to aid
I'll smash your prologues with a bottle of oil.

EURIPIDES. You mine with a bottle of oil?

AESCHYLUS.   With only one.
You frame your prologues so that each and all
Fit in with a "bottle of oil," or "coverlet-skin,"
Or "reticule-bag." I'll prove it here, and now.

EURIPIDES. You'll prove it? You?

AESCHYLUS.   I will.

DIONYSUS. Well then, begin.

EURIPIDES. *Aegyptus, sailing with his fifty sons,*
As ancient legends mostly tell the tale,
Touching at Argos

AESCHYLUS. Lost his bottle of oil.

EURIPIDES. Hang it, what's that? Confound that bottle of oil!

DIONYSUS. Give him another: let him try again.

EURIPIDES. *Bacchus, who, clad in fawnskins, leaps and bounds*
With torch and thyrsus in the choral dance
Along Parnassus

AESCHYLUS. Lost his bottle of oil.

DIONYSUS. Ah me, we are stricken—with that bottle again!

EURIPIDES. Pooh, pooh, that's nothing. I've a prologue here,
He'll never tack his bottle of oil to this:
No man is blest in every single thing.
One is of noble birth, but lacking means.
Another, baseborn,

AESCHYLUS. Lost his bottle of oil.

DIONYSUS. Euripides!

EURIPIDES. Well?

DIONYSUS. Lower your sails, my boy;
This bottle of oil is going to blow a gale.

EURIPIDES. O, by Demeter, I don't care one bit;
Now from his hands I'll strike that bottle of oil.

DIONYSUS. Go on then, go: but ware the bottle of oil.

EURIPIDES. *Once Cadmus, quitting the Sidonian town,*
Agenor's offspring

AESCHYLUS. Lost his bottle of oil.

DIONYSUS. O pray, my man, buy off that bottle of oil,
Or else he'll smash our prologues all to bits.

EURIPIDES. I buy of *him?*

DIONYSUS. If *my* advice you'll take.

EURIPIDES. No, no, I've many a prologue yet to say,
To which he can't tack on his bottle of oil.
Pelops, the son of Tantalus, while driving
His mares to Pisa

AESCHYLUS.   Lost his bottle of oil.

DIONYSUS. There! he tacked on the bottle of oil again.
O for heaven's sake, pay him its price, dear boy;
You'll get it for an obol, spick and span.

EURIPIDES. Not yet, by Zeus; I've plenty of prologues left.
Oeneus once reaping

AESCHYLUS.   Lost his bottle of oil.

EURIPIDES. Pray let me finish one entire line first.
Oeneus once reaping an abundant harvest,
Offering the firstfruits

AESCHYLUS.   Lost his bottle of oil.

DIONYSUS. What in the act of offering? Fie! Who stole it?

EURIPIDES. O don't keep bothering! Let him try with this!
Zeus, as by Truth's own voice the tale is told,

DIONYSUS. No, he'll cut in with "Lost his bottle of oil!"
Those bottles of oil on all your prologues seem
To gather and grow, like styes upon the eye.
Turn to his melodies now, for goodness' sake.

EURIPIDES. O I can easily show that he's a poor
Melody-maker; makes them all alike.

CHORUS. What, O what will be done!
Strange to think that he dare
Blame the bard who has won,
More than all in our days,
Fame and praise for his lays,
Lays so many and fair.
Much I marvel to hear
What the charge he will bring
'Gainst our tragedy king;
Yea for himself do I fear.

EURIPIDES. Wonderful lays! O yes, you'll see directly.
I'll cut down all his metrical strains to one.

DIONYSUS. And I, I'll take some pebbles, and keep count.

(*A slight pause, during which the music of a flute is
heard. The music continues to the end of the following
passage as an accompaniment to the recitative.*)

EURIPIDES. Lord of Phthia, Achilles, *why hearing the voice of
the hero-dividing*

Hah! smiting! approachest thou not to the rescue?
We, by the lake who *abide, are adoring our ancestor*
    Hermes.
    Hah! smiting! approachest thou not to the rescue?

DIONYSUS. O Aeschylus, twice art thou smitten!

EURIPIDES. Hearken to me, great king; yea, hearken *Atreides,*
    thou noblest of all the Achaeans.
    Hah! smiting! approachest thou not to the rescue?

DIONYSUS. Thrice, Aeschylus, thrice art thou smitten!

EURIPIDES. Hush! the bee-wardens are here: they *will quickly*
    the Temple of Artemis open.
    Hah! smiting! approachest thou not to the rescue?
I will expound (for *I know it) the omen the chieftains*
    encountered.
    Hah! smiting! approachest thou not to the rescue?

DIONYSUS. O Zeus and King, the terrible lot of smitings!
    I'll to the bath: I'm very sure my kidneys
    Are quite inflamed and swoln with all these smitings.

EURIPIDES. Wait till you've heard another batch of lays
    Culled from his lyre-accompanied melodies.

DIONYSUS. Go on then, go: but no more smitings, please.

EURIPIDES. How the twin-throned powers of *Achaea, the lords*
    of the mighty Hellenes.
        O phlattothrattophlattothrat!
    Sendeth *the Sphinx, the unchancy, the chieftainness*
        bloodhound.
        O phlattothrattophlattothrat!
    Launcheth fierce with brand *and hand the avengers the*
        terrible eagle.
        O phlattothrattophlattothrat!
    So for the swift-*winged hounds of the air he provided a*
        booty.
        O phlattothrattophlattothrat!
    The throng down-bearing on Aias.
        O phlattothrattophlattothrat!

DIONYSUS. Whence comes that phlattothrat? From Marathon,
    or
    Where picked you up these cable-twister's strains?

AESCHYLUS. From noblest source for noblest ends I brought
    them,
  Unwilling in the Muses' holy field
  The self-same flowers as Phrynichus to cull.
  But *he* from all things rotten draws his lays,
  From Carian flutings, catches of Meletus,[74]
  Dance-music, dirges. You shall hear directly.
  Bring me the lyre. Yet wherefore need a lyre
  For songs like these? Where's she that bangs and jangles
  Her castanets? Euripides's Muse,
  Present yourself: fit goddess for fit verse.

DIONYSUS. The Muse herself can't be a wanton? No!

AESCHYLUS. Halcyons, who by the ever-rippling
    Waves of the sea are babbling,
    Dewing your plumes with the drops that fall
    From wings in the salt spray dabbling.

    Spiders, ever with twir-r-r-r-rling fingers
    Weaving the warp and the woof,
    Little, brittle, network, fretwork,
    Under the coigns of the roof.

    The minstrel shuttle's care.

    Where in the front of the dark-prowed ships
    Yarely the flute-loving dolphin skips.

    Races here and oracles there.

    And the joy of the young vines smiling,
    And the tendril of grapes, care-beguiling.

    O embrace me, my child, O embrace me.
    (*To* DIONYSUS). You see this foot?

DIONYSUS.   I do.

AESCHYLUS. And this?

DIONYSUS.   And that one too.

AESCHYLUS (*to* EURIPIDES). You, such stuff who compile,
    Dare my songs to upbraid;
    You, whose songs in the style
    Of Cyrene's embraces are made.[75]
  So much for them: but still I'd like to show

The way in which your monodies are framed.
  "O darkly-light mysterious Night,
  What may this Vision mean,
  Sent from the world unseen
  With baleful omens rife;
  A thing of lifeless life,
  A child of sable night,
  A ghastly curdling sight,
  In black funereal veils,
With murder, murder in its eyes,
  And great enormous nails?
Light ye the lanterns, my maidens, and dipping your jugs
    in the stream,
Draw me the dew of the water, and heat it to boiling and
    steam;
So will I wash me away the ill effects of my dream.
  God of the sea!
  My dream's come true.
  Ho, lodgers, ho,
  This portent view.
Glyce has vanished, carrying off my cock,
  My cock that crew!
  O Mania, help! O Oreads of the rock
  Pursue! pursue!
For I, poor girl, was working within,
Holding my distaff heavy and full,
Twir-r-r-r-r-rling my hand as the threads I spin,
Weaving an excellent bobbin of wool;
Thinking 'To-morrow I'll go to the fair,
In the dusk of the morn, and be selling it there.'
But he to the blue upflew, upflew,
On the lightliest tips of his wings outspread;
To me he bequeathed but woe, but woe,
And tears, sad tears, from my eyes o'erflow,
Which I, the bereaved, must shed, must shed.
O children of Ida, sons of Crete,
Grasping your bows to the rescue come;
Twinkle about on your restless feet,
Stand in a circle around her home.
O Artemis, thou maid divine,

> Dictynna, huntress, fair to see,
> O bring that keen-nosed pack of thine,
> And hunt through all the house with me.
> O Hecate, with flameful brands,
> O Zeus's daughter, arm thine hands,
> Those swiftliest hands, both right and left;
> Thy rays on Glyce's cottage throw
> That I serenely there may go,
> And search by moonlight for the theft."

DIONYSUS. Enough of both your odes.

AESCHYLUS. Enough for me.
> Now would I bring the fellow to the scales.
> That, that alone, shall test our poetry now,
> And prove whose words are weightiest, his or mine.

DIONYSUS. Then both come hither, since I needs must weigh
> The art poetic like a pound of cheese.

(Whilst the CHORUS *are singing the following ode, a large balance is brought out and placed upon the stage.)*

CHORUS. O the labour these wits go through!
> O the wild, extravagant, new,
> Wonderful things they are going to do!
> Who but they would ever have thought of it?
> Why, if a man had happened to meet me
> Out in the street, and intelligence brought of it,
> I should have thought he was trying to cheat me;
> Thought that his story was false and deceiving.
> That were a tale I could never believe in.

DIONYSUS. Each of you stand beside his scale.

AESCHYLUS.
EURIPIDES. } We're here.

DIONYSUS. And grasp it firmly whilst ye speak your lines,
> And don't let you go until I cry "Cuckoo."

AESCHYLUS.
EURIPIDES. } Ready!

DIONYSUS. Now speak your lines into the scale.

EURIPIDES. *O that the Argo had not winged her way—*

AESCHYLUS. *River Spercheius, cattle-grazing haunts—*

DIONYSUS. Cuckoo! let go. O look, by far the lowest
His scale sinks down.

EURIPIDES. Why, how came that about?

DIONYSUS. He threw a river in, like some wool-seller
Wetting his wool, to make it weigh the more.
But *you* threw in a light and wingèd word.

EURIPIDES. Come, let him match another verse with mine.

DIONYSUS. Each to his scale.

AESCHYLUS. }
EURIPIDES. } We're ready.

DIONYSUS. Speak your lines.

EURIPIDES. *Persuasion's only shrine is eloquent speech.*

AESCHYLUS. *Death loves not gifts, alone amongst the gods.*

DIONYSUS. Let go, let go. Down goes his scale again.
He threw in Death, the heaviest ill of all.

EURIPIDES. And I Persuasion, the most lovely word.

DIONYSUS. A vain and empty sound, devoid of sense.
Think of some heavier-weighted line of yours,
To drag your scale down: something strong and big.

EURIPIDES. Where have I got one? Where? Let's see.

DIONYSUS. I'll tell you.
"Achilles threw two singles and a four."
Come, speak your lines: this is your last set-to.

EURIPIDES. *In his right hand he grasped an iron-clamped mace.*

AESCHYLUS. *Chariot on chariot, corpse on corpse was hurled.*

DIONYSUS. There now! again he has done you.

EURIPIDES. Done me? How?

DIONYSUS. He threw two chariots and two corpses in;
Five-score Egyptians could not lift that weight.

AESCHYLUS. No more of "line for line"; let him—himself,
His children, wife, Cephisophon—get in,
With all his books collected in his arms,
Two lines of mine shall overweigh the lot.

DIONYSUS. Both are my friends; I can't decide between them:
I don't desire to be at odds with either:
One is so clever, one delights me so.

PLUTO. Then you'll effect nothing for which you came?

DIONYSUS. And how, if I decide?

PLUTO.   Then take the winner;
  So will your journey not be made in vain.

DIONYSUS. Heaven bless your Highness! Listen, I came down
  After a poet.

EURIPIDES.   To what end?

DIONYSUS.   That so
  The city, saved, may keep her choral games.
  Now then, whichever of you two shall best
  Advise the city, *he* shall come with me.
  And first of Alcibiades, let each[76]
  Say what he thinks; the city travails sore.

EURIPIDES. What does she think herself about him?

DIONYSUS.   What?
  She loves, and hates, and longs to have him back.
  But give me *your* advice about the man.

EURIPIDES. I loathe a townsman who is slow to aid,
  And swift to hurt, his town: who ways and means
  Finds for himself, but finds not for the state.

DIONYSUS. Poseidon, but that's smart! (*To* AESCHYLUS.) And
        what say *you*?

AESCHYLUS. 'Twere best to rear no lion in the state:
  But having reared, 'tis best to humour him.

DIONYSUS. By Zeus the Saviour, still I can't decide.
  One is so clever, and so clear the other.
  But once again. Let each in turn declare
  What plan of safety for the state ye've got.

EURIPIDES. First with Cinesias wing Cleocritus,[77]
  Then zephyrs waft them o'er the watery plain.

DIONYSUS. A funny sight, I own: but where's the sense?

EURIPIDES. If, when the fleets engage, they holding cruets
  Should rain down vinegar in the foemen's eyes,
  I know, and I can tell you.

DIONYSUS.   Tell away.

EURIPIDES. When things, mistrusted now, shall trusted be,
  And trusted things, mistrusted.

DIONYSUS. How! I don't
Quite comprehend. Be clear, and not so clever.

EURIPIDES. If we mistrust those citizens of ours
Whom now we trust, and those employ whom now
We don't employ, the city will be saved.
If on our present tack we fail, we surely
Shall find salvation in the opposite course.

DIONYSUS. Good, O Palamedes! Good, you genius you.[78]
Is this *your* cleverness or Cephisophon's?

EURIPIDES. This is my own: the cruet-plan was his.

DIONYSUS (*to* AESCHYLUS.) Now, you.

AESCHYLUS. But tell me whom the city uses.
The good and useful?

DIONYSUS. What are you dreaming of?
She hates and loathes them.

AESCHYLUS. Does she love the bad?

DIONYSUS. Not love them, no: she uses them perforce.

AESCHYLUS. How can one save a city such as this,
Whom neither frieze nor woollen tunic suits?

DIONYSUS. O, if to earth you rise, find out some way.

AESCHYLUS. There will I speak: I cannot answer here.

DIONYSUS. Nay, nay; send up your guerdon from below.

AESCHYLUS. When they shall count the enemy's soil their
own,[79]
And theirs the enemy's: when they know that ships
Are their true wealth, their so-called wealth delusion.

DIONYSUS. Aye, but the justices suck that down, you know.

PLUTO. Now then, decide.

DIONYSUS. I will; and thus I'll do it.
I'll choose the man in whom my soul delights.

EURIPIDES. O, recollect the gods by whom you swore
You'd take me home again; and choose your friends.

DIONYSUS. 'Twas my tongue swore; my choice is—Aeschylus.[80]

EURIPIDES. Hah! what have you done?

DIONYSUS. Done? Given the victor's prize
To Aeschylus; why not?

EURIPIDES.   And do you dare
    Look in my face, after that shameful deed?

DIONYSUS. What's shameful, if the audience think not so?[81]

EURIPIDES. Have you no heart? Wretch, would you leave me
      dead?

DIONYSUS. Who knows if death be life, and life be death,
    And breath be mutton broth, and sleep a sheepskin?

PLUTO. Now, Dionysus, come ye in.

DIONYSUS.   What for?

PLUTO. And sup before ye go.

DIONYSUS.   A bright idea.
    I' faith, I'm nowise indisposed for that.

(All the actors go out.)

CHORUS. Blest the man who possesses a
        Keen intelligent mind.
        This full often we find.
        He, the bard of renown,
        Now to earth reascends,
        Goes, a joy to his town,
        Goes, a joy to his friends,
        Just because he possesses a
        Keen intelligent mind.
        Right it is and befitting,
        Not, by Socrates sitting,
        Idle talk to pursue,
        Stripping tragedy-art of
        All things noble and true.
        Surely the mind to school
        Fine-drawn quibbles to seek,
        Fine-set phrases to speak,
        Is but the part of a fool!

(Enter PLUTO and AESCHYLUS.)

PLUTO. Farewell then, Aeschylus, great and wise,
      Go, save our state by the maxims rare
    Of thy noble thought; and the fools chastise,
      For many a fool dwells there.

And *this* to Cleophon give, my friend (*handing him a
  halter*).[82]
And *this* to the revenue-raising crew,
Nicomachus, Myrmex, next I send,
  And *this* to Archenomus too.
And bid them all that without delay,
To my realm of the dead they hasten away.
For if they loiter above, I swear
I'll come myself and arrest them there.
And branded and fettered the slaves shall go
With the vilest rascal in all the town,
Adeimantus, son of Leucolophus, down,
  Down, down to the darkness below.

AESCHYLUS. I take the mission. This chair of mine
  Meanwhile to Sophocles here commit,
(For I count him next in our craft divine,)
  Till I come once more by thy side to sit.
But as for that rascally scoundrel there,
That low buffoon, that worker of ill,
O let him not sit in my vacant chair,
  Not even against his will.

PLUTO (*to the* CHORUS). Escort him up with your mystic
  throngs,
  While the holy torches quiver and blaze.
Escort him up with his own sweet songs,
  And his noble festival lays.

CHORUS. First, as the poet triumphant is passing away to the
  light,
Grant him success on his journey, ye powers that are ruling
  below.
Grant that he find for the city good counsels to guide her
  aright;
So we at last shall be freed from the anguish, the fear, and
  the woe,
Freed from the onsets of war. Let Cleophon now and his
  band
Battle, if they must, far away in their own fatherland.

1. *That comical joke.* The irresistibly funny jest was doubtless sufficiently indicated by gestures.

2. *Phrynichus* and *Ameipsias.* Old rivals of Aristophanes. Of *Lycis* we know nothing but the name.

3. *Pipkin.* The word for *wine jar* (*stamnos*) is introduced instead of the expected word.

4. *Why didn't I fight at sea?* If Xanthias had fought at the great battle of Arginusae, he would have received enfranchisement, and been as good a man as his master.

5. *Cleisthenes.* Of Cleisthenes, whose vile and effeminate vices had been lashed by Aristophanes for (at least) twenty years, we shall hear again in the same degraded character.

6. *The Andromeda.* A tragedy by Euripides.

7. *Molon.* A tragic actor of large stature. Therefore "to be as little as Molon" means to be, in fact, of unusual magnitude.

8. *"For some are not . . ."* Dionysus is quoting his favourite poet. The line is from the *Oeneus* of Euripides.

9. *Iophon.* The son of Sophocles. Dionysus admits Iophon to be a possible exception, if indeed the plays which he has exhibited are not, altogether or in part, the handiwork of his illustrious father. Iophon wrote many tragedies.

10. *Agathon, Xenocles,* and *Pythangelus.* Tragic poets.

11. *Who get one chorus.* Merely to obtain a chorus, to be one of the three tragedians selected to exhibit their plays, free of all expense to themselves, in public at the Athenian Dionysia, was no small triumph for a young dramatist, even if his play did not ultimately win the prize.

12. *Air, Zeus's chamber.* As examples of the hazardous ventures in which his soul delights, he cites, or travesties,

three passages of Euripides. The third is an expansion of a famous line in the *Hippolytus*.

13. *The Cerameicus*. Where torch-races began at the Panathenaean festival.

14. *An enormous lake*. This is the Acherusian lake which was deemed, says Lucian, the first stage in the passage to the realms below.

15. *An ancient mariner*. Charon.

16. *Morsimus*. A tragedian, who is also ridiculed in *The Knights* and *The Peace*.

17. *Cinesias*. A dithyrambic poet and musician, a favourite subject for Aristophanes' satire.

18. Charon calls out the various destinations for which he is ready to receive passengers. He will take passengers bound for (1) the Resting-place from cares and troubles; (2) the plain through which Lethe, the water of Oblivion, flows; (3) the Donkey-shearings, the equivalent of Nothingness; (4) the Cerberians, a name which is formed from Cerberus. An entrance to Hades was at (5) Taenarum, whilst (6) the Ravens is to be taken in the sense in which it is used constantly in Aristophanes, of absolute ruin.

19. *Salaminian*. The people of Salamis were constantly ferrying over from their island to the Athenian harbours.

20. *Nysaean*. An epithet of Dionysus. The place-name *Nysa* really arose from the latter half of the name *Dionysos*.

21. *Empusa*. A frightful hobgoblin, specially noted for its incessant changes of shape.

22. *My priest*. In these dramatic contests, which were part of the religious festival of the Dionysia, the priest of Dionysus was, so to say, the chairman who presided over the proceedings. He sat in a conspicuous seat or throne in the centre of the front row.

23. *A new fine wether*. In the *Orestes* of Euripides, the hero, recovering from a paroxysm of frenzy, says *After the storm I see afresh fine weather*. Hegelochus, who acted the part, when reciting the line made a slight involuntary pause, so that in Greek, the sense became *I see a cat*.

24. *O Iacchus!* Though Iacchus, the associate of Demeter and

Persephone, was originally quite distinct from the Theban Dionysus, yet their attributes were in some respects so similar that the process of identification had commenced long before the exhibition of *The Frogs*.

25. *Diagoras.* A lyric poet.

26. (*The calling forth of Iacchus.*) Throughout the following scene, the Chorus are represented as rehearsing in the world below the early stages of that great annual procession from the Cerameicus to Eleusis in which they themselves, when alive, had been accustomed to participate. The Chorus must be supposed to have mustered in the great building provided for the marshalling of these and similar processions, and they are now calling Iacchus to come from the adjoining Temple of the Eleusinian deities and be their divine companion on the long twelve-mile journey. It was this torch-bearing Iacchus whom they escorted from the splendid temple where he dwelt at Athens along the Sacred Way to the sanctuary at Eleusis. The statue is brought out, all evil-doers are warned off, and then the procession commences, the Chorus singing hymns to each of the Eleusinian deities in turn, Persephone, Demeter, Iacchus, as they pass through the Cerameicus and out by the Eleusinian gate to the bridge over the Cephisus, where a little chaffing takes place, and whence they disappear from our sight on their way to the flower-enamelled Thriasian plain. It must, of course, be remembered that all these phases of the procession are shown only by the dances and gestures of the Chorus in the orchestra.

27. *What a jolly whiff of pork!* An allusion to the sacrifice of pigs, which was an important part of the ceremony of initiation.

28. *Cratinus.* A comic poet, and hence a votary of Dionysus.

29. *Thorycion.* Of this unpatriotic toll-gatherer we know nothing beyond what is mentioned here.

30. *The Cyclian singer.* Cinesias.

31. As they depart from the city, they sing three hymns in succession, one to each of the Eleusinian deities, Persephone, Demeter, and Iacchus.

32. *The bridge of Cephisus.* Here the procession made a pause, and the processionists fell to abusing and jeering each other.

33. *Archedemus, Cleisthenes, Callias.* The Chorus now attack three unworthy Athenians, Archedemus, Cleisthenes, and Callias. Archedemus is ridiculed as an alien. He had been unable to prove his right to Athenian citizenship. But this meaning is conveyed in language which refers to a child not cutting his second teeth at the age of seven.

34. *"Zeus's Corinth."* A proverbial expression, applicable either to tedious iteration, as in the present passage, or to high-flown language with no corresponding results.

35. *Aeacus.* He was generally regarded as a member of the august tribunal for judging the dead, with Minos and Rhadamanthus for his colleagues. But Aristophanes assigns him the humbler post of doorkeeper in the hall of Pluto.

36. *The Tartesian Lamprey.* A reference to a great delicacy is unexpectedly inserted in a passage listing the dread topography and tortures of Hades.

37. *Melite.* A deme of Athens, the site of a temple of Heracles.

38. *Theramenes.* An Athenian politician, one of the leaders of the antidemocratic revolution which had established the Council of the Four Hundred (Thucydides, viii, 68.). He was famous for his changes of allegiance.

39. *Baskets and all.* In making cheese, the curd was introduced into a wicker basket, and pressed until all the whey was strained out and nothing remained but the dried cheese.

40. *Cleon and Hyperbolus.* Aeacus had threatened Dionysus with all sorts of mythological horrors; the hostesses threaten him with dead demagogues.

41. *The deadman's pit.* This was the pit or chasm at Athens into which the corpses of slain malefactors were cast.

42. *The Diomeian feast.* This festival of Heracles seems to have been celebrated with an abundance of buffoonery which would be dear to the soul of Xanthias; and doubtless at some stage of the proceedings the cry of *iattatai*

(here translated "Good gracious!") was raised by the assembled worshippers.

43. *Hipponax.* A poet of the sixth century B.C.

44. *Cleophon.* The political folly of this demagogic lyre-maker it attacked at the close of the play. Here the satire turns on the strain of Thracian blood which he derived from his mother.

45. *Phrynichus.* An Athenian general, leader of the antidemocratic Revolution of the Four Hundred, in 411 B.C.

46. *Battle on the waves.* The victory at Arginusae in 406 B.C. The slaves who fought at Arginusae were admitted to Athenian citizenship, as were the Plataeans, after the destruction of their city in 427 B.C.

47. *Cleigenes.* Utterly unknown.

48. *Kin-god Zeus.* Zeus was invoked under that name, not only between brothers, but between any members of the same family or kindred. Here Xanthias, delighted with the similarity of sentiment which he discovers between Aeacus and himself, speaks as if they were both members of one great slave family.

49. *Cleidemides.* An associate of Sophocles, probably the chief actor in his plays.

50. *The garden quean.* Aeschylus parodies a line of Euripides, and alludes to Euripides' mother, Cleito, who was by avocation a seller of herbs.

51. *A black-fleeced ewe.* As a sacrificial offering to avert a storm.

52. *Tales of incest.* Here he is referring to such marriages as those of Macareus and Canace in the *Aeolus.*

53. *Telephus.* One of Euripides' tragic heroes, who appeared disguised as a beggar.

54. *Phrynichus.* One of the early tragic poets, whose tragedies were of an essentially lyrical character.

55. *Achilles, . . . or Niobe.* He is specially referring to two lost tragedies of Aeschylus, the *Phrygians* (or the *Ransom of Hector*) and the *Niobe.*

56. *The tawny cock-horse.* This imaginary animal was intro-

duced in the *Myrmidons* of Aeschylus, as the painted figurehead of a ship.

57. *Eryxis.* Doubtless there was something in the appearance or character of Eryxis to give point to this allusion.

58. *Cephisophon.* He seems to have been a slave born in the house of Euripides. He was popularly credited with having a hand in the composition of his master's tragedies.

59. *Your record is not . . . particularly good.* Dionysus is referring to the antidemocratic tendencies of the school to which Euripides belonged. His pupils mentioned below, Theramenes and Cleitophon, were both active promoters of the establishment of the Four Hundred.

60. *Cycnuses or Memnons.* Cycnus the son of Poseidon, and Memnon the son of the Morning, were allies of Priam in the Trojan war. We do not know in which of his tragedies Aeschylus introduced Cycnus: but Memnon was represented in two tragedies, the *Memnon* and the *Psychostasia.*

61. *Megaenetus* and *Phormisius.* Of Megaenetus nothing is known. Phormisius was a politician of some note at this period.

62. *Cleitophon.* A well-known politician of those days, who took an active part in the establishment of the Four Hundred.

63. *"A Kian with a kappa, sir . . ."* If his faction were defeated he would devise some subtle distinction which would enable him to escape.

64. *Mammacouth.* A vulgar nickname for a babyish fool like our "mammy-suck" or "molly-coddle."

65. *All this thou beholdest . . .* This, the Scholiast tell us, is the first line of the *Myrmidons* of Aeschylus.

66. *Lamachus.* An Athenian general, one of the commanders of the Sicilian expedition.

67. *Phaedras and Stheneboeas.* The incestuous love of Phaedra for her stepson Hippolytus is the subject of the extant *Hippolytus* of Euripides; the adulterous love of Stheneboea for Bellerophon was doubtless told in the same poet's lost *Stheneboea.*

68. *Yourself she cast to the ground* . . . Aeschylus refers to the reported infidelity of Euripides' two wives.

69. *Lycabettuses.* Lycabettus, now Mount St. George, is a rocky peak at a little distance from Athens.

70. *"Rhyppapae."* The rhythmical cry to which the oars kept time.

71. *With the torch in his hand at the races.* The allusion is to the torch race at the Panathenaea and probably at some other festivals.

72. *A happy man was Oedipus at first.* Euripides quotes the opening of his *Antigone.*

73. *Erasinides.* One of the generals who was put to death after Arginusae. The meaning of this little speech is not quite clear, but in my opinion Dionysus is alluding to the last preceding words of Aeschylus. For had he been blind, he would not have joined the fleet; would not have won the battle of Arginusae; would not have fallen a victim, as Erasinides did, to the madness of the Athenian people.

74. *Catches of Meletus.* These were apparently erotic.

75. *Cyrene.* A famous courtesan.

76. *Alcibiades.* No more urgent problem could have been propounded than this. Alcibiades was now for the second time in exile, and was residing on his private estate in the Chersonese. Would it be wise to recall him? His genius, both in council and in war, was so transcendent that it might possibly even yet pull the Athenians through their troubles; but the man himself was so wayward and meteoric that it might be unsafe to entrust him with the supreme command.

77. *Cleocritus.* A gawky misshapen Athenian, who from some peculiarity of appearance or gait was thought to resemble an ostrich.

78. *O Palamedes!* Addressed to Euripides as a compliment to his amazing cleverness. The artfulness of Palamedes foiled even the craft of Odysseus when the latter feigned madness to avoid going to Troy, and Palamedes saw through the ruse.

79. *"When they shall count the enemy's soil their own . . ."*

etc. This was the counsel which was given by Pericles at the commencement of the Peloponnesian War (Thucydides, i, 140–44).

80. *'Twas my tongue swore . . .* Dionysus parodies a famous line from the *Hippolytus* of Euripides.

81. *"What's shameful, if the audience think not so?"* Again a parody of Euripides; as is the next line of Dionysus: "Who knows if death be life, and life be death?"

82. *And this to Cleophon give.* Aeschylus is to present halters to several obnoxious citizens, who are to terminate their existence therewith without unnecessary delay.

THE CLOUDS

The Clouds was exhibited at the Great Dionysia celebrated in the month of March, 423 B.C. The three competitors for the prize of comedy were Aristophanes with
The Clouds, Cratinus with *The Wine-flagon,* and Ameipsias
with the *Connos.* The prize was awarded to Cratinus;
Ameipsias was placed second; and Aristophanes third and
last. But *The Clouds* so exhibited and defeated was not in
all respects precisely identical with the existing play. Indignant at what he considered the unmerited slur cast upon
his most brilliant achievement, Aristophanes carefully revised the entire comedy. It is this revised edition, never
exhibited, which we have in our hands.

In *The Clouds* Aristophanes is attacking the subtle and
insidious disease which was sapping the very life of the old
Athenian character; which for a money payment taught
men to argue not for truth, but for victory; to assail all
traditional beliefs; and to pride themselves on their ability
to take up a bad cause and make it triumph over the right.
Indeed, the worse the cause, the more creditable the victory. In other words, the comedy of *The Clouds* was aimed
at the Sophistical system of education.

In the great central discussion between the two sys-
tems under the names of the Right Logic and the Wrong
Logic, the former expounds the ancient system in which
the men of Marathon had been trained; its efforts to foster
in the minds of the young sentiments of reverence, honour,
and modesty; an instinctive shrinking from whatever is
base, ignoble, or unclean; a willingness to endure hardships for their country and their own honour's sake. In the
Sophistical teaching, on the other hand, the idea of duty
was altogether eliminated. There was no special appeal to
the conscience; no recognition of the immutable distinction

between right and wrong. Everything was a matter of argument.

Socrates was precisely the figurehead which the poet required for the Sophistical system—a native Athenian universally known, whose demeanour and habits lent themselves readily to caricature, and who might reasonably be considered a Sophist, since the avowed object of his teaching was to make young men *sophous*. What matter if he did not in all respects conform to the type which Aristophanes was setting himself to combat; if he kept no school or Phrontisterion, took no money from his pupils, had not (like the Wrong Logic) risen from poverty to affluence, had not taught Hyperbolus, and so on? The suggestion (which every Athenian would know to be unfounded) that Socrates did these things was as purely farcical as the presentation of the philosopher himself suspended in a basket betwixt heaven and earth.

Characters of the Drama

STREPSIADES

PHEIDIPPIDES, *his son*

SERVANT-BOY *of Strepsiades*

STUDENTS *of Socrates*

SOCRATES

CHORUS OF CLOUDS

RIGHT LOGIC

WRONG LOGIC

PASIAS, *a creditor*

AMYNIAS, *another creditor*

A WITNESS

CHAEREPHON

THE CLOUDS

*There are two buildings at the back of the stage, the resi-
dence of* STREPSIADES, *and the Phrontisterion, or thinking-
establishment of the Sophists. The opening scene discloses
the interior of the house of* STREPSIADES. STREPSIADES *and
his son* PHEIDIPPIDES *are lying within, each on his own
pallet. It is still dark, but day is about to dawn.*

STREPSIADES. O dear! O dear!
    O Lord! O Zeus! these nights, how long they are.
    Will they ne'er pass? will the day never come?
    Surely I heard the cock crow, hours ago.
    Yet my servants still snore. These are new customs.
    O 'ware of war for many various reasons;
    One fears in war even to flog one's servants.
    And here's this hopeful son of mine wrapped up
    Snoring and sweating under five thick blankets.
    Come, we'll wrap up and snore in opposition.

                                (Tries to sleep.)

    But I can't sleep a wink, devoured and bitten
    By ticks, and bugbears, duns, and race-horses,
    All through this son of mine. *He* curls his hair,
    And sports his thoroughbreds, and drives his tandem;
    Even in dreams he rides: while I—I'm ruined,
    Now that the Moon has reached her twentieths,[1]
    And paying-time comes on. Boy! light a lamp,
    And fetch my ledger: now I'll reckon up
    Who are my creditors, and what I owe them.
    Come, let me see then. *Fifty pounds to Pasias!*
    Why fifty pounds to Pasias? what were they for?
    O, for the hack from Corinth. O dear! O dear!
    I wish my eye had been hacked out before—

PHEIDIPPIDES (*in his sleep*). You are cheating, Philon; keep to your own side.

STREPSIADES. Ah! there it is! that's what has ruined me!
Even in his very sleep he thinks of horses.

PHEIDIPPIDES (*in his sleep*). How many heats do the war-chariots run?

STREPSIADES. A pretty many heats you have run your father.
Now then, what debt assails me after Pasias?
A curricle and wheels. Twelve pounds. Amynias.

PHEIDIPPIDES (*in his sleep*). Here, give the horse a roll, and take him home.

STREPSIADES. You have rolled me *out* of house and home, my boy,
Cast in some suits already, while some swear
They'll seize my goods for payment.

PHEIDIPPIDES.   Good, my father,
What makes you toss so restless all night long?

STREPSIADES. There's a bumbailiff from the mattress bites me.

PHEIDIPPIDES. Come now, I prithee, let me sleep in peace.

STREPSIADES. Well then, you sleep: only be sure of this,
These debts will fall on your own head at last.
Alas, alas! For ever cursed be that same matchmaker,
Who stirred me up to marry your poor mother.
Mine in the country was the pleasantest life,
Untidy, easy-going, unrestrained,
Brimming with olives, sheepfolds, honey-bees.
Ah! then I married—I a rustic—her
A fine town-lady, niece of Megacles.
A regular, proud, luxurious, Coesyra.
This wife I married, and we came together,
I rank with wine-lees, fig-boards, greasy woolpacks;
She all with scents, and saffron, and tongue-kissings,
Feasting, expense, and lordly modes of loving.
She was not idle though, she was too fast.
I used to tell her, holding out my cloak,
Threadbare and worn; *Wife, you're too fast by half.*

SERVANT-BOY. Here's no more oil remaining in the lamp.

STREPSIADES. O me! what made you light the tippling lamp?
Come and be whipp'd.

SERVANT-BOY.   Why, what would you whip me for?

STREPSIADES. Why did you put one of those thick wicks in?
    Well, when at last to me and my good woman
    This hopeful son was born, our son and heir,
    Why then we took to wrangle on the name.
    She was for giving him some knightly name,
    "Callippides," "Xanthippus," or "Charippus:"
    I wished "Pheidonides," his grandsire's name.
    Thus for some time we argued: till at last
    We compromised it in Pheidippides.
    This boy she took, and used to spoil him, saying,
    Oh! when you are driving to the Acropolis, clad
    Like Megacles, in your purple; whilst I said
    Oh! when the goats you are driving from the fells,
    Clad like your father, in your sheepskin coat.
    Well, he cared nought for my advice, but soon
    A galloping consumption caught my fortunes.
    Now cogitating all night long, I've found
    One way, one marvellous transcendent way,
    Which if he'll follow, we may yet be saved.
    So,—but, however, I must rouse him first;
    But how to rouse him kindliest? that's the rub.
    Pheidippides, my sweet one.

PHEIDIPPIDES.   Well, my father.

STREPSIADES. Shake hands, Pheidippides, shake hands and kiss
    me.

PHEIDIPPIDES. There; what's the matter?

STREPSIADES.   Dost thou love me, boy?

PHEIDIPPIDES. Ay! by Poseidon there, the God of horses.[2]

STREPSIADES. No, no, not that: miss out the God of horses,
    That God's the origin of all my evils.
    But if you love me from your heart and soul,
    My son, obey me.

PHEIDIPPIDES.   Very well: what in?

STREPSIADES. Strip with all speed, strip off your present habits,
    And go and learn what I'll advise you to.

    (*Here the two leave the bedroom and come out upon the*
    stage.)

PHEIDIPPIDES. Name your commands.

STREPSIADES.   Will you obey?

PHEIDIPPIDES.   I will,
By Dionysus!

STREPSIADES. Well then, look this way.
See you that wicket and the lodge beyond?

PHEIDIPPIDES. I see: and prithee what is that, my father?

STREPSIADES. That is the thinking-house of sapient souls.[3]
There dwell the men who teach—aye, who persuade us,
That Heaven is one vast fire-extinguisher
Placed round about us, and that we're the cinders.
Aye, and they'll teach (only they'll want some money,)
How one may speak and conquer, right or wrong.

PHEIDIPPIDES. Come, tell their names.

STREPSIADES.   Well, I can't quite remember
But they're deep thinkers, and true gentlemen.

PHEIDIPPIDES. Out on the rogues! I know them. Those rank
            pedants,
Those palefaced, barefoot vagabonds you mean:
That Socrates, poor wretch, and Chaerephon.

STREPSIADES. Oh! Oh! hush! hush! don't use those foolish
            words;
But if the sorrows of my barley touch you,
Enter their Schools and cut the Turf for ever.

PHEIDIPPIDES. I wouldn't go, so help me Dionysus,
For all Leogoras's breed of Phasians![5]

STREPSIADES. Go, I beseech you, dearest, dearest son,
Go and be taught.

PHEIDIPPIDES.   And what would you have me learn?

STREPSIADES. 'Tis known that in their Schools they keep two
            Logics,[6]
The Worse, Zeus save the mark, the Worse and Better.
This Second Logic then, I mean the Worse one,
They teach to talk unjustly and—prevail.
Think then, you only learn that Unjust Logic,
And all the debts, which I have incurred through you,—
I'll never pay, no, not one farthing of them.

PHEIDIPPIDES. I will not go. How could I face the knights
    With all my colour worn and torn away!

STREPSIADES. O! then, by Earth, you have eat your last of
        mine,
    You, and your coach-horse, and your sigma-brand:
    Out with you! Go to the crows, for all I care.

PHEIDIPPIDES. But uncle Megacles won't leave me long
    Without a horse: I'll go to him: good-bye.

    (*Exit* PHEIDIPPIDES.)

STREPSIADES. I'm thrown, by Zeus, but I won't long lie pros-
        trate.
    I'll pray the Gods and send myself to school:
    I'll go at once and try their thinking-house.
    Stay: how can I, forgetful, slow, old fool,
    Learn the nice hair-splittings of subtle Logic?
    Well, go I must. 'Twont do to linger here.
    Come on, I'll knock the door. Boy! Ho there, boy!

STUDENT (*within*). O, hang it all! who's knocking at the door?

    (*Opens the door.*)

STREPSIADES. Me! Pheidon's son: Strepsiades of Cicynna.

STUDENT. Why, what a clown you are! to kick our door,
    In such a thoughtless, inconsiderate way!
    You've made my cogitation to miscarry.[7]

STREPSIADES. Forgive me: I'm an awkward country fool.
    But tell me, what was that I made miscarry?

STUDENT. 'Tis not allowed: Students alone may hear.

STREPSIADES. O that's all right: you may tell *me*: I'm come
    To be a student in your thinking-house.

STUDENT. Come then. But they're high mysteries, remember.
    'Twas Socrates was asking Chaerephon,
    How many feet of its own a flea could jump.
    For one first bit the brow of Chaerephon,
    Then bounded off to Socrates's head.

STREPSIADES. How did he measure this?

STUDENT.   Most cleverly.
    He warmed some wax, and then he caught the flea,
    And dipped its feet into the wax he'd melted:

  Then let it cool, and there were Persian slippers!
  These he took off, and so he found the distance.

STREPSIADES. O Zeus and king, what subtle intellects!

STUDENT. What would you say then if you heard another,
  Our Master's own?

STREPSIADES.   O come, do tell me that.

STUDENT. Why, Chaerephon was asking him in turn,
  Which theory did he sanction; that the gnats
  Hummed through their mouth, or backwards, through the
     tail?

STREPSIADES. Aye, and what said your Master of the gnat?

STUDENT. He answered thus: the entrail of the gnat
  Is small: and through this narrow pipe the wind
  Rushes with violence straight towards the tail;
  There, close against the pipe, the hollow rump
  Receives the wind, and whistles to the blast.

STREPSIADES. So then the rump is trumpet to the gnats!
  O happy, happy in your entrail-learning
  Full surely need he fear nor debts nor duns,
  Who knows about the entrails of the gnats.

STUDENT. And yet last night a mighty thought we lost
  Through a green lizard.

STREPSIADES.   Tell me, how was that?

STUDENT. Why, as Himself, with eyes and mouth wide open
  Mused on the moon, her paths and revolutions,
  A lizard from the roof squirted full on him.

STREPSIADES. He, he, he, he. I like the lizard's spattering
  Socrates.

STUDENT. Then yesterday, poor we, we'd got no dinner.

STREPSIADES. Hah! what did he devise to do for barley?

STUDENT. He sprinkled on the table—some fine ash—[8]
  He bent a spit—he grasped it compass-wise—
  And—filched a mantle from the Wrestling School.

STREPSIADES. Good heavens! Why Thales was a fool to this![9]
  O open, open, wide the study door,
  And show me, show me, show me Socrates.
  I die to be a student. Open, open!

(The entire front of the house is wheeled round, bringing out, and exposing to the view of the audience, the inner court of the Phrontisterion. High up in the air we behold SOCRATES *suspended in a basket, whilst below are a number of miserable half-starved wretches, all stooping forward as if anxiously examining something on the ground. They look so little like ordinary specimens of humanity, that* STREPSIADES *invokes Heracles the destroyer of monsters.)*

O Heracles, what kind of beasts are these!

STUDENT. Why, what's the matter? what do you think they're like?

STREPSIADES. Like? why those Spartans whom we brought from Pylus:[10]
What makes them fix their eyes so on the ground?

STUDENT. They seek things underground.

STREPSIADES.   O! to be sure,
Truffles! You there, don't trouble about that!
I'll tell you where the best and finest grow.
Look! why do those stoop down so very much?

STUDENT. They're diving deep into the deepest secrets.

STREPSIADES. Then why's their rump turned up towards the sky?

STUDENT. It's taking private lessons on the stars.
(To the other Students.) Come, come: get in: *he'll* catch us presently.

STREPSIADES. Not yet! not yet! just let them stop one moment,
While I impart a little matter to them.

STUDENT. No, no: they must go in: 'twould never do
To expose themselves too long to the open air.

STREPSIADES. O! by the Gods, now, what are these? do tell me.[11]

STUDENT. This is Astronomy.

STREPSIADES.   And what is this?

STUDENT. Geometry.

STREPSIADES.   Well, what's the use of that?

STUDENT. To mete out lands.

STREPSIADES.   What, for allotment grounds?

STUDENT. No, but all lands.

STREPSIADES.   A choice idea, truly.
   Then every man may take his choice, you mean.

STUDENT. Look; here's a chart of the whole world. Do you
      see?
   This city's Athens.

STREPSIADES.   Athens? I like that.
   I see no dicasts sitting. That's not Athens.[12]

STUDENT. In very truth, this is the Attic ground.

STREPSIADES. And where then are my townsmen of Cicynna?

STUDENT. Why, thereabouts; and here, you see, Euboea:
   Here, reaching out a long way by the shore.

STREPSIADES. Yes, overreached by us and Pericles.
   But now, where's Sparta?

STUDENT.   Let me see: O, here.

STREPSIADES. Heavens! how near us. O do please manage this,
   To shove her off from us, a long way further.

STUDENT. We can't do that, by Zeus.

STREPSIADES.   The worse for you.
   Hallo! who's that? that fellow in the basket?

STUDENT. That's *he*.

STREPSIADES.   Who's *he*?

STUDENT.   Socrates.

STREPSIADES.   Socrates!
   You sir, call out to him as loud as you can.

STUDENT. Call him yourself: I have not leisure now.

                       (*Exit* STUDENT.)

STREPSIADES.   Socrates! Socrates!
   Sweet Socrates!

SOCRATES.   Mortal! why call'st thou me?

STREPSIADES. O, first of all, please tell me what you are doing.

SOCRATES. I walk on air, and contem-plate the Sun.

STREPSIADES. O then from a basket you contemn the Gods,
   And not from the earth, at any rate?

SOCRATES.   Most true.
   I could not have searched out celestial matters
   Without suspending judgement, and infusing
   My subtle spirit with the kindred air.
   If from the ground I were to seek these things,
   I could not find: so surely doth the earth
   Draw to herself the essence of our thought.
   The same too is the case with water-cress.[13]

STREPSIADES. Hillo! what's that?
   Thought draws the essence into water-cress?
   Come down, sweet Socrates, more near my level,
   And teach the lessons which I come to learn.

                        (SOCRATES *descends*.)

SOCRATES. And wherefore art thou come?

STREPSIADES.   To learn to speak.
   For owing to my horrid debts and duns,
   My goods are seized, I'm robbed, and mobbed, and plun-
      dered.

SOCRATES. How did you get involved with your eyes open?

STREPSIADES. A galloping consumption seized my money.
   Come now: do let me learn the unjust Logic
   That can shirk debts: now do just let me learn it.
   Name your own price, by all the Gods I'll pay it.

SOCRATES. The Gods! why you must know the Gods with us
   Don't pass for current coin.

STREPSIADES.   Eh? what do you use then?
   Have you got iron, as the Byzantines have?

SOCRATES. Come, would you like to learn celestial matters,
   How their truth stands?

STREPSIADES.   Yes, if there's any truth.

SOCRATES. And to hold intercourse with yon bright Clouds,
   Our virgin Goddesses?

STREPSIADES.   Yes, that I should.

SOCRATES. Then sit you down upon that sacred bed.

STREPSIADES. Well, I am sitting.

SOCRATES.   Here then, take this chaplet.

STREPSIADES. Chaplet? why? why? now, never, Socrates:
Don't sacrifice poor me, like Athamas.[14]

SOCRATES. Fear not: our entrance-services require
All to do this.

STREPSIADES.   But what am I to gain?

SOCRATES. You'll be the flower of talkers, prattlers, gossips:
Only keep quiet.

STREPSIADES.   Zeus! your words come true!
I shall be flour indeed with all this peppering.[15]

SOCRATES. Old man sit you still, and attend to my will, and
hearken in peace to my prayer,
O Master and King, holding earth in your swing, O meas-
ureless infinite Air;
And thou glowing Ether, and Clouds who enwreathe her
with thunder, and lightning, and storms,
Arise ye and shine, bright Ladies Divine, to your student
in bodily forms.

STREPSIADES. No, but stay, no, but stay, just one moment I
pray, while my cloak round my temples I wrap.
To think that I've come, stupid fool, from my home, with
never a waterproof cap!

SOCRATES. Come forth, come forth, dread Clouds, and to earth
your glorious majesty show;
Whether lightly ye rest on the time-honoured crest of
Olympus environed in snow,
Or tread the soft dance 'mid the stately expanse of Ocean,
the nymphs to beguile,
Or stoop to enfold with your pitchers of gold, the mystical
waves of the Nile,
Or around the white foam of Maeotis ye roam, or Mimas
all wintry and bare,
O hear while we pray, and turn not away from the rites
which your servants prepare.

CHORUS (*Heard approaching from a distance.*) Clouds of all
hue,
Rise we aloft with our garments of dew.
Come from old Ocean's unchangeable bed,
Come, till the mountain's green summits we tread,
Come to the peaks with their landscapes untold,

Gaze on the Earth with her harvests of gold,
Gaze on the rivers in majesty streaming,
　Gaze on the lordly, invincible Sea,
Come, for the Eye of the Ether is beaming,
　Come, for all Nature is flashing and free.
　　Let us shake off this close-clinging dew
　　From our members eternally new,
　　And sail upwards the wide world to view.
　　　Come away! Come away!

SOCRATES. O Goddesses mine, great Clouds and divine, ye
　　have heeded and answered my prayer.
Heard ye their sound, and the thunder around, as it
　　thrilled through the tremulous air?

STREPSIADES. Yes, by Zeus, and I shake, and I'm all of a quake,
　　and I fear I must sound a reply,
Their thunders have made my soul so afraid, and those
　　terrible voices so nigh:
So if lawful or not, I must run to a pot, by Zeus, if I stop
　　I shall die.

SOCRATES. Don't act in our schools like those Comedy-fools
　　with their scurrilous scandalous ways.
Deep silence be thine: while this Cluster divine their soul-
　　stirring melody raise.

CHORUS.　　　Come then with me,
　　Daughters of Mist, to the land of the free.
　　Come to the people whom Pallas hath blest,
　　Come to the soil where the Mysteries rest;
　　Come, where the glorified Temple invites
　　The pure to partake of its mystical rites:
　　Holy the gifts that are brought to the Gods,
　　　Shrines with festoons and with garlands are crowned,
　　Pilgrims resort to the sacred abodes,
　　　Gorgeous the festivals all the year round.
　　　　And the Bromian rejoicings in Spring,[16]
　　　　When the flutes with their deep music ring,
　　　　And the sweetly-toned Choruses sing
　　　　　Come away! Come away!

STREPSIADES. O Socrates pray, by all the Gods, say, for I ear-
　　nestly long to be told,

Who are these that recite with such grandeur and might
    are they glorified mortals of old?

SOCRATES. No mortals are there, but Clouds of the air, grea
    Gods who the indolent fill:

These grant us discourse, and logical force, and the art o
    persuasion instil,

And periphrasis strange, and a power to arrange, and
    marvellous judgement and skill.

STREPSIADES. So then when I heard their omnipotent word
    my spirit felt all of a flutter,

And it yearns to begin subtle cobwebs to spin and abou
    metaphysics to stutter,

And together to glue an idea or two, and battle away i
    replies:

So if it's not wrong, I earnestly long to behold them mysel
    with my eyes.

SOCRATES. Look up in the air, towards Parnes out there, for
    see they will pitch before long
These regions about.

STREPSIADES.   Where? point me them out.

SOCRATES.   They are drifting, an infinite throng
And their long shadows quake over valley and brake.

STREPSIADES.   Why, whatever's the matter to-day
    I can't see, I declare.

SOCRATES.   By the Entrance; look there![17]

STREPSIADES.   Ah, I just got a glimpse, by the way.

(During the following conversation the CLOUDS silently
take their places in the orchestra, nor do they break silence
until STREPSIADES earnestly begs them to speak.)

SOCRATES. There, now you must see how resplendent they be,
    or your eyes must be pumpkins, I vow.

STREPSIADES. Ah! I see them proceed; I should think so in-
    deed: great powers! they fill everything now.

SOCRATES. So then till this day that celestials were they, you
    never imagined or knew?

STREPSIADES. Why, no, on my word, for I always had heard
    they were nothing but vapour and dew.

SOCRATES. O, then I declare, you can't be aware that 'tis these
who the sophists protect,
Prophets sent beyond sea, quacks of every degree, fops
signet-and-jewel-bedecked,
Astrological knaves, and fools who their staves of dithyrambs proudly rehearse—
'Tis the Clouds who all these support at their ease, because they exalt them in verse.

STREPSIADES. 'Tis for this then they write of "the on-rushin'
might o' the light-stappin' rain-drappin' Cloud,"
And the "thousand black curls whilk the Tempest-lord
whirls," and the "thunder-blast stormy an' loud,"
And "birds o' the sky floatin' upwards on high," and "air-
water leddies" which "drown
Wi' their saft falling dew the gran' Ether sae blue," and
then in return they gulp down
Huge gobbets o' fishes an' bountifu' dishes o' mavises
prime in their season.

SOCRATES. And is it not right such praise to requite?

STREPSIADES. Ah, but tell me then what is the reason
That if, as you say, they are Clouds, they to-day as women
appear to our view?
For the ones in the air are not women, I swear.

SOCRATES. Why, what do they seem then to you?

STREPSIADES. I can't say very well, but they straggle and swell
like fleeces spread out in the air;
Not like women they flit, no, by Zeus, not a bit, but these
have got noses to wear.

SOCRATES. Well, now then, attend to this question, my friend.

STREPSIADES. Look sharp, and propound it to me.

SOCRATES. Didst thou never espy a Cloud in the sky, which a
centaur or leopard might be,
Or a wolf, or a cow?

STREPSIADES. Very often, I vow: and show me the
cause, I entreat.

SOCRATES. Why, I tell you that these become just what they
please, and whenever they happen to meet
One shaggy and wild, like the tangle-haired child of old
Xenophantes, their rule[18]

Is at once to appear like Centaurs, to jeer the ridiculous
 look of the fool.

STREPSIADES. What then do they do if Simon they view, that
 fraudulent harpy to shame?[19]

SOCRATES. Why, his nature to show to us mortals below, a
 wolfish appearance they frame.

STREPSIADES. O, they then I ween having yesterday seen
 Cleonymus quaking with fear,[20]

(Him who threw off his shield as he fled from the field),
 metamorphosed themselves into deer.

SOCRATES. Yes, and now they espy soft Cleisthenes nigh, and
 therefore as women appear.

STREPSIADES. O then without fail, All hail! and All hail! my
 welcome receive; and reply

With your voices so fine, so grand and divine, majestical
 Queens of the Sky!

CHORUS. Our welcome to thee, old man, who wouldst see the
 marvels that science can show:

And thou, the high-priest of this subtlety feast, say what
 would you have us bestow?

Since there is not a sage for whom we'd engage our wonders more freely to do,

Except, it may be, for Prodicus: he for his knowledge may
 claim them, but you,[21]

For that sideways you throw your eyes as you go, and are
 all affectation and fuss;

No shoes will you wear, but assume the grand air on the
 strength of your dealings with us.

STREPSIADES. Oh Earth! what a sound, how august and profound! it fills me with wonder and awe.

SOCRATES. These, these then alone, for true Deities own, the
 rest are all God-ships of straw.

STREPSIADES. Let Zeus be left out: He's a God beyond doubt:
 come, that you can scarcely deny.

SOCRATES. Zeus, indeed! there's no Zeus: don't you be so
 obtuse.

STREPSIADES. No Zeus up aloft in the sky!

Then, you first must explain, who it is sends the rain; or
 I really must think you are wrong.

SOCRATES. Well then, be it known, these send it alone: I can
    prove it by arguments strong.
Was there ever a shower seen to fall in an hour when the
    sky was all cloudless and blue?
Yet on a fine day, when the Clouds are away, he might
    send one, according to you.

STREPSIADES. Well, it must be confessed, that chimes in with
    the rest: your words I am forced to believe.
Yet before, I had dreamed that the rain-water streamed
    from Zeus and his chamber-pot sieve.
But whence then, my friend, does the thunder descend?
    that does make me quake with affright!

SOCRATES. Why 'tis they, I declare, as they roll through the
    air.

STREPSIADES. What the Clouds? did I hear you aright?

SOCRATES. Ay: for when to the brim filled with water they
    swim, by Necessity carried along,
They are hung up on high in the vault of the sky, and so
    by Necessity strong
In the midst of their course, they clash with great force,
    and thunder away without end.

STREPSIADES. But is it not He who compels this to be? does
    not Zeus this Necessity send?

SOCRATES. No Zeus have we there, but a Vortex of air.[22]

STREPSIADES.   What! Vortex? that's something, I own.
I knew not before, that Zeus was no more, but Vortex was
    placed on his throne!
But I have not yet heard to what cause you referred the
    thunder's majestical roar.

SOCRATES. Yes, 'tis they, when on high full of water they fly,
    and then, as I told you before,
By Compression impelled, as they clash, are compelled a
    terrible clatter to make.

STREPSIADES. Come, how can that be? I really don't see.

SOCRATES.   Yourself as my proof I will take.
Have you never then eat the broth-puddings you get
    when the Panathenaea comes round,
And felt with what might your bowels all night in turbu-
    lent tumult resound?

STREPSIADES. By Apollo, 'tis true, there's a mighty to-do, and
my belly keeps rumbling about;

And the puddings begin to clatter within and kick up a
wonderful rout:

Quite gently at first, papapax, papapax, but soon pappapappax away,

Till at last, I'll be bound, I can thunder as loud, papapap-
pappapappax, as They.

SOCRATES. Shalt thou then a sound so loud and profound from
thy belly diminutive send,

And shall not the high and the infinite Sky go thundering
on without end?

For both, you will find, on an impulse of wind and similar
causes depend.

STREPSIADES. Well, but tell me from Whom comes the bolt
through the gloom, with its awful and terrible
flashes;

And wherever it turns, some it singes and burns, and some
it reduces to ashes!

For this 'tis quite plain, let who will send the rain, that
Zeus against perjurers dashes.

SOCRATES. And how, you old fool of a dark-ages school, and
an antediluvian wit,

If the perjured they strike, and not all men alike, have
they never Cleonymus hit?

Then of Simon again, and Theorus explain: known perjurers, yet they escape.[23]

But he smites his own shrine with his arrows divine, and
"Sunium, Attica's cape,"

And the ancient gnarled oaks: now what prompted those
strokes? *They* never forswore I should say.

STREPSIADES. Can't say that they do: your words appear true.
Whence comes then the thunderbolt, pray?

SOCRATES. When a wind that is dry, being lifted on high, is
suddenly pent into these,

It swells up their skin, like a bladder, within, by Necessity's changeless decrees:

Till, compressed very tight, it bursts them outright, and
away with an impulse so strong,

That at last by the force and the swing of its course, it
    takes fire as it whizzes along.

STREPSIADES. That's exactly the thing that I suffered one
    Spring, at the great feast of Zeus, I admit:

I'd a paunch in the pot, but I wholly forgot about making
    the safety-valve slit.

So it spluttered and swelled, while the saucepan I held,
    till at last with a vengeance it flew:

Took me quite by surprise, dung-bespattered my eyes,
    and scalded my face black and blue!

CHORUS. O thou who wouldst fain great wisdom attain, and
    comest to us in thy need,

All Hellas around shall thy glory resound, such a pros-
    perous life thou shalt lead:

So thou art but endued with a memory good, and accus-
    tomed profoundly to think,

And thy soul wilt inure all wants to endure, and from no
    undertaking to shrink,

And art hardy and bold, to bear up against cold, and
    with patience a supper thou losest:

Nor too much dost incline to gymnastics and wine, but all
    lusts of the body refusest:

And esteemest it best, what is always the test of a truly
    intelligent brain,

To prevail and succeed whensoever you plead, and hosts
    of tongue-conquests to gain.

STREPSIADES. But as far as a sturdy soul is concerned and a hor-
    rible restless care,

And a belly that pines and wears away on the wretchedest,
    frugalest fare,

You may hammer and strike as long as you like; I am quite
    invincible there.

SOCRATES. Now then you agree in rejecting with me the Gods
    you believed in when young,

And *my* creed you'll embrace "I believe in wide Space, in
    the Clouds, in the eloquent Tongue."

STREPSIADES. If I happened to meet other Gods in the street,
    I'd show the cold shoulder, I vow.

No libation I'll pour: not one victim more on their altars
    I'll sacrifice now.

CHORUS. Now be honest and true, and say what we shall do:
    since you never shall fail of our aid,
  If you hold us most dear in devotion and fear, and will
    ply the philosopher's trade.

STREPSIADES. O Ladies Divine, small ambition is mine: I only
    most modestly seek,
  Out and out for the rest of my life to be best of the chil-
    dren of Hellas to speak.

CHORUS. Say no more of your care, we have granted your
    prayer: and know from this moment, that none
  More acts shall pass through in the People than you: such
    favour from us you have won.

STREPSIADES. Not acts, if you please: I want nothing of these:
    this gift you may quickly withdraw;
  But I wish to succeed, just enough for my need, and to
    slip through the clutches of law.

CHORUS. This then you shall do, for your wishes are few: not
    many nor great your demands,
  So away with all care from henceforth, and prepare to be
    placed in our votaries' hands.

STREPSIADES. This then will I do, confiding in you, for Neces-
    sity presses me sore,
  And so sad is my life, 'twixt my cobs and my wife, that I
    cannot put up with it more.
    So now, at your word, I give and afford
    My body to these, to treat as they please,
    To have and to hold, in squalor, in cold,
    In hunger and thirst, yea by Zeus, at the worst,
    To be flayed out of shape from my heels to my nape
    So along with my hide from my duns I escape,
    And to men may appear without conscience or fear,
    Bold, hasty, and wise, a concocter of lies,
    A rattler to speak, a dodger, a sneak,
    A regular claw of the tables of law,
    A shuffler complete, well worn in deceit,
    A supple, unprincipled, troublesome cheat;
    A hang-dog accurst, a bore with the worst,
    In the tricks of the jury-courts thoroughly versed.
    If all that I meet this praise shall repeat,

Work away as you choose, I will nothing refuse,
Without any reserve, from my head to my shoes.
You shan't see me wince though my gutlets you mince,
And these entrails of mine for a sausage combine,
Served up for the gentlemen students to dine.

CHORUS. Here's a spirit bold and high Ready-armed for any strife.

(*To* STREPSIADES.) If you learn what I can teach Of the mysteries of speech,

Your glory soon shall reach To the summit of the sky.

STREPSIADES. And what am I to gain?

CHORUS.   With the Clouds you will obtain
The most happy, the most enviable life.

STREPSIADES. Is it possible for me Such felicity to see?

CHORUS. Yes, and men shall come and wait In their thousands at your gate,

Desiring consultations and advice

On an action or a pleading From the man of light and leading,

And you'll pocket many talents in a trice.

(*To* SOCRATES.) Here, take the old man, and do all that you can, your new-fashioned thoughts to instil,

And stir up his mind with your notions refined, and test him with judgement and skill.

SOCRATES. Come now, you tell me something of your habits:
For if I don't know them, I can't determine
What engines I must bring to bear upon you.

STREPSIADES. Eh! what? Not going to storm me, by the Gods?

SOCRATES. No, no: I want to ask you a few questions.
First: is your memory good?

STREPSIADES.   Two ways, by Zeus:
If I'm owed anything, I'm mindful, very:
But if I owe, (Oh, dear!) forgetful, very.

SOCRATES. Well then: have you the gift of speaking in you?

STREPSIADES. The gift of speaking, no: of cheating, yes.

SOCRATES. No? how then can you learn?

STREPSIADES.   O, well enough.

SOCRATES. Then when I throw you out some clever notion
    About the laws of nature, you must catch it.

STREPSIADES. What! must I snap up sapience, in dog-fashion?

SOCRATES. O! why the man's an ignorant old savage:
    I fear, my friend, that you'll require the whip.
    Come, if one strikes you, what do you do?

STREPSIADES.   I'm struck:
    Then in a little while I call my witness:
    Then in another little while I summon him.

SOCRATES. Put off your cloak.

STREPSIADES.   Why, what have I done wrong?

SOCRATES. O, nothing, nothing: all go in here naked.

STREPSIADES. Well, but I have not come with a search-war-
        rant.[24]

SOCRATES. Fool! throw it off.

STREPSIADES.   Well, tell me this one thing;
    If I'm extremely careful and attentive,
    Which of your students shall I most resemble?

SOCRATES. Why Chaerephon. You'll be his very image.

STREPSIADES. What! I shall be half-dead! O luckless me!

SOCRATES. Don't chatter there, but come and follow me;
    Make haste now, quicker, here.

STREPSIADES.   O, but do first
    Give me a honied cake: Zeus! how I tremble,
    To go down there, as if to see Trophonius.[25]

SOCRATES. Go on! why keep you pottering round the door.

(*Exeunt* SOCRATES *and* STREPSIADES.)

CHORUS. Yes! go, and farewell; as your courage is great,
        So bright be your fate.
    May all good fortune his steps pursue,
        Who now, in his life's dim twilight haze,
    Is game such venturesome things to do,
    To steep his mind in discoveries new,
        To walk, a novice, in wisdom's ways.

O Spectators, I will utter honest truths with accents free,
Yea! by mighty Dionysus, Him who bred and nurtured me.

So may I be deemed a poet, and this day obtain the prize,
As till that unhappy blunder I had always held you wise,
And of all my plays esteeming this the wisest and the best,
Served it up for your enjoyment, which had, more than all
   the rest,
Cost me thought, and time, and labour: then most scan-
   dalously treated,
I retired in mighty dudgeon, by unworthy foes defeated.
This is why I blame your critics, for whose sake I framed
   the play:
Yet the clever ones amongst you even now I won't betray.
No! for ever since from judges unto whom 'tis joy to speak,
Brothers Profligate and Modest gained the praise we
   fondly seek,[26]
When, for I was yet a Virgin, and it was not right to bear,
I exposed it, and Another did the foundling nurse with
   care,[26a]
But 'twas ye who nobly nurtured, ye who brought it up
   with skill;—
From that hour I proudly cherish pledges of your sure
   good will.
Now then comes its sister hither, like Electra in the play,[27]
Comes in earnest expectation kindred minds to meet to-
   day;
She will recognize full surely, if she find, her brother's
   tress.
And observe how pure her morals: who, to notice first her
   dress,
Enters not with filthy symbols on her modest garments
   hung,
Jeering bald-heads, dancing ballets, for the laughter of
   the young.
In this play no wretched grey-beard with a staff his fellow
   pokes,
So obscuring from the audience all the poorness of his
   jokes.
No one rushes in with torches, no one groans, *"Oh, dear!
   Oh, dear!"*
Trusting in its genuine merits comes this play before you
   here.

Yet, though such a hero-poet, I, the bald-head, do not grow

Curling ringlets: neither do I twice or thrice my pieces show.

Always fresh ideas sparkle, always novel jests delight,

Nothing like each other, save that all are most exceeding bright.

I am he who floored the giant, Cleon, in his hour of pride,

Yet when down I scorned to strike him, and I left him when he died!

But the others, when a handle once Hyperbolus did lend,

Trample down the wretched caitiff, and his mother, without end.[28]

In his Maricas the Drunkard, Eupolis the charge began,

Shamefully my Knights distorting, as he is a shameful man,[29]

Tacking on the tipsy beldame, just the ballet-dance to keep,

Phrynichus's prime invention, eat by monsters of the deep.

Then Hermippus on the caitiff opened all his little skill,

And the rest upon the caitiff are their wit exhausting still;

And my simile to pilfer "of the Eels" they all combine.[30]

Whoso laughs at their productions, let him not delight in mine.

But for you who praise my genius, you who think my writings clever,

Ye shall gain a name for wisdom, yea! for ever and for ever.

O mighty god, O heavenly King,
First unto Thee my prayer I bring,
    O come, Lord Zeus, to my choral song;—
And Thou, dread Power, whose resistless hand
Heaves up the sea and the trembling land,
    Lord of the trident, stern and strong;—
And Thou who sustainest the life of us all
Come, Ether, our parent, O come to my call;—
And Thou who floodest the world with light,
Guiding thy steeds through the glittering sky,
To men below and to Gods on high
    A Potentate heavenly-bright!

O most sapient wise spectators, hither turn attention due,
We complain of sad ill-treatment, we've a bone to pick
    with you:
We have ever helped your city, helped with all our might
    and main;
Yet you pay us no devotion, that is why we now complain.
We who always watch around you. For if any project
    seems
Ill-concocted, then we thunder, then the rain comes down
    in streams.
And, remember, very lately, how we knit our brows
    together,
"Thunders crashing, lightnings flashing," never was such
    awful weather;
And the Moon in haste eclipsed her, and the Sun in anger
    swore
He would curl his wick within him and give light to you
    no more,
Should you choose that mischief-worker, Cleon, whom the
    Gods abhor,
Tanner, Slave, and Paphlagonian, to lead out your hosts
    to war.
Yet you chose him! yet you chose him! For they say that
    Folly grows
Best and finest in this city, but the gracious Gods dispose
Always all things for the better, causing errors to succeed:
And how this sad job may profit, surely he who runs may
    read.
Let the Cormorant be convicted, in command, of bribes
    and theft,
Let us have him gagged and muzzled, in the pillory
    chained and left,
Then again, in ancient fashion, all that ye have erred of
    late,
Will turn out your own advantage, and a blessing to the
    State.

"Phoebus, my king, come to me still,"
Thou who holdest the Cynthian hill,
    The lofty peak of the Delian isle;—

And Thou, his sister, to whom each day
Lydian maidens devoutly pray
   In Thy stately gilded Ephesian pile;—
And Athene, our Lady, the queen of us all,
With the Aegis of God, O come to my call;—
And Thou whose dancing torches of pine
Flicker, Parnassian glades along,
Dionysus, Star of Thy Maenad throng,
   Come, Reveller most divine!

We, when we had finished packing, and prepared our
   journey down,
Met the Lady Moon, who charged us with a message for
   your town.
First, All hail to noble Athens, and her faithful true Allies;
Then, she said, your shameful conduct made her angry
   passions rise,
Treating her so ill who always aids you, not in words, but
   clearly;
Saves you, first of all, in torchlight every month a drachma
   nearly,
So that each one says, if business calls him out from home
   by night,
"Buy no link, my boy, this evening, for the Moon will lend
   her light."
Other blessings too she sends you, yet you will not mark
   your days
As she bids you, but confuse them, jumbling them all sorts
   of ways.
And, she says, the Gods in chorus shower reproaches on
   her head,
When in bitter disappointment, they go supperless to bed,
Not obtaining festal banquets duly on the festal day;
Ye are badgering in the law-courts when ye should arise
   and slay!
And full oft when we celestials some strict fast are duly
   keeping,
For the fate of mighty Memnon, or divine Sarpedon weep-
   ing,[31]
Then you feast and pour libations: and Hyperbolus of late

Lost the crown he wore so proudly as Recorder of the
    Gate,[32]
Through the wrath of us immortals: so perchance he'll
    rather know
Always all his days in future by the Lady Moon to go.

(*Enter* SOCRATES.)

SOCRATES. Never by Chaos, Air, and Respiration,
    Never, no never have I seen a clown
    So helpless, and forgetful, and absurd!
    Why if he learns a quirk or two he clean
    Forgets them ere he has learnt them: all the same,
    I'll call him out of doors here to the light.
    Take up your bed, Strepsiades, and come!

(*Enter* STREPSIADES.)

STREPSIADES. By Zeus, I can't: the bugs make such resistance.

SOCRATES. Make haste. There, throw it down, and listen.

STREPSIADES.   Well!

SOCRATES. Attend to me: what shall I teach you first
    That you've not learnt before? Which will you have,
    Measures or rhythms or the right use of words?

STREPSIADES. O! measures to be sure: for very lately
    A grocer swindled me of full three pints.

SOCRATES. I don't mean that: but which do you like the best
    Of all the measures; six feet, or eight feet?

STREPSIADES. Well, I like nothing better than the yard.

SOCRATES. Fool! don't talk nonsense.

STREPSIADES.   What will you bet me now
    That two yards don't exactly make six feet?

SOCRATES. Consume you! what an ignorant clown you are!
    Still, perhaps you can learn tunes more easily.

STREPSIADES. But will tunes help me to repair my fortunes?

SOCRATES. They'll help you to behave in company:
    If you can tell which kind of tune is best
    For the sword-dance, and which for finger music.[33]

STREPSIADES. For fingers! aye, but I know that.

SOCRATES.   Say on, then.

STREPSIADES. What is it but this finger? though before,
   Ere this was grown, I used to play with that.

SOCRATES. Insufferable dolt!

STREPSIADES.   Well but, you goose,
   I don't want to learn this.

SOCRATES.   What *do* you want then?

STREPSIADES. Teach me the Logic! teach me the unjust Logic!

SOCRATES. But you must learn some other matters first:
   As, what are males among the quadrupeds.

STREPSIADES. I should be mad indeed not to know that.
   The Ram, the Bull, the Goat, the Dog, the Fowl.

SOCRATES. Ah! there you are! there's a mistake at once!
   You call the male and female fowl the same.

STREPSIADES. How! tell me how.

SOCRATES.   Why fowl and fowl of course.

STREPSIADES. That's true though! what then shall I say in
      future?

SOCRATES. Call one a fowless and the other a fowl.

STREPSIADES. A fowless? Good! Bravo! Bravo! by Air.
   Now for that one bright piece of information.
   I'll give you a barley bumper in your trough.

SOCRATES. Look there, a fresh mistake; you called it trough,
   Masculine, when it's feminine.

STREPSIADES.   How, pray?
   How did I make it masculine?

SOCRATES.   Why "trough,"
   Just like "Cleonymus."

STREPSIADES.   I don't quite catch it.

SOCRATES. Why "trough," "Cleonymus," both masculine.

STREPSIADES. Ah, but Cleonymus has got no trough,
   His bread is kneaded in a rounded mortar:
   Still, what must I say in future?

SOCRATES.   What! why call it
   A "troughess," female, just as one says "an actress."

STREPSIADES. A "troughess," female?

SOCRATES.   That's the way to call it.

STREPSIADES. O "troughess" then and Miss Cleonymus.

SOCRATES. Still you must learn some more about these names;
   Which are the names of men and which of women.

STREPSIADES. Oh, I know which are women.

SOCRATES.   Well, repeat some.

STREPSIADES. Demetria, Cleitagora, Philinna.

SOCRATES. Now tell me some men's names.

STREPSIADES.   O yes, ten thousand.
   Philon, Melesias, Amynias.[34]

SOCRATES. Hold! I said men's names: these are women's
   names.

STREPSIADES. No, no, they're men's.

SOCRATES.   They are *not* men's, for how
   Would you address Amynias if you met him?

STREPSIADES. How? somehow thus: "Here, here, Amynia!"

SOCRATES. Amynia! a woman's name, you see.

STREPSIADES. And rightly too; a sneak who shirks all service!
   But all know this: let's pass to something else.

SOCRATES. Well, then, you get into the bed.

STREPSIADES.   And then?

SOCRATES. Excogitate about your own affairs.

STREPSIADES. Not there: I do beseech, not there: at least
   Let me excogitate on the bare ground.

SOCRATES. There is no way but this.

STREPSIADES.   O luckless me!
   How I shall suffer from the bugs to-day.

   (STREPSIADES *gets into bed.*)

SOCRATES. Now then survey in every way, with airy judge-
            ment sharp and quick:
      Wrapping thoughts around you thick:
      And if so be in one you stick,
      Never stop to toil and bother,
         Lightly, lightly, lightly leap,
      To another, to another;
         Far away be balmy sleep.

STREPSIADES. Ugh! Ugh! Ugh! Ugh! Ugh!

CHORUS. What's the matter? where's the pain?

STREPSIADES. Friends! I'm dying. From the bed
Out creep bugbears scantly fed,
And my ribs they bite in twain,
And my life-blood out they suck,
And my manhood off they pluck,
And my loins they dig and drain,
And I'm dying, once again.

CHORUS. O take not the smart so deeply to heart.

STREPSIADES.   Why, what can I do?
Vanished my skin so ruddy of hue,
Vanished my life-blood, vanished my shoe,
Vanished my purse, and what is still worse
As I hummed an old tune till my watch should be past,
I had very near vanished myself at the last.

SOCRATES. Hallo there, are you pondering?

STREPSIADES.   Eh! what? I?
Yes to be sure.

SOCRATES.   And what have your ponderings come to?

STREPSIADES. Whether these bugs will leave a bit of me.

SOCRATES. Consume you, wretch!

STREPSIADES.   Faith, I'm consumed already.

SOCRATES. Come, come, don't flinch: pull up the clothes again:
Search out and catch some very subtle dodge
To fleece your creditors.   •

STREPSIADES.   O me, how can I
Fleece any one with all these fleeces on me?

(*Puts his head under the clothes.*)

SOCRATES. Come, let me peep a moment what he's doing.
Hey! he's asleep!

STREPSIADES.   No, no! no fear of that!

SOCRATES. Caught anything?

STREPSIADES.   No, nothing.

SOCRATES.   Surely, something.

STREPSIADES. Well, I had something in my hand, I'll own.

SOCRATES. Pull up the clothes again, and go on pondering.

STREPSIADES. On what? now do please tell me, Socrates.

SOCRATES. What is it that you want? first tell me that.

STREPSIADES. You have heard a million times what 'tis I want:
My debts! my debts! I want to shirk my debts.

SOCRATES. Come, come, pull up the clothes: refine your thoughts
With subtle wit: look at the case on all sides:
Mind you divide correctly.

STREPSIADES.   Ugh! O me.

SOCRATES. Hush: if you meet with any difficulty
Leave it a moment: then return again
To the same thought: then lift and weigh it well.

STREPSIADES. O, here, dear Socrates!

SOCRATES.   Well, my old friend.

STREPSIADES. I've found a notion how to shirk my debts.

SOCRATES. Well then, propound it.

STREPSIADES.   What do you think of this?
Suppose I hire some grand Thessalian witch
To conjure down the Moon, and then I take it
And clap it into some round helmet-box,
And keep it fast there, like a looking-glass,—

SOCRATES. But what's the use of that?

STREPSIADES.   The use, quotha:
Why if the Moon should never rise again,
I'd never pay one farthing.

SOCRATES.   No! why not?

STREPSIADES. Why, don't we pay our interest by the month?[35]

SOCRATES. Good! now I'll proffer you another problem.
Suppose an action: damages, five talents:
Now tell me how you can evade that same.

STREPSIADES. How! how! can't say at all: but I'll go seek.

SOCRATES. Don't wrap your mind for ever round yourself,
But let your thoughts range freely through the air,
Like chafers with a thread about their feet.

STREPSIADES. I've found a bright evasion of the action:
Confess yourself, 'tis glorious.

SOCRATES. But what is it?

STREPSIADES. I say, haven't you seen in druggists' shops
That stone, that splendidly transparent stone,
By which they kindle fire?

SOCRATES. The burning glass?

STREPSIADES. That's it: well then, I'd get me one of these,
And as the clerk was entering down my case,
I'd stand, like this, some distance towards the sun,
And burn out every line.

SOCRATES. By my Three Graces,
A clever dodge!

STREPSIADES. O me, how pleased I am
To have a debt like that clean blotted out.

SOCRATES. Come, then, make haste and snap up this.

STREPSIADES. Well, what?

SOCRATES. How to prevent an adversary's suit
Supposing you were sure to lose it; tell me.

STREPSIADES. O, nothing easier.

SOCRATES. How, pray?

STREPSIADES. Why thus,
While there was yet one trial intervening,
Ere mine was cited, I'd go hang myself.

SOCRATES. Absurd!

STREPSIADES. No, by the Gods, it isn't though:
They could not prosecute me were I dead.

SOCRATES. Nonsense! Be off: I'll try no more to teach you.

STREPSIADES. Why not? do, please: now, please do, Socrates.

SOCRATES. Why you forget all that you learn, directly.
Come, say what you learnt first: there's a chance for you.

STREPSIADES. Ah! what was first?—Dear me: whatever was
it?—
Whatever's that we knead the barley in?—
Bless us, what was it?

SOCRATES. Be off, and feed the crows,
You most forgetful, most absurd old dolt!

STREPSIADES. O me! what will become of me, poor wretch!

I'm clean undone: I haven't learnt to speak.—
O gracious Clouds, now do advise me something.

CHORUS. Our counsel, ancient friend, is simply this,
To send your son, if you have one at home,
And let him learn this wisdom in your stead.

STREPSIADES. Yes! I've a son, quite a fine gentleman:
But he won't learn, so what am I to do?

CHORUS. What! is he master?

STREPSIADES.   Well: he's strong and vigorous,
And he's got some of the Coesyra blood within him:[36]
Still I'll go for him, and if he won't come
By all the Gods I'll turn him out of doors.
Go in one moment, I'll be back directly.

(STREPSIADES *goes into his house*.)

CHORUS. Dost thou not see how bounteous we our favours free
            Will shower on you,
        Since whatsoe'er your will prepare
        This dupe will do.
But now that you have dazzled and elated so your man,
Make haste and seize whate'er you please as quickly as
    you can,
For cases such as these, my friend, are very prone to
    change and bend.

(*Exit* SOCRATES. *Enter* STREPSIADES *and* PHEIDIPPIDES.)

STREPSIADES. Get out! you shan't stop here: so help me Mist!
Be off, and eat up Megacles's columns.[37]

PHEIDIPPIDES. How now, my father? what's i'the wind to-day?
You're wandering; by Olympian Zeus, you are.

STREPSIADES. Look there! Olympian Zeus! you blockhead you,
Come to *your* age, and yet believe in Zeus!

PHEIDIPPIDES. Why prithee, what's the joke?

STREPSIADES.   'Tis so preposterous
When babes like you hold antiquated notions.
But come and I'll impart a thing or two,
A wrinkle, making you a man indeed.
But, mind: don't whisper this to any one.

PHEIDIPPIDES. Well, what's the matter?

STREPSIADES.   Didn't you swear by Zeus?

PHEIDIPPIDES. I did.

STREPSIADES.   See now, how good a thing is learning.
There is no Zeus, Pheidippides.

PHEIDIPPIDES.   Who then?

STREPSIADES. Why Vortex reigns, and he has turned out Zeus.

PHEIDIPPIDES. Oh me, what stuff.

STREPSIADES.   Be sure that this is so.

PHEIDIPPIDES. Who says so, pray?

STREPSIADES.   The Melian—Socrates,[38]
And Chaerephon, who knows about the flea-tracks.

PHEIDIPPIDES. And are you come to such a pitch of madness
As to put faith in brain-struck men?

STREPSIADES.   O hush!
And don't blaspheme such very dexterous men
And sapient too: men of such frugal habits
They never shave, nor use your precious ointment,
Nor go to baths to clean themselves: but you
Have taken *me* for a corpse and cleaned me out.
Come, come, make haste, do go and learn for me.

PHEIDIPPIDES. What can one learn from them that is worth
              knowing?

STREPSIADES. Learn! why whatever's clever in the world:
And you shall learn how gross and dense you are.
But stop one moment: I'll be back directly.

(*Exit* STREPSIADES.)

PHEIDIPPIDES. O me! what must I do with my mad father?
Shall I indict him for his lunacy,
Or tell the undertakers of his symptoms?

(*Enter* STREPSIADES *carrying a cock and a hen.*)

STREPSIADES. Now then! you see this, don't you? what do you
              call it?

PHEIDIPPIDES. That? why a fowl.

STREPSIADES.   Good! now then, what is this?

PHEIDIPPIDES. That's a fowl too.

STREPSIADES.   What both! Ridiculous!
  Never say that again, but mind you always
  Call this a fowless and the other a fowl.

PHEIDIPPIDES. A fowless! These then are the mighty secrets
  You have picked up amongst those earth-born fellows.

STREPSIADES. And lots besides: but everything I learn
  I straight forget: I am so old and stupid.

PHEIDIPPIDES. And this is what you have lost your mantle for?

STREPSIADES. It's very absent sometimes: 'tisn't lost.

PHEIDIPPIDES. And what have you done with your shoes, you
              dotard you!

STREPSIADES. Like Pericles, all for the best, I've lost them.[39]
  Come, come; go with me: humour me in this,
  And then do what you like. Ah! I remember
  How I to humour you, a coaxing baby,
  With the first obol which my judgeship fetched me
  Bought you a go-cart at the great Diasia.[40]

PHEIDIPPIDES. The time will come when you'll repent of this.

  (*Enter* SOCRATES.)

STREPSIADES. Good boy to obey me. Hallo! Socrates.
  Come here; come here; I've brought this son of mine,
  Trouble enough, I'll warrant you.

SOCRATES.   Poor infant
  Not yet aware of my suspension-wonders.

PHEIDIPPIDES. You'd make a wondrous piece of ware, sus-
              pended.

STREPSIADES. Hey! Hang the lad! Do you abuse the Master?

SOCRATES. And look, "suthspended!" In what foolish fashion
  He mouthed the word with pouting lips agape.
  How can *he* learn evasion of a suit,
  Timely citation, damaging replies?
  Hyperbolus, though, learnt them for a talent.

STREPSIADES. O never fear! he's very sharp, by nature.
  For when he was a little chap, *so* high,
  He used to build small baby-houses, boats,
  Go-carts of leather, darling little frogs
  Carved from pomegranates, you can't think how nicely!

So now, I prithee, teach him both your Logics,
The Better, as you call it, and the Worse
Which with the worse cause can defeat the Better;
Or if not both, at all events the Worse.

SOCRATES. Aye, with his own ears he shall hear them argue.
I shan't be there.

STREPSIADES.   But please remember this,
Give him the knack of reasoning down all Justice.

(*Exit* SOCRATES. *Enter* RIGHT LOGIC *and* WRONG LOGIC.)

RIGHT LOGIC. Come show yourself now with your confident
brow.
   —To the stage, if you dare!

WRONG LOGIC. "Lead on where you please:" I shall smash you
with ease,
If an audience be there.

RIGHT LOGIC. *You'll* smash me, you say! And who are *you*,
pray?

WRONG LOGIC. A Logic, like you.

RIGHT LOGIC.   But the Worst of the two.

WRONG LOGIC. Yet you I can drub whom my Better they dub.

RIGHT LOGIC. By what artifice taught?

WRONG LOGIC.   By original thought.

RIGHT LOGIC. Aye truly your trade so successful is made
By means of these noodles of ours, I'm afraid.

WRONG LOGIC. Not noodles, but wise.

RIGHT LOGIC.   I'll smash you and your lies!

WRONG LOGIC. By what method, forsooth?

RIGHT LOGIC.   By speaking the Truth.

WRONG LOGIC. Your words I will meet, and entirely defeat:
There never *was* Justice or Truth, I repeat.

RIGHT LOGIC. No Justice! you say?

WRONG LOGIC.   Well, where does it stay?

RIGHT LOGIC. With the Gods in the air.

WRONG LOGIC.   If Justice be there,
How comes it that Zeus could his father reduce,
Yet live with their Godships unpunished and loose?

RIGHT LOGIC. Ugh! Ugh! These evils come thick, I feel awfully sick,
  A basin, quick, quick!

WRONG LOGIC. You're a useless old drone with one foot in the grave!

RIGHT LOGIC. You're a shameless, unprincipled, dissolute knave!

WRONG LOGIC. Hey! a rosy festoon.

RIGHT LOGIC.   And a vulgar buffoon!

WRONG LOGIC. What! Lilies from *you?*

RIGHT LOGIC.   And a parricide too!

WRONG LOGIC. 'Tis with gold (you don't know it) you sprinkle my head.

RIGHT LOGIC. O gold is it now? but it used to be lead!

WRONG LOGIC. But now it's a grace and a glory instead.

RIGHT LOGIC. You're a little too bold.

WRONG LOGIC.   You're a good deal too old.

RIGHT LOGIC. 'Tis through you I well know not a stripling will go
  To attend to the rules which are taught in the Schools;
  But Athens one day shall be up to the fools.

WRONG LOGIC. How squalid your dress!

RIGHT LOGIC.   Yours is fine, I confess,
  Yet of old, I declare, but a pauper you were;
  And passed yourself off, our compassion to draw
    As a Telephus, (Euripidéan)[41]
  Well pleased from a beggarly wallet to gnaw
    At inanities Pandeletéan.

WRONG LOGIC. O me! for the wisdom you've mentioned in jest!

RIGHT LOGIC. O me! for the folly of you, and the rest
  Who you to destroy their children employ!

WRONG LOGIC. *Him* you never shall teach; you are quite out of date.

RIGHT LOGIC. If not, he'll be lost, as he'll find to his cost:
  Taught nothing by you but to chatter and prate.

WRONG LOGIC. He raves, as you see: let him be, let him be.

RIGHT LOGIC. Touch him if you dare! I bid you beware.

CHORUS. Forbear, forbear to wrangle and scold!
    Each of you show
You what you taught their fathers of old,
    You let us know
Your system untried, that hearing each side
From the lips of the Rivals the youth may decide
    To which of your schools he will go.

RIGHT LOGIC. This then will I do.

WRONG LOGIC.   And so will I too.

CHORUS. And who will put in his claim to begin?

WRONG LOGIC. If *he* wishes, he may: I kindly give way:
    And out of his argument quickly will I
Draw facts and devices to fledge the reply
Wherewith I will shoot him and smite and refute him.
And at last if a word from his mouth shall be heard
My sayings like fierce savage hornets shall pierce
    His forehead and eyes,
Till in fear and distraction he yields and he—dies!

CHORUS. With thoughts and words and maxims pondered well
    Now then in confidence let both begin:
Try which his rival can in speech excel:
    Try which this perilous wordy war can win,
Which all my votaries' hopes are fondly centred in.
O Thou who wert born our sires to adorn with characters
    blameless and fair,
Say on what you please, say on and to these your glorious
    Nature declare.

RIGHT LOGIC. To hear then prepare of the Discipline rare
    which flourished in Athens of yore
When Honour and Truth were in fashion with youth and
    Sobriety bloomed on our shore;
First of all the old rule was preserved in our school that
    "boys should be seen and not heard:"
And then to the home of the Harpist would come decorous
    in action and word
All the lads of one town, though the snow peppered down,
    in spite of all wind and all weather:

And they sung an old song as they paced it along, not
    shambling with thighs glued together:
"O the dread shout of War how it peals from afar," or
    "Pallas the Stormer adore,"
To some manly old air all simple and bare which their
    fathers had chanted before.
And should any one dare the tune to impair and with
    intricate twistings to fill,
Such as Phrynis is fain, and his long-winded train, per-
    versely to quaver and trill,[42]
Many stripes would he feel in return for his zeal, as to
    genuine Music a foe.
And every one's thigh was forward and high as they sat
    to be drilled in a row,
So that nothing the while indecent or vile the eye of a
    stranger might meet;
And then with their hand they would smooth down the
    sand whenever they rose from their seat,
To leave not a trace of themselves in the place for a vigi-
    lant lover to view.
They never would soil their persons with oil but were in-
    artificial and true.
Nor tempered their throat to a soft mincing note and sighs
    to their lovers addressed:
Nor laid themselves out, as they strutted about, to the
    wanton desires of the rest:
Nor would any one dare such stimulant fare as the head
    of the radish to wish:
Nor to make over bold with the food of the old, the anise,
    and parsley, and fish:
Nor dainties to quaff, nor giggle and laugh, nor foot within
    foot to enfold.
WRONG LOGIC. Faugh! this smells very strong of some musty
    old song, and Chirrupers mounted in gold;[43]
And Slaughter of beasts, and old-fashioned feasts.
RIGHT LOGIC.   Yet these are the precepts which taught
The heroes of old to be hardy and bold, and the Men who
    at Marathon fought!
But now must the lad from his boyhood be clad in a Man's
    all-enveloping cloak:

So that, oft as the Panathenaea returns, I feel myself ready
to choke

When the dancers go by with their shields to their thigh,
not caring for Pallas a jot.

You therefore, young man, choose me while you can; cast
in with my Method your lot;

And then you shall learn the forum to spurn, and from
dissolute baths to abstain,

And fashions impure and shameful abjure, and scorners
repel with disdain:

And rise from your chair if an elder be there, and respect-
fully give him your place,

And with love and with fear your parents revere, and
shrink from the brand of Disgrace,

And deep in your breast be the Image imprest of Modesty,
simple and true,

Nor resort any more to a dancing-girl's door, nor glance
at the harlotry crew,

Lest at length by the blow of the Apple they throw from
the hopes of your Manhood you fall.[44]

Nor dare to reply when your Father is nigh, nor "musty
old Japhet" to call[45]

In your malice and rage that Sacred Old Age which lov-
ingly cherished your youth!

WRONG LOGIC. Yes, yes, my young friend, if to him you attend,
by Bacchus I swear of a truth

You will scarce with the sty of Hippocrates vie, as a
mammy-suck known even there![46]

RIGHT LOGIC. But then you'll excel in the games you love well,
all blooming, athletic and fair:

Not learning to prate as your idlers debate with marvellous prickly dispute,

Not dragged into Court day by day to make sport in some
small disagreeable suit:

But you will below to the Academe go, and under the
olives contend[47]

With your chaplet of reed, in a contest of speed with some
excellent rival and friend:

All fragrant with woodbine and peaceful content, and the
leaf which the lime blossoms fling,

When the plane whispers love to the elm in the grove in
    the beautiful season of Spring.
If then you'll obey and do what I say,
And follow with me the more excellent way,
Your chest shall be white, your skin shall be bright,
Your arms shall be tight, your tongue shall be slight,
And everything else shall be proper and right.
But if you pursue what men nowadays do,
You will have, to begin, a cold pallid skin,
Arms small and chest weak, tongue practised to speak,
Special laws very long, and the symptoms all strong
Which show that your life is licentious and wrong.
And your mind he'll prepare so that foul to be fair
And fair to be foul you shall always declare;
And you'll find yourself soon, if you listen to him,
With the filth of Antimachus filled to the brim![48]

CHORUS. O glorious Sage! with loveliest Wisdom teeming!
    Sweet on thy words does ancient Virtue rest!
    Thrice happy they who watched thy Youth's bright
        beaming!
    Thou of the vaunted genius, do thy best;
    This man has gained applause: His Wisdom stands
        confest.
And you with clever words and thoughts must needs your
    case adorn
Else he will surely win the day, and you retreat with
    scorn.

WRONG LOGIC. Aye, say you so? why I have been half-burst;
    I do so long
To overthrow his arguments with arguments more strong.
I am the Lesser Logic? True: these Schoolmen call me so,
Simply because I was the first of all mankind to show
How old established rules and laws might contradicted be:
And this, as you may guess, is worth a thousand pounds
    to me,
To take the feebler cause, and yet to win the disputation.
And mark me now, how I'll confute his boasted Education!
You said that always from warm baths the stripling must
    abstain:

Why must he? on what grounds do you of these warm
baths complain?

RIGHT LOGIC. Why it's the worst thing possible, it quite un-
strings a man.

WRONG LOGIC. Hold there: I've got you round the waist:
escape me if you can.

And first: of all the sons of Zeus which think you was the
best?

Which was the manliest? which endured more toils than
all the rest?

RIGHT LOGIC. Well, I suppose that Heracles was bravest and
most bold.

WRONG LOGIC. And are the baths of Heracles so wonderfully
cold?[49]

Aha! you blame warm baths, I think.

RIGHT LOGIC.   This, this is what they say:
This is the stuff our precious youths are chattering all the
day!

This is what makes them haunt the baths, and shun the
manlier Games!

WRONG LOGIC. Well then, we'll take the Forum next: I praise
it, and he blames.

But if it *was* so bad, do you think old Homer would have
made

Nestor and all his worthies ply a real forensic trade?

Well: then he says a stripling's tongue should always idle
be:

I say it should be used of course: so there we disagree.

And next he says you must be chaste. A most preposterous
plan!

Come, tell me did you ever know one single blessed man

Gain the least good by chastity? come, prove I'm wrong:
make haste.

RIGHT LOGIC. Yes, many, many! Peleus gained a sword by
being chaste.[50]

WRONG LOGIC. A sword indeed! a wondrous meed the unlucky
fool obtained.

Hyperbolus the Lamp-maker hath many a talent gained

    By knavish tricks which I have taught: but not a sword, no, no!

RIGHT LOGIC. Then Peleus did to his chaste life the bed of Thetis owe.

WRONG LOGIC. And then she cut and ran away! for nothing so engages

    A woman's heart as forward warmth, old shred of those dark Ages!

    For take this chastity, young man: sift it inside and out:

    Count all the pleasures, all the joys, it bids you live without:

    No kind of dames, no kind of games, no laughing, feasting, drinking,—

    Why life itself is little worth without these joys, I'm thinking.

    Well I must notice now the wants by Nature's self implanted;

    You love, seduce, you can't help that, you're caught, convicted. Granted.

    You're done for; you can't say one word: while if you follow me

    Indulge your genius, laugh and quaff, hold nothing base to be.

    Why if you're in adultery caught, your pleas will still be ample:

    You've done no wrong, you'll say, and then bring Zeus as your example.

    He fell before the wondrous powers by Love and Beauty wielded:

    And how can you, the Mortal, stand, where He, the Immortal, yielded?

RIGHT LOGIC. Aye, but suppose in spite of all, he must be wedged and sanded:[51]

    Won't he be probed, or else can you prevent it? now be candid.

WRONG LOGIC. And what's the damage if it should be so?

RIGHT LOGIC. What greater damage can the young man know?

WRONG LOGIC. What will you do, if this dispute I win?

RIGHT LOGIC. I'll be for ever silent.

WRONG LOGIC. Good, begin.
The Counsellor: from whence comes he?

RIGHT LOGIC. From probed adulterers.

WRONG LOGIC. I agree.
The Tragic Poets: whence are they?

RIGHT LOGIC. From probed adulterers.

WRONG LOGIC. So I say.
The Orators: what class of men?

RIGHT LOGIC. All probed adulterers.

WRONG LOGIC. Right again.
You feel your error, I'll engage,
But look once more around the stage,
Survey the audience, which they be,
Probed or not Probed.

RIGHT LOGIC. I see, I see.

WRONG LOGIC. Well, give your verdict.

RIGHT LOGIC. It must go
For probed adulterers: him I know,
And him, and him: the Probed are most.

WRONG LOGIC. How stand we then?

RIGHT LOGIC. I own, I've lost.
O Cinaeds, Cinaeds, take my robe!
Your words have won, to you I run
To live and die with glorious Probe!

(*Enter* SOCRATES *and* STREPSIADES, *the former from the Phrontisterion, the latter from his own house, to see how his son's education is progressing.*)

SOCRATES. Well, what do you want? to take away your son
At once, or shall I teach him how to speak?

STREPSIADES. Teach him, and flog him, and be sure you well
Sharpen his mother wit, grind the one edge
Fit for my little law-suits, and the other
Why make that serve for more important matters.

SOCRATES. O, never fear! He'll make a splendid sophist.

STREPSIADES. Well, well, I hope he'll be a poor pale rascal.

(*Exeunt* SOCRATES *and* STREPSIADES.)

CHORUS. Go: but in us the thought is strong, you will repent
of this ere long.

Now we wish to tell the Judges all the blessings they shall
gain

If, as Justice plainly warrants, we the worthy prize obtain.

First, whenever in the Season ye would fain your fields
renew,

All the world shall wait expectant till we've poured our
rain on you:

Then of all your crops and vineyards we will take the
utmost care

So that neither drought oppress them, nor the heavy rain
impair.

But if any one amongst you dare to treat our claims with
scorn,

Mortal he, the Clouds immortal, better had he ne'er been
born!

He from his estates shall gather neither corn, nor oil, nor
wine,

For whenever blossoms sparkle on the olive or the vine

They shall all at once be blighted: we will ply our slings
so true.

And if ever we behold him building up his mansions new,

With our tight and nipping hailstones we will all his tiles
destroy.

But if he, his friends or kinsfolk, would a marriage-feast
enjoy,

All night long we'll pour in torrents: so perchance he'll
rather pray

To endure the drought of Egypt, than decide amiss to-
day!

(*The preceding Chorus represents a period of time long
enough for* PHEIDIPPIDES *to have gone through his entire
course of training.*)

(*Enter* STREPSIADES.)

STREPSIADES. The fifth, the fourth, the third, and then the
second,

And then that day which more than all the rest

I loathe and shrink from and abominate,

Then comes at once that hateful Old-and-New day.[52]
And every single blessed dun has sworn
He'll stake his gage, and ruin and destroy me.
And when I make a modest small request,
"O my good friend, part don't exact at present,
And part defer, and part remit," they swear
So they shall never touch it, and abuse me
As a rank swindler, threatening me with actions.
Now let them bring their actions! Who's afraid?
Not I: if these have taught my son to speak.
But here's the door: I'll knock and soon find out.
Boy! Ho there, boy!

(*Enter* SOCRATES.)

SOCRATES.   I clasp Strepsiades.

STREPSIADES. And I clasp you: but take this meal-bag first.
'Tis meet and right to glorify one's Tutors.
But tell me, tell me, has my son yet learnt
That Second Logic which he saw just now?

SOCRATES. He hath.

STREPSIADES.   Hurrah! great Sovereign Knavery!

SOCRATES. You may escape whatever suit you please.

STREPSIADES. What, if I borrowed before witnesses?

SOCRATES. Before a thousand, and the more the merrier.

STREPSIADES. "Then shall my song be loud and deep."
    Weep, obol-weighers, weep, weep, weep,
Ye, and your principals, and compound interests,
For ye shall never pester me again.
    Such a son have I bred,
    (He is within this door),
Born to inspire my foemen with dread,
    Born his old father's house to restore:
Keen and polished of tongue is he,
He my Champion and Guard shall be,
He will set his old father free,
Run you, and call him forth to me.
"O my child! O my sweet! come out, I entreat;[53]
    'Tis the voice" of your sire.

(*Enter* PHEIDIPPIDES.)

SOCRATES. Here's the man you require.

STREPSIADES. Joy, joy of my heart!

SOCRATES. Take your son and depart.

STREPSIADES. O come, O come, my son, my son,
      O dear! O dear!
    O joy, to see your beautiful complexion!
    Aye now you have an aspect Negative
    And Disputative, and our native query
    Shines forth there "What d'ye say?" You've the true face
    Which rogues put on, of injured innocence.
    You have the regular Attic look about you.
    So now, you save me, for 'twas you undid me.

PHEIDIPPIDES. What is it ails you?

STREPSIADES.   Why the Old-and-New day.

PHEIDIPPIDES. And is there such a day as Old-and-New?

STREPSIADES. Yes: that's the day they mean to stake their
      gages.

PHEIDIPPIDES. They'll lose them if they stake them. What! do
      you think
    That one day can be two days, both together?

STREPSIADES. Why, can't it be so?

PHEIDIPPIDES.   Surely not; or else
    A woman might at once be old and young.

STREPSIADES. Still, the law says so.

PHEIDIPPIDES.   True: but I believe
    They don't quite understand it.

STREPSIADES.   You explain it.

PHEIDIPPIDES. Old Solon had a democratic turn.

STREPSIADES. Well, but that's nothing to the Old-and-New.

PHEIDIPPIDES. Hence then he fixed that summonses be issued
    For these two days, the old one and the new one,
    So that the gage be staked on the New-month.

STREPSIADES. What made him add "the old" then?

PHEIDIPPIDES.   I will tell you
    He wished the litigants to meet on *that* day
    And compromise their quarrels: if they could not,
    Then let them fight it out on the New-month.

STREPSIADES. Why then do Magistrates receive the stakes
On the Old-and-New instead of the New-month?

PHEIDIPPIDES. Well, I believe they act like the Foretasters.[54]
They wish to bag the gage as soon as possible,
And thus they gain a whole day's foretaste of it.

STREPSIADES. Aha! poor dupes, why sit ye mooning there,
Game for us Artful Dodgers, you dull stones,
You ciphers, lambkins, butts piled up together!
O! my success inspires me, and I'll sing
Glad eulogies on me and thee, my son.
   "Man, most blessed, most divine,
   What a wondrous wit is thine,
   What a son to grace thy line,"
      Friends and neighbors day by day
         Thus will say,
When with envious eyes my suits they see you win:
But first I'll feast you, so come in, my son, come in.

(*Exeunt* STREPSIADES *and* PHEIDIPPIDES. *Enter* PASIAS *and
a* WITNESS.)

PASIAS. What! must a man lose his own property!
No: never, never. Better have refused
With a bold face, than be so plagued as this.
See! to get paid my own just debts, I'm forced
To drag you to bear witness, and what's worse
I needs must quarrel with my townsman here.
Well, I won't shame my country, while I live,
I'll go to law, I'll summon him.

(*Enter* STREPSIADES.)

STREPSIADES.   Hallo!

PASIAS. To the next Old-and-New.

STREPSIADES.   Bear witness, all!
He named two days. You'll summon me; what for?

PASIAS. The fifty pounds I lent you when you bought
That iron-grey.

STREPSIADES.   Just listen to the fellow!
The whole world knows that I detest all horses.

PASIAS. I swear you swore by all the Gods to pay me.

STREPSIADES. Well, now I swear I won't: Pheidippides
  Has learnt since then the unanswerable Logic.

PASIAS. And will you therefore shirk my just demand?

STREPSIADES. Of course I will: else why should he have learnt
      it?

PASIAS. And will you dare forswear it by the Gods?

STREPSIADES. The Gods indeed! What Gods?

PASIAS. Poseidon, Hermes, Zeus.

STREPSIADES.   By Zeus I would,
  Though I gave twopence halfpenny for the privilege.

PASIAS. O then confound you for a shameless rogue!

STREPSIADES. Hallo! this butt should be rubbed down with salt.

PASIAS. Zounds! you deride me!

STREPSIADES.   Why 'twill hold four gallons.

PASIAS. You 'scape me not, by Mighty Zeus, and all
  The Gods!

STREPSIADES. I wonderfully like the Gods;
  An oath by Zeus is sport to knowing ones.

PASIAS. Sooner or later you'll repent of this.
  Come do you mean to pay your debts or don't you?
  Tell me, and I'll be off.

STREPSIADES. Now do have patience;
  I'll give you a clear answer in one moment.

PASIAS. What do you think he'll do?

WITNESS.   I think he'll pay you.

STREPSIADES. Where is that horrid dun? O here: now tell me
  What you call this.

PASIAS.   What I call that? a trough.

STREPSIADES. Heavens! what a fool: and do *you* want your
      money?
  I'd never pay one penny to a fellow
  Who calls my troughess, trough. So there's your answer.

PASIAS. Then you won't pay me?

STREPSIADES.   No, not if I know it.
  Come put your best foot forward, and be off:
  March off, I say, this instant!

PASIAS.   May I die
  If I don't go at once and stake my gage!

STREPSIADES. No don't: the fifty pounds are loss enough:
  And really on my word I would not wish you
  To lose this too just for one silly blunder.

(*Exeunt* PASIAS *and* WITNESS. *Enter* AMYNIAS, *limping.*)

AMYNIAS. Ah me! Oh! Oh! Oh!

STREPSIADES. Hallo! who's that making that horrible noise?
  Not one of Carcinus's snivelling Gods?

AMYNIAS. Who cares to know what I am? what imports it?
  An ill-starred man.

STREPSIADES.   Then keep it to yourself.

AMYNIAS. "O heavy fate!" "O Fortune, thou hast broken
  My chariot wheels!" "Thou hast undone me, Pallas!"

STREPSIADES. How! has Tlepolemus been at you, man?

AMYNIAS. Jeer me not, friend, but tell your worthy son
  To pay me back the money which I lent him:
  I'm in a bad way and the times are pressing.

STREPSIADES. What money do you mean?

AMYNIAS.   Why what he borrowed.

STREPSIADES. You *are* in a bad way, I really think.

AMYNIAS. Driving my four-wheel out I fell, by Zeus.

STREPSIADES. You rave as if you'd fall'n times out-of-mind.

AMYNIAS. I rave? how so? I only claim my own.

STREPSIADES. You can't be quite right, surely.

AMYNIAS.   Why what mean you?

STREPSIADES. I shrewdly guess your brain's received a shake.

AMYNIAS. I shrewdly guess that you'll receive a summons
  If you don't pay my money.

STREPSIADES.   Well then tell me,
  Which theory do you side with, that the rain
  Falls fresh each time, or that the Sun draws back
  The same old rain, and sends it down again?

AMYNIAS. I'm very sure I neither know nor care.

STREPSIADES. Not care! good heavens! And do *you* claim your
    money,
  So unenlightened in the Laws of Nature?

AMYNIAS. If you're hard up then, pay me back the Interest
  At least.

STREPSIADES. Int-er-est? what kind of a beast is that?

AMYNIAS. What else than day by day and month by month
  Larger and larger still the silver grows
  As time sweeps by.

STREPSIADES.   Finely and nobly said.
  What then! think you the Sea is larger now
  Than 'twas last year?

AMYNIAS.   No surely, 'tis no larger:
  It is not right it should be.

STREPSIADES.   And do you then,
  Insatiable grasper! when the Sea,
  Receiving all these Rivers, grows no larger,
  Do you desire your silver to grow larger?
  Come now, you prosecute your journey off!
  Here, fetch the whip.

AMYNIAS.   Bear witness, I appeal.

STREPSIADES. Be off! what won't you? Gee up, sigma-brand!

AMYNIAS. I say! a clear assault!

STREPSIADES.   You won't be off?
  I'll stimulate you; Zeus! I'll goad your haunches.
  Aha! you run: I thought I'd stir you up
  You and your phaetons, and wheels, and all!

(*Exeunt* AMYNIAS *and* STREPSIADES.)

CHORUS. What a thing it is to long for matters which are
    wrong!
    For you see how this old man
    Is seeking, if he can
    His creditors trepan:
    And I confidently say
    That he will this very day
      Such a blow
  Amid his prosperous cheats receive, that he will deeply
    deeply grieve.

For I think that he has won what he wanted for his son,
And the lad has learned the way
All justice to gainsay,
Be it what or where it may:
That he'll trump up any tale,
Right or wrong, and so prevail.
    This I know.
Yea! and perchance the time will come when he shall
    wish his son were dumb.

(*Enter* STREPSIADES *and* PHEIDIPPIDES.)

STREPSIADES.   Oh! Oh!
Help! Murder! Help! O neighbours, kinsfolk, townsmen,
Help, one and all, against this base assault,
Ah! Ah! my cheek! my head! O luckless me!
Wretch! do you strike your father?

PHEIDIPPIDES.   Yes, Papa.

STREPSIADES. See! See! he owns he struck me.

PHEIDIPPIDES.   To be sure.

STREPSIADES. Scoundrel! and parricide! and house-breaker!

PHEIDIPPIDES. Thank you: go on, go on: do please go on.
    I am quite delighted to be called such names!

STREPSIADES. O probed Adulterer.

PHEIDIPPIDES.   Roses from your lips.

STREPSIADES. Strike you your father?

PHEIDIPPIDES.   O dear yes: what's more,
    I'll prove I struck you justly.

STREPSIADES.   Struck me justly!
Villain! how can you strike a father justly?

PHEIDIPPIDES. Yes, and I'll demonstrate it, if you please.

STREPSIADES. Demonstrate this?

PHEIDIPPIDES.   O yes, quite easily.
    Come, take your choice, which Logic do you choose?

STREPSIADES. Which what?

PHEIDIPPIDES.   Logic: the Better or the Worse?

STREPSIADES. Ah, then, in very truth I've had you taught
    To reason down all Justice, if you think

You can prove this, that it is just and right
That fathers should be beaten by their sons!

PHEIDIPPIDES. Well, well, I think I'll prove it, if you'll listen,
So that even you won't have one word to answer.

STREPSIADES. Come, I should like to hear what you've to say.

CHORUS. 'Tis yours, old man, some method to contrive
    This fight to win:
He would not without arms wherewith to strive
    So bold have been.
    He knows, be sure, whereon to trust.
    His eager bearing proves he must.

So come and tell us from what cause this sad dispute
        began;
Come, tell us how it first arose: do tell us if you can.

STREPSIADES. Well from the very first I will the whole conten-
        tion show:
'Twas when I went into the house to feast him, as you
        know,
I bade him bring his lyre and sing, the supper to adorn,
Some lay of old Simonides, as, how the Ram was shorn:
But he replied, to sing at meals was coarse and obsolete;
Like some old beldame humming airs the while she grinds
        her wheat.

PHEIDIPPIDES. And should you not be thrashed who told your
        son, from food abstaining
To sing! as though you were, forsooth, cicalas entertain-
        ing.[55]

STREPSIADES. You hear him! so he said just now or e'er high
        words began:
And next he called Simonides a very sorry man.
And when I heard him, I could scarce my rising wrath
        command;
Yet so I did, and him I bid take myrtle in his hand
And chant some lines from Aeschylus, but he replied with
        ire,
"Believe me, I'm not one of those who Aeschylus admire,
That rough, unpolished, turgid bard, that mouther of
        bombast!"

When he said this, my heart began to heave extremely
    fast;

Yet still I kept my passion down, and said, "Then prithee
    you,

Sing one of those new-fangled songs which modern strip-
    lings do."

And he began the shameful tale Euripides has told[56]

How a brother and a sister lived incestuous lives of old.

Then, then I could no more restrain, but first I must con-
    fess

With strong abuse I loaded him, and so, as you may guess,

We stormed and bandied threat for threat: till out at last
    he flew,

And smashed and thrashed and thumped and bumped and
    bruised me black and blue.

PHEIDIPPIDES. And rightly too, who coolly dared Euripides to
    blame,

Most sapient bard.

STREPSIADES. Most sapient bard! you, what's your fitting name?
    Ah! but he'll pummel me again.

PHEIDIPPIDES.   He will: and justly too.

STREPSIADES. What! justly, heartless villain! when 'twas I who
    nurtured you.

I knew your little lisping ways, how soon, you'd hardly
    think,

If you cried "bree!" I guessed your wants, and used to
    give you drink:

If you said "mamm!" I fetched you bread with fond dis-
    cernment true,

And you could hardly say "Cacca!" when through the door
    I flew

And held you out a full arm's length your little needs
    to do:

    But now when I was crying

    That I with pain was dying,

    You brute! you would not tarry

    Me out of doors to carry,

    But choking with despair

    I've been and done it there.

CHORUS. Sure all young hearts are palpitating now
　　　　To hear him plead,
　　Since if those lips with artful words avow
　　　　The daring deed,
　　And once a favouring verdict win,
　　A fig for every old man's skin.

　　O thou! who rakest up new thoughts with daring hands
　　　　profane,
　　Try all you can, ingenious man, that verdict to obtain.

PHEIDIPPIDES. How sweet it is these novel arts, these clever
　　　　words to know,
　　And have the power established rules and laws to over-
　　　　throw.
　　Why in old times when horses were my sole delight, 'twas
　　　　wonder
　　If I could say a dozen words without some awful blunder!
　　But now that he has made me quit that reckless mode of
　　　　living,
　　And I have been to subtle thoughts my whole attention
　　　　giving,
　　I hope to prove by logic strict 'tis right to beat my father.

STREPSIADES. O! buy your horses back, by Zeus, since I would
　　　　ten times rather
　　Have to support a four-in-hand, so I be struck no more.

PHEIDIPPIDES. Peace. I will now resume the thread where I
　　　　broke off before.
　　And first I ask: when I was young, did you not strike me
　　　　then?

STREPSIADES. Yea: for I loved and cherished you.

PHEIDIPPIDES. 　　　　　　　　　　Well, solve me this again,
　　Is it not just that I your son should cherish you alike,
　　And strike you, since, as you observe, to cherish means to
　　　　strike?
　　What! must my body needs be scourged and pounded
　　　　black and blue
　　And yours be scathless? was not I as much freeborn as
　　　　you?
　　"Children are whipped, and shall not sires be whipped?"⁵⁷

Perhaps you'll urge that children's minds alone are taught
 by blows:—

Well: Age is Second Childhood then: that everybody
 knows.

And as by old experience Age should guide its steps more
 clearly,

So when they err, they surely should be punished more
 severely.

STREPSIADES. But Law goes everywhere for me: deny it, if you
 can.

PHEIDIPPIDES. Well was not he who made the law, a man, a
 mortal man,

As you or I, who in old times talked over all the crowd?

And think you that to you or me the same is not allowed,

To change it, so that sons by blows should keep their
 fathers steady?

Still, we'll be liberal, and blows which we've received
 already

We will forget, we'll have no ex-post-facto legislation.

—Look at the game-cocks, look at all the animal creation,

Do not *they* beat their parents? Aye: I say then, that in fact

They are as we, except that they no special laws enact.

STREPSIADES. Why don't you then, if always where the game-
 cock leads you follow,

Ascend your perch to roost at night, and dirt and ordure
 swallow?

PHEIDIPPIDES. The case is different there, old man, as Socrates
 would see.

STREPSIADES. Well then you'll blame yourself at last, if you
 keep striking me.

PHEIDIPPIDES. How so?

STREPSIADES. Why, if it's right for me to punish you my son,
You can, if you have got one, yours.

PHEIDIPPIDES.   Aye, but suppose I've none.
Then having gulled me you will die, while I've been
 flogged in vain.

STREPSIADES. Good friends! I really think he has some reason
 to complain.

I must concede he has put the case in quite a novel light:
I really think we should be flogged unless we act aright!

PHEIDIPPIDES. Look to a fresh idea then.

STREPSIADES.   He'll be my death I vow.

PHEIDIPPIDES. Yet then perhaps you will not grudge ev'n what
          you suffer now.

STREPSIADES. How! will you make me like the blows which
          I've received to-day?

PHEIDIPPIDES. Yes, for I'll beat my mother too.

STREPSIADES.   What! What is that you say!
     Why this is worse than all.

PHEIDIPPIDES.   But what, if as I proved the other,
     By the same Logic I can prove 'tis right to beat my mother?

STREPSIADES. Aye! what indeed! if this you plead,
          If this you think to win,
          Why then, for all I care, you may
          To the Accursed Pit convey[58]
          Yourself with all your learning new,
          Your master, and your Logic too,
               And tumble headlong in.
     O Clouds! O Clouds! I owe all this to you!
     Why did I let you manage my affairs!

CHORUS. Nay, nay, old man, you owe it to yourself.
     Why didst thou turn to wicked practices?

STREPSIADES. Ah, but ye should have asked me that before,
     And not have spurred a poor old fool to evil.

CHORUS. Such is our plan. We find a man
               On evil thoughts intent,
     Guide him along to shame and wrong,
               Then leave him to repent.

STREPSIADES. Hard words, alas! yet not more hard than just.
     It was not right unfairly to keep back
     The money that I borrowed. Come, my darling,
     Come and destroy that filthy Chaerephon
     And Socrates; for they've deceived us both!

PHEIDIPPIDES. No. I will lift no hand against my Tutors.

STREPSIADES. Yes do, come, reverence Paternal Zeus.

PHEIDIPPIDES. Look there! Paternal Zeus! what an old fool.
Is there a Zeus?

STREPSIADES.   There is.

PHEIDIPPIDES.   There is *no* Zeus.
Young Vortex reigns, and he has turned out Zeus.

STREPSIADES. No Vortex reigns: that was my foolish thought
All through this vortex here. Fool that I was,
To think a piece of earthenware a God.[59]

PHEIDIPPIDES. Well rave away, talk nonsense to yourself.

STREPSIADES. O! fool, fool, fool, how mad I must have been
To cast away the Gods, for Socrates.
Yet Hermes, gracious Hermes, be not angry
Nor crush me utterly, but look with mercy
On faults to which his idle talk hath led me.
And lend thy counsel; tell me, had I better
Plague them with lawsuits, or how else annoy them.

(*Affects to listen.*)

Good: your advice is good: I'll have no lawsuits,
I'll go at once and set their house on fire,
The prating rascals. Here, here, Xanthias,
Quick, quick here, bring your ladder and your pitchfork,
Climb to the roof of their vile thinking-house,
Dig at their tiles, dig stoutly, an' thou lovest me,
Tumble the very house about their ears.
And some one fetch me here a lighted torch,
And I'll soon see if, boasters as they are,
They won't repent of what they've done to me.

STUDENT 1. O dear! O dear!

STREPSIADES. Now, now, my torch, send out a lusty flame.

STUDENT 1. Man! what are you at there?

STREPSIADES.   What am I at? I'll tell you.
I'm splitting straws with your house-rafters here.

STUDENT 2. Oh me! who's been and set our house on fire?

STREPSIADES. Who was it, think you, that you stole the cloak
                from?

STUDENT 3. O murder! Murder!

STREPSIADES.   That's the very thing,
　　Unless this pick prove traitor to my hopes,
　　Or I fall down, and break my blessed neck.

SOCRATES. Hallo! what are you at, up on our roof?

STREPSIADES. I walk on air, and contemplate the Sun.

SOCRATES. O! I shall suffocate. O dear! O dear!

CHAEREPHON. And I, poor devil, shall be burnt to death.

STREPSIADES. For with what aim did ye insult the Gods,
　　And pry around the dwellings of the Moon?
　　Strike, smite them, spare them not, for many reasons,
　　But most because they have blasphemed the Gods!

CHORUS. Lead out of the way: for I think we may say
　　We have acted our part very fairly to-day.

1. *Her twentieths.* Two thirds of the month have passed; interest was payable monthly.

2. *By Poseidon.* The implication is that there was on the scene some shrine or statuette of Poseidon. Its presence there was doubtless due to the young man's passion for horses.

3. *Thinking-house.* The word Phrontisterion (thinking-establishment, or thinking-house) was apparently the invention of Aristophanes. Neither it nor any of its surroundings has any real connection with Socrates, who founded no school, gave no lectures, and had no regular pupils, but was merely willing to converse at any time and in any place, in season or out of season, with anybody who was willing to converse with him.

4. The Sophistical teachers required a money payment. Socrates never did. This is repeatedly insisted upon by both Plato and Xenophon; perhaps the more frequently on account of the suggestion here.

5. *Breed of Phasians.* Probably horses.

6. "The art of making the worse appear the better cause" received Protagoras of Abdera as its first exponent in Greece. It was he who introduced the custom of teaching his disciples to argue for and against a given thesis with equal plausibility and ingenuity.

7. *You've made . . . to miscarry.* This phraseology was probably in use before the time of Socrates, but it cannot be better illustrated than by the passage in Plato's *Theaetetus* (148–151) in which Socrates describes himself as a midwife of ideas.

8. *Some fine ash.* Socrates goes to the palaestra, one of his usual haunts. Spreading charcoal ashes over the table, he

takes a spit and bends it into the form of a compass, and, instead of working out, as was expected, some geometrical problem, he contrives to angle away a garment which some athlete had thrown aside, and the sale of which will furnish the Phrontists with the means of obtaining their dinner.

9. *Thales* of Miletus, one of the seven wise men, was constantly spoken of as the embodiment of wisdom.

10. *Pylus.* The Laconians captured in Sphacteria were thrown into prison and kept in chains under strict watch and ward.

11. *What are these?* The eye of Strepsiades is attracted by two figures standing in the court. They represent, the one Astronomy, the other Geometry.

12. *Dicasts.* Members of the Athenian jury system.

13. *Water-cress.* An allusion to the homely imagery of Socrates.

14. *Athamas* was married to a Nephele (cloud). In a play of Sophocles called *Athamas,* he is brought in with a chaplet on his head to be sacrificed: Strepsiades fears lest *his* connection with the Clouds is to end in the same way.

15. *Flour.* This was another point of resemblance between the ritual of initiation and the ritual of sacrifice. Socrates seems to be sprinkling grain of some sort on the head of Strepsiades here.

16. *Bromian rejoicings.* The two Dionysian festivals with the competitions of the Choruses, the Tragic, the Comic, and the Dithyrambic.

17. *The Entrance* by which the Chorus made their way into the orchestra.

18. *Child of old Xenophantes.* Hieronymus, a poet with shaggy hair.

19. *Simon.* Unknown.

20. *Cleonymus.* Repeatedly attacked for his cowardice, Cleisthenes is another constant butt of the poet. There is scarcely a comedy in which he is not satirized for his gross effeminacy.

21. *Prodicus* of Ceos. A famous sophist.

22. *Vortex.* It was the theory of Anaxagoras, says Diogenes Laertius.

23. *Theorus.* This is doubtless the Theorus of whom we hear so much in *The Wasps*, chiefly as a hanger-on of Cleon.

24. *Search-warrant.* When one man charged another with a theft and went to search his house, he was bound to lay aside his upper garments lest he privately convey into the dwelling of the accused the thing asserted to be stolen.

25. *Trophonius.* They who went to consult the famous oracle of Trophonius took honied cakes in their hand to appease the serpents which haunted the spot.

26. *Brothers Profligate and Modest.* Aristophanes is referring to his first comedy, *The Banqueters*, which told of two brothers, one of whom was sent for his education into Athens and there imbibed not only the sharpness but also the dissolute principles of the rhetoricians, the sophists, and the demagogues, while the other, remaining with his father in the country, grew up a plain, honest countryman.

26a. *Another did the foundling nurse.* The Banqueters was exhibited in the name of Callistratus.

27. *Electra* in *The Choephoroe* of Aeschylus.

28. *Hyperbolus and his mother.* Hyperbolus was a dema-gogue. As to his mother, we know that she was a money-lender. Eupolis seems to have brought her on the stage drunk and dancing, for she is doubtless the person de-scribed three lines below.

29. *My Knights.* A reference to Aristophanes' comedy *The Knights* (424 B.C.). Eupolis, Phrynichus, and Hermippus were rival comic poets.

30. *"The Eels."* This is the famous simile in *The Knights* in which Aristophanes compares the demagogues troubling the city to eel-fishers who can catch nothing while the water is clear, but, when they have troubled the water and made it muddy and turbid, then make their catch.

31. *Memnon* and *Sarpedon.* These both fell before Troy, the former by the hand of Achilles, the latter by that of Patroclus. Sarpedon was the son of Zeus, whose grief at his

death is forcibly depicted in the sixteenth book of the *Iliad;* Memnon was the son of the Morning.

32. *Recorder of the Gate.* This would mean as an official at the meeting of the Amphictyonic Council.

33. *Finger music.* Dactylic metre, so named from *dactylos,* finger. Strepsiades takes the expression literally.

34. *Amynias.* This is no doubt the long-haired fop of whom we hear more in *The Wasps.*

35. *By the month.* Interest, as we are repeatedly reminded in this play, was payable at the New Moon.

36. *Coesyra blood.* He means that his son coming, on his mother's side, from the aspiring ladies of the great Alcmaeonid family, is full, like them, of soaring and lofty notions.

37. *Megacles' columns.* Pheidippides had relied on his uncle Megacles, and now to his uncle Megacles he shall go, and eat (if he will) the marble columns which adorn the palace of his noble relatives.

38. *The Melian.* Diagoras the Melian was a well-known sceptic. As there would be few Melians known at Athens, the application of the epithet to Socrates would at once be understood to refer to the sceptical philosopher.

39. *All for the best.* The reference is to a deliberately vague phrase used by Pericles to explain an expenditure to the Assembly. See Plutarch, Pericles, 23.

40. *The great Diasia.* A festival of Zeus in Athens.

41. *Telephus.* Appeared as a beggar in Euripides' play. Euripides is accused here of borrowing some of the sayings of Pandeletus.

42. *Phrynis.* The celebrated musician of Mitylene, who was doubtless alive when this comedy was written.

43. *Chirrupers.* Athenians of an earlier age had worn golden cicalas, or "chirrupers," in their hair.

44. *The blow of the Apple.* Throwing an apple was the recognized love-challenge amongst the Greeks and Romans.

45. *Japhet.* Iapetus the Titan was the father of Atlas, Menoetius, Prometheus, and Epimetheus.

46. *Hippocrates.* This Hippocrates is generally identified with the Athenian general, the nephew of Pericles.

47. *The Academe.* The Academy, the most famous "recreation ground" of Athens.

48. *Antimachus.* Otherwise unknown.

49. *The baths of Heracles.* Warm springs were called baths of Heracles, because, according to the legend, the first sprang up at Thermopylae to refresh Heracles when he was tired and weary after one of his labours.

50. *Peleus.* The husband of Thetis and father of Achilles, who resisted the advances of the wife of Acastus and was given a sword by the gods.

51. *Wedged and sanded.* The reference is to an ancient punishment for adultery, also alluded to in Rogers' phrase "probed adulterers."

52. *Old-and-New day.* The last day of the month, between the old moon and the new, in the old lunar calendar.

53. *"O my child!"* These two lines are parodied from Euripides' *Hecuba,* where Hecuba is calling her daughter Polyxena from the tent.

54. *The Foretasters.* It seems clear that at Athens these were an organized body, whose duty it was to taste the viands about to be served up at a public banquet, for the purpose of seeing that everything was well cooked and wholesome.

55. *Cicalas.* These little creatures were supposed to live upon dew. A person who was entertaining cicalas might reasonably expect that they would be singing all the time and would require no food.

56. *The shameful tale.* The incestuous marriage of Macareus and Canace, the children of Aeolus, as presented in the *Aeolus* of Euripides.

57. *"Children are whipped . . ."* A parody of a famous line in the *Alcestis* of Euripides.

58. *The Accursed Pit.* The chasm at Athens into which the bodies of criminals were thrown.

59. *A piece of earthenware.* The Greek word translated Vortex (*dinos*) also means a large earthenware pot or bowl.

THE WASPS

The Wasps was exhibited at the Lenaean festival in the year 422 B.C. The didascalia which records the result of that competition has come down to us in a corrupt form; but we can gather from it that *The Wasps*, exhibited by Aristophanes in his own name, obtained the prize; that *The Rehearsal*, also the work of Aristophanes, but exhibited in the name of Philonides, was placed second; and that the comedy placed third was *The Ambassadors* of Leucon.

The Wasps was merely one phase in the combat which the poet was waging against the demagogues. It had for its object the rupture of the alliance which existed between the demagogues on the one hand and the dicasts (justices in the Athenian jury system), who constituted their main support and stay in the popular assemblies, on the other. And this object Aristophanes endeavours to compass by showing that while the demagogues affected to flatter and patronize the dicastic system, they in reality reserved to themselves all the substantial benefits and fruits of the alliance and left the dicasts to pine and starve in a state of abject and degraded poverty.

Characters of the Drama

PHILOCLEON, *an old dicast*

BDELYCLEON, *his son*

SOSIAS,
XANTHIAS, } *two slaves*

CHORUS OF DICASTS, *dressed up as* WASPS

BOYS, *sons of the* CHORUS

CUR,
LABES, } *two dogs representing* CLEON *and* LACHES

A FLUTE-GIRL *named* DARDANIS, *a mute*

A GUEST

A BAKING-GIRL

A COMPLAINANT

THE WASPS

Before daybreak. The house in the background is enveloped in nets, and two drowsy slaves are watching at the doors.

SOSIAS. You ill-starred Xanthias, what's the matter now?

XANTHIAS. The nightly watch I'm studying to relieve.

SOSIAS. Why then, your ribs will have a score against you.
Do you forget what sort of beast we're guarding?

XANTHIAS. No, but I'd fain just drowse dull care away.

SOSIAS. Well, try your luck: for I too feel a sort
Of drowsy sweetness settling o'er my eyes.

XANTHIAS. Sure you're a maniac or a Corybant.

SOSIAS (*producing a wine flask*). Nay 'tis a sleep from great
Sabazius holds me.[1]

XANTHIAS (*producing another*). Aha! and I'm your fellow-
votary there.
My lids too felt just now the fierce assault
Of a strong Median nod-compelling sleep.
And then I dreamed a dream; such a strange dream!

SOSIAS. And so did I: the strangest e'er I heard of.
But tell yours first.

XANTHIAS.   Methought a monstrous eagle
Came flying towards the market-place, and there
Seized in its claws a wriggling brassy shield,
And bore it up in triumph to the sky,
And then—Cleonymus fled off and dropped it.[2]

SOSIAS. Why then, Cleonymus is quite a riddle.

XANTHIAS. How so?

SOSIAS.   A man will ask his boon companions,

> *What is that brute which throws away its shield*
> *Alike in air, in ocean, in the field?*

XANTHIAS. O what mishap awaits me, that have seen
So strange a vision?

SOSIAS.   Take it not to heart,
'Twill be no harm, I swear it by the Gods.

XANTHIAS. No harm to see a man throw off his shield!
But now tell yours.

SOSIAS.   Ah, mine's a big one, mine is;
About the whole great vessel of the state.

XANTHIAS. Tell us at once the keel of the affair.

SOSIAS. 'Twas in my earliest sleep methought I saw
A flock of sheep assembled in the Pnyx,
Sitting close-packed, with little cloaks and staves;[3]
Then to these sheep I heard, or seemed to hear,
An all-receptive grampus holding forth[4]
In tone and accents like a scalded pig.

XANTHIAS. Pheugh!

SOSIAS.   Eh?

XANTHIAS.   Stop, stop, don't tell us any more.
Your dream smells horribly of putrid hides.

SOSIAS. Then the vile grampus, scales in hand, weighed out
Bits of fat beef, cut up.

XANTHIAS.   Woe worth the day!
He means to cut our city up in bits.

SOSIAS. Methought beside him, on the ground, I saw
Theorus seated, with a raven's head.
Then Alcibiades lisped out to me,
Cwemark! Theocwus has a cwaven's head.[5]

XANTHIAS. Well lisped! and rightly, Alcibiades!

SOSIAS. But is not this ill-omened, that a man
Turn to a crow?

XANTHIAS.   Nay, excellent.

SOSIAS.   How?

XANTHIAS.   How!
Being a man he straight becomes a crow:
Is it not obvious to conjecture that
He's going to leave us, going to the crows?[6]

SOSIAS. Shall I not pay two obols then, and hire
    One who so cleverly interprets dreams?

XANTHIAS. Come, let me tell the story to the audience
    With just these few remarks, by way of preface.
    Expect not from us something mighty grand,
    Nor yet some mirth purloined from Megara.
    We have no brace of servants here, to scatter
    Nuts from their basket out among the audience,
    No Heracles defrauded of his supper,
    Nor yet Euripides besmirched again;
    No, nor though Cleon shine, by fortune's favour,
    Will we to mincemeat chop the man again.
    Ours is a little tale, with meaning in it,
    Not too refined and exquisite for you,
    Yet wittier far than vulgar comedy.
    You see that great big man, the man asleep
    Up on the roof, aloft: well, that's our master.
    He keeps his father here, shut up within,
    And bids us guard him that he stir not out.
    For he, the father, has a strange disease,
    Which none of you will know, nor yet conjecture,
    Unless we tell: else, if you think so, guess.
    Amynias there, the son of Pronapes,
    Says he's a dice-lover: but he's quite out.

SOSIAS. Ah, he conjectures from his own disease.

XANTHIAS. Nay, but the word does really end with -lover.
    Then Sosias here observes to Dercylus,
    That 'tis a *drink*-lover.

SOSIAS.   Confound it, no:
    That's the disease of honest gentlemen.

XANTHIAS. Then next, Nicostratus of Scambon says,
    It is a sacrifice- or stranger-lover.

SOSIAS. What, like Philoxenus? No, by the dog,
    Not quite so lewd, Nicostratus, as that.

XANTHIAS. Come, you waste words: you'll never find it out,
    So all keep silence if you want to know.
    I'll tell you the disease old master has.
    He is a *lawcourt*-lover, no man like him.

Judging is what he dotes on, and he weeps
Unless he sit on the front bench of all.
At night he gets no sleep, no, not one grain,
Or if he doze the tiniest speck, his soul
Flutters in dreams around the water-clock.[7]
So used he is to holding votes, he wakes
With thumb and first two fingers closed, as one
That offers incense on a new moon's day.
If on a gate is written *Lovely Demus*,
Meaning the son of Pyrilamp, he goes
And writes beside it *Lovely Verdict-box*.
The cock which crew from eventide, he said,
Was tampered with, he knew, to call him late,
Bribed by officials whose accounts were due.
Supper scarce done, he clamours for his shoes,
Hurries ere daybreak to the Court, and sleeps
Stuck like a limpet to the doorpost there.
So sour he is, the long condemning line
He marks for all, then homeward like a bee
Laden with wax beneath his finger-nails.
Lest he lack votes, he keeps, to judge withal,
A private pebble-beach secure within.
Such is his frenzy, and the more you chide him
The more he judges: so with bolts and bars
We guard him straitly that he stir not out.
For ill the young man brooks his sire's disease.
And first he tried by soft emollient words
To win him over, not to don the cloak
Or walk abroad: but never a jot he yielded.
He washed and purged him then: but never a jot.
A Corybant next he made him, but old master,
Timbrel and all, into the New Court bursts
And there sits judging. So when these rites failed,
We cross the Strait, and, in Aegina, place him,
To sleep the night inside Asclepius' temple:[8]
Lo! with the dawn he stands at the Court rails!
Then, after that, we let him out no more.
But he! he dodged along the pipes and gutters,
And so made off: we block up every cranny,
Stopping and stuffing them with clouts of rag:

Quick he drove pegs into the wall, and clambered
Up like an old jackdaw, and so hopped out.
Now then, we compass all the house with nets,
Spreading them round, and mew him safe within.
Well, sirs, Philocleon is the old man's name;
Ay truly; and the son's, Bdelycleon:[9]
A wondrous high-and-mighty mannered man.

BDELYCLEON (*from the house-top*). Xanthias and Sosias! are
   ye fast asleep?

XANTHIAS. O dear!

SOSIAS.   What now?

XANTHIAS.   Bdelycleon is up.

BDELYCLEON. One of you two run hither instantly,
For now my father's got into the kitchen,
Scurrying, mouselike, somewhere. Mind he don't
Slip through the hole for turning off the water.
And you, keep pressing at the door.

SOSIAS.   Ay, ay, sir.

BDELYCLEON. O heavens! what's that? what makes the chimney rumble?
Hallo, sir! who are you?

PHILOCLEON (*from the chimney*). I'm smoke escaping.

BDELYCLEON. Smoke? of what wood?

PHILOCLEON.   I'm of the fig-tree panel.

BDELYCLEON. Ay, and there's no more stinging smoke than
   that.
Come, trundle back: what, won't you? where's the board?
In with you! nay, I'll clap this log on too.
There now, invent some other stratagem.
But I'm the wretchedest man that ever was;
They'll call me now the son of Chimney-smoked.

SOSIAS. He's at the door now, pushing.

BDELYCLEON.   Press it back then
With all your force: I'm coming there directly.
And O be careful of the bolt and bar,
And mind he does not nibble off the door-pin.

(BDELYCLEON *descends to the ground.*)

PHILOCLEON (*within*). Let me out, villains! let me out to
  judge.
What, shall Dracontides escape unpunished?

BDELYCLEON. What if he should?

PHILOCLEON.   Why once, when I consulted
The Delphian oracle, the God replied,
That I should wither if a man escaped me.

BDELYCLEON. Apollo shield us, what a prophecy!

PHILOCLEON. O let me out, or I shall burst, I shall.

BDELYCLEON. No, by Poseidon! no, Philocleon, never!

PHILOCLEON. O then by Zeus I'll nibble through the net.

BDELYCLEON. You've got no teeth, my beauty.

PHILOCLEON.   Fire and fury!
How shall I slay thee, how? Give me a sword,
Quick, quick, or else a damage-cessing tablet.

BDELYCLEON. Hang it, he meditates some dreadful deed.

PHILOCLEON. O no, I don't: I only want to take
And sell the donkey and his panniers too.
'Tis the new moon to-day.

BDELYCLEON.   And if it is,
Cannot I sell them?

PHILOCLEON.   Not so well as I.

BDELYCLEON. No, but much better: drive the donkey out.

XANTHIAS. How well and craftily he dropped the bait
To make you let him through.

BDELYCLEON.   But he caught nothing
That haul at least, for I perceived the trick.
But I will in, and fetch the donkey out.
No, no; he shan't come slipping through again.
Donkey, why grieve? at being sold to-day?
Gee up! why grunt and groan, unless you carry
Some new Odysseus there?

XANTHIAS.   And, in good truth,
Here *is* a fellow clinging on beneath.

BDELYCLEON. Who? where?

XANTHIAS.   Why here.

BDELYCLEON.   Why what in the world is this?
Who are you, sirrah?

PHILOCLEON.   Noman I, by Zeus.

BDELYCLEON. Where from?

PHILOCLEON.   From Ithaca, son of Runaway.

BDELYCLEON. Noman I promise to no good you'll be.
Drag him out there from under. O the villain,
The place he had crept to! Now he seems to me
The very image of a sompnour's foal.

PHILOCLEON. Come now, hands off: or you and I shall fight.

BDELYCLEON. Fight! what about?

PHILOCLEON.   About a donkey's shadow.

BDELYCLEON. You're a born bad one, with your tricks and
        fetches.

PHILOCLEON. Bad! O my gracious! then you don't know yet
How good I am: but wait until you taste
The seasoned paunchlet of a prime old judge.

BDELYCLEON. Get along in, you and your donkey too.

PHILOCLEON. O help me, fellow-dicasts: help me, Cleon!

BDELYCLEON. Bellow within there when the door is shut.
Now pile a heap of stones against the door,
And shoot the door-pin home into the bar,
And heave the beam athwart it, and roll up,
Quick, the great mortar-block.

SOSIAS (starting).   Save us! what's that?
Whence fell that clod of dirt upon my head?

XANTHIAS. Belike some mouse dislodged it from above.

SOSIAS. A mouse? O, no, a rafter-haunting dicast,
Wriggling about behind the tiling there.

BDELYCLEON. Good lack! the man is changing to a sparrow.
Sure he'll fly off: where, where's the casting-net?
Shoo! shoo there! shoo! 'Fore Zeus, 'twere easier work
To guard Scione than a sire like this.[10]

SOSIAS. Well but at last we have fairly scared him in,
He can't slip out, he can't elude us now,
So why not slumber just a—just a—drop?

BDELYCLEON. Slumber, you rogue! when in a little while

His fellow-justices will come this way
Calling him up.

SOSIAS. Why sir, 'tis twilight yet.

BDELYCLEON. Why then, by Zeus, they are very late to-day.
Soon after midnight is their usual time
To come here, carrying lights, and warbling tunes
Sweet-charming-old-Sidono-Phrynichéan[11]
Wherewith they call him out.

SOSIAS. And if they come,
Had we not better pelt them with some stones?

BDELYCLEON. Pelt them, you rogue! you might as well provoke
A nest of wasps as anger these old men.
Each wears beside his loins a deadly sting,
Wherewith they smite, and on with yells and cries
They leap, and strike at you, like sparks of fire.

SOSIAS. Tut, never trouble, give me but some stones,
I'll chase the biggest wasps-nest of them all.

(*The actors retire to their respective posts, and after a
short pause the* CHORUS *make their appearance. They are
dressed up to resemble* WASPS, *and are armed with formidable stings. The Coryphaeus is encouraging his troop.*)

CHORUS. Step out, step out, my comrades stout: no loitering,
Comias, pound along,
You're shirking now, you used, I vow, to pull as tough as
leathern thong,
Yet now, with ease, Charinades can walk a brisker pace
than you.
Ho! Strymodore of Conthylè, the best of all our dicast
crew,
Has old Euergides appeared, and Chabes too from Phlya,
pray?
Ah! here it strains, the poor remains, alas! alas! alack the
day,
Of that mad set, I mind it yet, when once we paced our
nightly round,
In years gone by, both you and I, along Byzantium's wall,
and found[12]
And stole away the baker's tray, and sliced it up, and
chopped it well,

A merry blaze therewith to raise, and so we cooked our
    pimpernel.

On, on again, with might and main: for Laches' turn is
    come to-day:[13]

Quick, look alive, a splendid hive of wealth the fellow's
    got, they say.

And Cleon too, our patron true, enjoined us each betimes
    to bring

Of anger sore, an ample store, a good three days' provi-
    sioning:

On all the man's unrighteous plans a vengeance well-
    deserved to take.

Come, every dear and tried compeer, come, quickly come,
    ere morning break,

And as you go, be sure you throw the light around on
    every side;

Lest somewhere nigh a stone may lie, and we therefrom
    be damnified.

BOY. O father, father, here's some mud! look sharp or in
    you'll go.

CHORUS. Pick up a stick, and trim the wick, a better light to
    show.

BOY. Nay, father, with my finger, thus, I choose to trim the
    lamp.

CHORUS. How dare you rout the wick about, you little waste-
    ful scamp,

And that with oil so scarce? but no, it don't disturb *your*
    quiet,

However dear the oil may be, when I have got to buy it.

BOY. If with your knuckles once again you 'monish us, I swear

We'll douse the light, and take to flight, and leave you
    floundering there.

Then wading on without the lamp in darkness, I'll be
    bound

You'll stir and splash the mud about, like snipes in marshy
    ground.

CHORUS. Ah, greater men than you, my boy, 'tis often mine to
    beat.

But, bless me, this is filth indeed I feel beneath my feet:

Ay, and within four days from this, or sooner, it is plain,
God will send down upon our town a fresh supply of rain:
So dense and thick around the wick these thieves collect
    and gather,
And that's, as everybody knows, a sign of heavy weather.
Well, well, 'tis useful for the fruits, and all the backward
    trees,
To have a timely fall of rain, and eke a good North breeze.
But how is this? Our friend not here! how comes it he's
    so slack?
By Zeus, he never used to be at all a hanger-back.
He always marched before us all, on legal cares intent,
And some old tune of Phrynichus he warbled as he went.
O he's a wonder for the songs! Come, comrades, one and
    all,
Come stand around the house, and sing, its master forth
    to call.
If once he hears me tuning up, I know it won't be long
Before he comes creep, creeping out, from pleasure at the
    song.

  How is it our friend is not here to receive us?
    Why comes he not forth from his dwelling?
  Can it be that he's had the misfortune to lose
    His one pair of shoes;
  Or striking his toe in the dark, by the grievous
  Contusion is lamed, and his ankle inflamed?
    Or his groin has, it may be, a swelling.
      He of us all, I ween,
    Was evermore the austerest, and most keen.
      Alone no prayers he heeded:
      Whene'er for grace they pleaded,
      He bent (like this) his head,
      You cook a stone, he said.

  Is it all of that yesterday's man who cajoled us,
    And slipped through our hands, the deceiver,
  Pretending a lover of Athens to be,
    Pretending that he
  Was the first, of the Samian rebellion that told us?[14]
  Our friend may be sick with disgust at the trick,

And be now lying ill of a fever.
That would be like him quite.
But now up, up, nor gnaw your soul with spite.
There comes a traitor base,
A wealthy rogue from Thrace.
Safe in our toils we've got him,
Up, up, old friend, and pot him!

On with you, boy, on with you.

BOY. Father, if a boon I pray,
Will you grant it, father, eh?

CHORUS. Certainly I will, my son.
Tell me what you'd have me buy.
Dibs, my son? Hey, my son?
Dibs it is, undoubtedly.

BOY. Dibs, my father! No, my father!
Figs! for they are sweeter far.

CHORUS. You be hanged first: yet you shall not
Have them, monkey, when you are.

BOY. Then, my father, woe betide you! Not another step I'll
guide you.

CHORUS. Is it not enough that I
With this paltry pay must buy
Fuel, bread, and sauce for three?
Must I needs buy figs for thee?

BOY. Father, if the Archon say
That the Court won't sit to-day,
Tell me truly, father mine,
Have we wherewithal to dine?
O my father, should not we
Then in "Straits of Helle" be?

CHORUS. Out upon it! out upon it!
Then, indeed, I should not know
For a little bit of supper
Whither in this world to go.

BOY. Why, my mother, didst thou breed me, giving nothing
else to feed me,
But a store of legal woe?

CHORUS. Empty scrip! O empty show,
      Bootless, fruitless ornament!

BOY. O! O! woe! woe!
      Ours to sorrow and lament.

PHILOCLEON (*appearing above*). Long my reins have been
      stirred,
      Long through chinks have I heard,
      Heard your voices below.
      Vain my efforts to sing,
      These forbid me to go.
      Vainly my sad heart yearns,
      Yearns to be marching with you,
      On to the judgement urns,
      There some mischief to do.
      O change to smoke by a lightning stroke,
      Dread-thundering Zeus! this body of mine,
      Till I'm like Proxenides, like the son
         Of Sellus, that false tree-vine.[15]
      O Sovereign, pity my woeful lot,
      Vouchsafe to grant me my heart's desire,
      Fry me in dust with a glittering, hot,
         Red bolt of celestial fire,
      Then take me up with thy hand divine,
      And puff me, and plunge me in scalding brine.
      Or turn me into the stone, whereon
      They count the votes when the trial is done.

CHORUS. Who is he that thus detains you?
      Who with bolted door restrains you?
        Tell us, you will speak to friends.

PHILOCLEON. 'Tis my son, but don't be bawling: for he's
      slumbering now at ease
  There, upon the roof before you: drop your tone a little,
    please.

CHORUS. What's his object, idle trifler, that he does such things
      as these?
      What's the motive he pretends?

PHILOCLEON. He will let me do no mischief, and no more a
      lawsuit try.
  True it is he'll feast and pet me, but with that I won't
    comply.

CHORUS. This the Demagogcleon blared
    Out against you, since you dared
    Truth about the fleet to show.
    He must be involved, I see,
    In some dark *conspiracy*,
    Else he durst not use you so.
 It is time some means of escape to find, some novel, in-
    genious plan, that so,
 Unseen of your son, you may get you down, alighting in
    safety here below.

PHILOCLEON. O what shall it be? consider it ye! I'm ready to
    do whatever is planned:
 So sorely I'm longing a circuit to go, through the lists of
    the Court, with a vote in my hand.

CHORUS. Can you find no cranny or secret run, through which,
    from within, your path to urge,
 And then like wily Odysseus, here, disguised in tatters
    and rags, emerge?

PHILOCLEON. Each cranny is barred: there's never a run, thro'
    which though it were but a midge could squeeze.
 You must think, if you can, of a likelier plan: I can't run
    out like a runnet cheese.

CHORUS. O don't you remember the old campaign, when you
    stole the spit, and let yourself down,
 And away by the side of the wall you hied? 'Twas when
    we had captured Naxos town.[16]

PHILOCLEON. Ah, well I remember! but what of that? it is
    quite another affair to-day.
 For then I was young, and then I could steal, and over
    myself I possessed full sway.
 And then none guarded my steps, but I
 Was free, wherever I chose, to fly;
 Whilst now, in every alley and street,
 Armed men with arms are stationed about,
 Watching with care that I steal not out.
 And there at the gate you may see those two
 Waiting with spits to spit me through,
 Like a cat that is running away with the meat.

CHORUS. Well but now be quickly shaping

Some contrivance for escaping;
Morning breaks, my honey-bee.

PHILOCLEON. Then the best that I can think of, is to gnaw these meshes through.

May Dictynna, queen of hunters, pardon me the deed I do.[17]

CHORUS. Spoken like a man whose efforts will salvation's goal ensue. Ply your jaw then lustily.

PHILOCLEON. There, I've gnawn them through completely—Ah! but do not raise a shout,

We must use the greatest caution, lest Bdelycleon find us out.

CHORUS. Fear not: fear not: if he speak,
He shall gnaw his heart, and seek
For his life to run amain.
We will quickly make him learn
Nevermore again to spurn
Th' holy statutes of the Twain.[18]

So now to the window lash the cord, and twine it securely your limbs around.

With all Diopeithes fill your soul, then let yourself cleverly down to the ground.[19]

PHILOCLEON. But suppose they catch me suspended here, and hoist me up by the line again,

And angle me into the house once more, say what ye will do to deliver me then.

CHORUS. Our hearts of oak we'll summon to aid, and all give battle at once for you.

'Twere vain to attempt to detain you more: such wonderful feats we are going to do.

PHILOCLEON. This then will I do, confiding in you: and if anything happens to me, I implore

That you take me up and bewail my fate, and bury me under the court-house floor.

CHORUS. O nothing, nothing will happen to you: keep up, old comrade, your heart and hope;

First breathe a prayer to your father's gods: then let yourself down by the trusty rope.

PHILOCLEON. O Lycus, neighbour and hero and lord! thou
　　lovest the selfsame pleasures as I;[20]

Day after day we both enjoy the suppliant's tears and his
　　wailing cry.

Thou camest here thine abode to fix, on purpose to listen
　　to sounds so sweet,

The only hero of all that deigns by the mourner's side to
　　assume his seat:

O pity thine old familiar friend: O save me and succour
　　me, Power Divine!

And never again will I do my needs by the osier matting
　　that guards thy shrine.

BDELYCLEON (from the house-top). Get up, get up.

SOSIAS. 　　　　　　　　　　　　　Why, what's in the wind?

BDELYCLEON. Some voice seems circling me round and round.

SOSIAS. Is the old man slipping away through a hole?

BDELYCLEON. No, by Zeus, but he lets himself down to the
　　ground

Tied on to the rope.

SOSIAS. You infamous wretch! what, won't you be quiet and
　　not come down?

BDELYCLEON. Climb up by the other window-sill, and wallop
　　him well with the harvest crown.

I warrant he'll speedily back stern first, when he's thrashed
　　with the branch of autumnal fruits.

PHILOCLEON. Help! help! all those whoever propose this year
　　to busy themselves with suits.

Smicythion, help! Tisiades, help! Pheredeipnus, Chremon,
　　the fray begin:

O now or never, assist your friend, before I'm carried
　　away within.

CHORUS. Wherefore slumbers, wherefore slumbers, that resent-
　　ment in our breast,

Such as when a rash assailant dares provoke our hornets-
　　nest?

　　　　Now protruding, now protruding,

　　　　Comes the fierce and dreadful sting,

　　　　Which we wield for punishing.

    Children, hold these garments for us: then away with all
            your speed,
    Shout and run and bawl to Cleon, tell him of this direful
            deed;
        Bid him quickly hither fly
        As against a city-hater,
        And a traitor doomed to die,
        One who actually proposes
        That we should no lawsuits try.

BDELYCLEON. Listen, worthy sirs, to reason: goodness! don't
    keep screaming so.

CHORUS. Scream! we'll scream as high as heaven.

BDELYCLEON.   I don't intend to let him go.

CHORUS. These be frightful things to see! This is open *tyranny!*
    Rouse the State!   Rouse the great   God-abhorred
        Sneak Theorus!
    And whoe'er   Else is there,   Fawning lord
        Ruling o'er us.

XANTHIAS. Heracles! they've stings beside them! Master, mas-
    ter, don't you see?

BDELYCLEON. Ay, which slew the son of Gorgias, Philip, with
    their sharp decree.[21]

CHORUS. You we'll also slay directly! Wheel about him, every
        one,
    Draw your stings, and, all together, in upon the fellow
        run.
    Close your ranks, collect your forces, brimming full of
        rage and hate,
    He shall know the sort of wasps-nest he has dared to
        irritate.

XANTHIAS. Now with such as these to combat is, by Zeus, a
    serious thing:
    Verily I quake and tremble, but to look upon their sting.

CHORUS. Let him go! Loose your hold! If you don't I declare
    You shall bless   Tortoise-backs   For the shells Which
        they wear.

PHILOCLEON. On then, on, my fellow-dicasts, brother wasps of
    heart severe,

Some fly in with angry buzzings, and attack them in the
rear,

Some surround them in a ring, and both their eyes and
fingers sting.

BDELYCLEON. Ho there! Midas! Phryx! Masyntias! hither!
hither! haste to me!

Take my father, guard him safely: suffer none to set him
free;

Else you both shall lunch off nothing, clapped in fetters
strong and stout.

There's a sound of many fig-leaves (well I know it) buzzed
about.

(BDELYCLEON *goes into the house with* XANTHIAS *and*
SOSIAS.)

CHORUS. This shall stand infixed within you if you will not let
him go.

PHILOCLEON. Mighty Cecrops! King and hero! Dragon-born
and -shaped below,[22]

Wilt thou let these rude barbarians vex and maul me at
their pleasure,

Me who heretofore have made them weep in full im-
perial measure?

CHORUS. Truly, of abundant evils, age is evermore the source:

Only see how these two scoundrels hold their ancient lord
perforce,

Clean forgetting how, aforetime, he their daily wants supplied,

Bought them little sleeveless jackets, bought them caps
and coats of hide,

Clean forgetting all the kindness, shown their feet in
wintry weather,

How from chill and cold he kept them: ah! but these
have altogether

Banished from their eyes the reverence owing to those
dear old brogues.

PHILOCLEON. Won't you even now unhand me, shameless villain, worst of rogues?

When the grapes I caught you stealing, O remember, if
you can,

How I tied you to the olive, and I flogged you like a man,
So that all beheld with envy: but a grateful soul you lack!
O, unhand me, you, and you, at once, before my son come
      back.

CHORUS. But a famous retribution ye for this shall undergo,
      One that will not lag nor linger; so that ye betimes shall
            know,
      Know the mood of angry-tempered, righteous, mustard-
            glancing men.

(BDELYCLEON *and the two slaves issue from the house,*
XANTHIAS *armed with a stick,* SOSIAS *carrying an apparatus
for smoking out wasps.*)

BDELYCLEON. Beat them, Xanthias, from the door-way; beat
      the wasps away again.

XANTHIAS. That I will, sir.

BDELYCLEON.   Fume them, Sosias, drive the smoke
      in dense and thick.
      Shoo there, shoo! be off, confound you. At them, Xanthias,
            with the stick!
      Smoke them, Sosias, smoke, infusing Aeschines, Selartius'
            son.

SOSIAS. So then we at last were going, as it seems, to make you
      run.

BDELYCLEON. But you never would have managed thus to beat
      them off with ease,
      Had it chanced that they had eaten of the songs of
            Philocles.[23]

CHORUS. Creeping o'er us, creeping o'er us,
            Here at least the poor can see
            Stealthy-creeping *tyranny!*
      If you from the laws debar us, which the city has or-
            dained,
      You, a curly-haired Amynias, you, a rascal double-grained,
            Not by words of wit persuading,
            Not for weighty reasons shown,
            But because, forsooth, you *will* it,
            Like an autocrat, alone.

BDELYCLEON. Can't we now, without this outcry, and this fierce denunciation,

Come to peaceful terms together, terms of reconciliation?

CHORUS. Terms with *thee*, thou people-hater, and with Brasidas, thou traitor,

Hand and glove!   You who dare   Woolly-fringed Clothes to wear,[24]

Yes, and show   Beard and hair   Left to grow Everywhere.

BDELYCLEON. O, by Zeus, I'd really liefer drop my father altogether

Than endure these daily conflicts, buffeting with waves and weather.

CHORUS. Why, as yet you've hardly entered on the parsley and the rue:[25]

(That we'll just throw in a sample of our three-quart words for you.)

Now you care not, wait a little, till the prosecutor trounce you,

Sluicing out these selfsame charges, and *conspirator* denounce you.

BDELYCLEON. O by all the gods I ask you, will ye never go away?

Are ye quite resolved to linger, thwacked and thwacking all the day?

CHORUS. Never more   Will I while   There's a grain   Left of me Leave your door   Traitor vile   Bent to gain   *Tyranny.*

BDELYCLEON. Ay "Conspiracy" and "Tyrant," these with you are all in all,

Whatsoe'er is brought before you, be the matter great or small.

Everywhere the name of Tyrant, now for fifty years unknown,

Is than cheap salt-fish at Athens commoner and cheaper grown.

Everywhere about the market it is bandied to and fro:

If you wish a bass to purchase, and without a pilchard go,

Straight the man who sells the pilchards grumbles from his stall hard by,

Here is plainly one that caters with a view to Tyranny.
If a leek, besides, you order, relish for your sprats per-
  chance,
Says the potherb-girl directly, eyeing you with looks
  askance,
*Leeks indeed! and leeks I prithee! what, with Tyranny in
  view?*
Athens must be taxed, you fancy, relish to supply for you!

XANTHIAS. Even so a naughty damsel yesternoon observed to
  me,
Just because I said her manners were a little bit too free,
She supposed that I was wishing Hippias's Tyranny.[26]

BDELYCLEON. Ay, by charges such as these our litigious friends
  they please.
Now because I'd have my father (quitting all this toil and
  strife,
This up-early-false-informing-troublesome-litigious life)
Live a life of ease and splendour, live like Morychus, you
  see[27]
Straight I'm charged with Tyrant leanings, charged with
  foul conspiracy.

PHILOCLEON. Yes, by Zeus, and very justly. Not for pigeon's
  milk in store
I the pleasant life would barter which you let me lead no
  more.
Nought I care for eels and rayfish: daintier food to me
  would seem
Just a little, tiny lawsuit, dished and stifled in its steam.

BDELYCLEON. Yes, for that's the sort of dainty you, by Zeus,
  have loved so long.
Yet I think I'll soon convince you that your mode of life
  is wrong,
If you can but once be silent, and to what I say give heed.

PHILOCLEON. I am wrong to be a dicast!

BDELYCLEON.   Laughed to utter scorn indeed,
Mocked by men you all but worship, for you can't their
  treachery see,
You're a slave, and yet don't know it.

PHILOCLEON. Name not slavery to me!
I am lord of all, I tell you.

BDELYCLEON. You're the veriest drudge, I vow,
Thinking that you're lord of all. For come, my father,
teach us now,
If you reap the fruits of Hellas, what's the benefit to you?

PHILOCLEON. Willingly. Let these be umpires.

BDELYCLEON. I'll accept their judgement too.
Now then all at once release him.

PHILOCLEON. And besides a sword supply,
If in this dispute I'm worsted, here upon this sword I'll
die.

BDELYCLEON. But suppose you won't their final (what's the
phrase) award obey?

PHILOCLEON. May I never drink thereafter, pure and neat,
good fortune's—pay.

CHORUS. Now must the champion, going
Out of our school, be showing
Keen wit and genius new.

BDELYCLEON. Bring forth my memorandum-book: bring forth
my desk to write in.
I'll quickly show you what you're like, if that's your style
of fighting.

CHORUS. In quite another fashion
To aught this youth can do.
Stern is the strife and anxious
For all our earthly good,
If he intends to conquer,
Which Heaven forfend he should.

BDELYCLEON. Now I'll observe his arguments, and take a note
of each.

PHILOCLEON. What would you say, if he to-day should make
the conquering speech?

CHORUS. Ah! should that mischance befall us,
Our old troop were nothing worth:
In the streets with ribald mirth
Idle boys would dotards call us,

> Fit for nought but olive-bearing,
> Shrivelled husks of counter swearing.

O friend upon whom it devolves to plead the cause of our
Sovereign Power to-day,

Now show us your best; now bring to the test each trick
that an eloquent tongue can play.

PHILOCLEON. Away, away, like a racer gay, I start at once
from the head of the lists,

To prove that no kinglier power than ours in any part of
the world exists.

Is there any creature on earth more blest, more feared and
petted from day to day,

Or that leads a happier, pleasanter life, than a Justice of
Athens, though old and gray?

For first when rising from bed in the morn, to the crimi-
nal Court betimes I trudge,

Great six-foot fellows are there at the rails, in anxious
haste to salute their Judge.

And the delicate hand, which has dipped so deep in the
public purse, he claps into mine,

And he bows before me, and makes his prayer, and softens
his voice to a pitiful whine:

O pity me, pity me, Sire, he cries, *if you ever indulged your
longing for pelf,*

*When you managed the mess on a far campaign, or served
some office of state yourself.*

The man would never have heard my name, if he had not
been tried and acquitted before.

BDELYCLEON (*writing*). I'll take a note of the point you make,
that *suppliant fellows your grace implore.*

PHILOCLEON. So when they have begged and implored me
enough, and my angry temper is wiped away

I enter in and I take my seat, and then I do none of the
things I say.

I hear them utter all sorts of cries design'd expressly to
win my grace,

What won't they utter, what don't they urge, to coax a
Justice who tries their case?

Some vow they are needy and friendless men, and over
their poverty wail and whine,

And reckon up hardships, false with true, till he makes
    them out to be equal to mine.

Some tell us a legend of days gone by, or a joke from
    Aesop witty and sage,

Or jest and banter, to make me laugh, that so I may doff
    my terrible rage.

And if all this fails, and I stand unmoved, he leads by the
    hand his little ones near,

He brings his girls and he brings his boys; and I, the
    Judge, am composed to hear.

They huddle together with piteous bleats: while trem-
    bling above them he prays to me,

Prays as to a God his accounts to pass, to give him a quit-
    tance, and leave him free.

If thou lovest a bleating male of the flock, O lend thine
    ear to this boy of mine:

Or pity this sweet little delicate girl, if thy soul delights in
    the squeaking of swine.

So then we relax the pitch of our wrath, and screw it down
    to a peg more low.

Is *this* not a fine dominion of mine, a derision of wealth
    with its pride and show?

BDELYCLEON (*writing*). A second point for my note-book that,
    a derision of wealth with its show and its pride.

Go on to mention the good you get by your empire of
    Hellas so vast and wide.

PHILOCLEON. 'Tis ours to inspect the Athenian youths, when
    we enter their names on the rolls of men.

And if ever Oeagrus gets into a suit, be sure that he'll
    never get out again[28]

Till he give us a speech from his Niobe part, selecting the
    best and the liveliest one.

And then if a piper gain his cause, he pays us our price
    for the kindness done,

By piping a tune with his mouth-band on, quick march as
    out of the Court we go.

And what if a father by will to a friend his daughter and
    heiress bequeath and bestow,

We care not a rap for the will, or the cap which is there
    on the seal so grand and sedate,

We bid them begone, and be hanged, and ourselves take
    charge of the girl and her worthy estate;

And we give her away to whoever we choose, to whoever
    may chance to persuade us: yet we,

Whilst other officials must pass an account, alone from con-
    trol and accounting are free.

BDELYCLEON. Ay that, and that only, of all you have said, I
    own is a privilege lucky and rare,

But uncapping the seal of the heiress's will seems rather a
    shabby and doubtful affair.

PHILOCLEON. And if ever the Council or People have got a
    knotty and difficult case to decide,

They pass a decree for the culprits to go to the able and
    popular Courts to be tried:

Evathlus, and He! the loser of shields, the fawning, the
    great Cowardonymus say[29]

"They'll always be fighting away for the mob," "the people
    of Athens they'll never betray."

And none in the People a measure can pass, unless he pro-
    pose that the Courts shall be free,

Dismissed and discharged for the rest of the day when
    once we have settled a single decree.

Yea, Cleon the Bawler and Brawler himself, at us, and us
    only, to nibble forbears,

And sweeps off the flies that annoy us, and still with a
    vigilant hand for our dignity cares.

You never have shown such attention as this, or displayed
    such a zeal in your father's affairs.

Yet Theorus, a statesman as noble and grand as lordly
    Euphemius, runs at our call

And whips out a sponge from his bottle, and stoops, to
    black and to polish the shoes of us all.

Such, such is the glory, the joy, the renown, from which
    you desire to retain and withhold me,

And *this* you will show, this Empire of mine, to be bond-
    age and slavery merely, you told me.

BDELYCLEON. Ay, chatter your fill, you will cease before long:
    and then I will show that your boasted success

Is just the success of a tail that is washed, going back to
    its filth and its slovenliness.

PHILOCLEON. But the nicest and pleasantest part of it all is this,
    which I'd wholly forgotten to say,
'Tis when with my fee in my wallet I come, returning
    home at the close of the day,
O then what a welcome I get for its sake; my daughter, the
    darling, is foremost of all,
And she washes my feet and anoints them with care, and
    above them she stoops, and a kiss lets fall,
Till at last by the pretty Papas of her tongue she angles
    withal my three-obol away.
Then my dear little wife, she sets on the board nice man-
    chets of bread in a tempting array,
And cosily taking a seat by my side, with loving entreaty
    constrains me to feed;
I beseech you taste this, I implore you try that. This, this I
    delight in, and ne'er may I need
To look to yourself and your pantler, a scrub who, when-
    ever I ask him my breakfast to set,
Keeps grumbling and murmuring under his breath. No!
    no! if he haste not a manchet to get,
Lo here my defence from the evils of life, my armour of
    proof, my impregnable shield.
And what if you pour me no liquor to drink, yet here's an
    old Ass, full of wine, that I wield,[30]
And I tilt him, and pour for myself, and imbibe; whilst
    sturdy old Jack, as a bumper I drain,
Lets fly at your goblet a bray of contempt, a mighty and
    masterful snort of disdain.
    Is *this* not a fine dominion of mine?
    Is it less than the empire of Zeus?
Why the very same phrases, so grand and divine,
    For me, as for Him, are in use.
For when we are raging loud and high
    In stormy, tumultuous din,
O Lord! O Zeus! say the passers-by,
    How thunders the Court within!
The wealthy and great, when my lightnings glare,
Turn pale and sick, and mutter a prayer.
You fear me too: I protest you do:

Yes, yes, by Demeter I vow 'tis true.
But hang me if I am afraid of you.

CHORUS. I never, no, I never
 Have heard so clear and clever
 And eloquent a speech—

PHILOCLEON. Ay, ay, he thought he'd steal my grapes, and
 pluck them undefended,
For well he knew that I'm in this particularly splendid.

CHORUS. No topic he omitted,
  But he duly went through each.
 I waxed in size to hear him
 Till with ecstasy possessed
 Methought I sat a-judging
 In the Islands of the Blest.

PHILOCLEON. See how uneasily he stands, and gapes, and shifts
 his ground.
I warrant, sir, before I've done, you'll look like a beaten
 hound.

CHORUS. You must now, young man, be seeking
 Every turn and every twist
 Which can your defence assist.
 To a youth against me speaking
 Mine's a heart 'tis hard to render
 (So you'll find it) soft and tender.
And therefore unless you can speak to the point, you
 must look for a millstone handy and good,
Fresh hewn from the rock, to shiver and shock the un-
 yielding grit of my resolute mood.

BDELYCLEON. Hard were the task, and shrewd the intent, for a
 Comedy-poet all too great
To attempt to heal an inveterate, old disease engrained in
 the heart of the state.
Yet, O dread Cronides, Father and Lord,

PHILOCLEON.   Stop, stop, don't talk in that father-me way,
Convince me at once that I'm only a slave, or else I protest you shall die this day,
Albeit I then must ever abstain from the holy flesh of the
 victims slain.

BDELYCLEON. Then listen my own little pet Papa, and smooth
    your brow from its frowns again.

And not with pebbles precisely ranged, but roughly thus
    on your fingers count

The tribute paid by the subject States, and just consider
    its whole amount;

And then, in addition to this, compute the many taxes and
    one-per-cents,

The fees and the fines, and the silver mines, the markets
    and harbours and sales and rents.

If you take the total result of the lot, 'twill reach two
    thousand talents or near.

And next put down the Justices' pay, and reckon the sums
    they receive a year:

Six thousand Justices, count them through, there dwell no
    more in the land as yet,

One hundred and fifty talents a year I think you will find
    is all they get.[31]

PHILOCLEON. Then not one tithe of our income goes to furnish
    forth the Justices' pay.

BDELYCLEON. No, certainly not.

PHILOCLEON.   And what becomes of all the
    rest of the revenue, pray?

BDELYCLEON. Why, bless you, it goes to the pockets of those,
    To the rabble of Athens I'll ever be true,
    I'll always battle away for the mob. O father, my father,
    'tis owing to you:

By such small phrases as these cajoled, you lift them over
    yourselves to reign.

And then, believe me, they soon contrive some fifty tal-
    ents in bribes to gain,

Extorting them out of the subject states, by hostile menace
    and angry frown:

Hand over, they say, *the tribute-pay, or else my thunders
    shall crush your town.*

You joy the while at the remnants vile, the trotters and
    tips of your power to gnaw.

So when our knowing, acute allies the rest, the scum of
    the Populace, saw

> On a vote-box pine, and on nothingness dine, and marked
> how lanky and lean ye grow,
> They count you all as a Connas's vote, and ever and ever
> on these bestow[32]
> Wines, cheeses, necklaces, sesamè fruit, and jars of pickle
> and pots of honey,
> Rugs, cushions, and mantles, and cups, and crowns, and
> health, and vigour, and lots of money.
> Whilst *you!* from out of the broad domain for which on
> the land and the wave you toiled,
> None gives you so much as a garlic head, to flavour the
> dish when your sprats are boiled.

PHILOCLEON. That's true no doubt, for I just sent out and
bought, myself, from Eucharides three;
But you wear me away by your long delay in proving my
bondage and slavery.

BDELYCLEON. Why *is* it not slavery pure and neat, when these
(themselves and their parasites too)
Are all in receipt of their pay, God wots, as high officials
of state: whilst you
Must thankful be for your obols three, those obols which
ye yourselves have won
In the battle's roar, by sea and by shore, 'mid sieges and
miseries many a one.
But O what throttles me most of all, is this, that under
constraint you go,
When some young dissolute spark comes in, some son of
a Chaereas, straddling—so[33]
With his legs apart, and his body poised, and a mincing,
soft, effeminate air,
And bids you Justices, one and all, betimes in the morn
to the Court repair,
For that any who after the signal come shall lose and
forfeit their obols three.
Yet come as late as he choose himself, he pockets his
drachma, "Counsel's fee."
And then if a culprit give him a bribe, he gets his fellow
the job to share,
And into each other's hands they play, and manage together the suit to square.

Just like two men at a saw they work, and one keeps
    pulling, and one gives way,
While you at the Treasurer stare and gape, and never
    observe the tricks they play.

PHILOCLEON. Is *that* what they do! O can it be true! Ah me,
    the depths of my being are stirred,
Your statements shake my soul, and I feel, I know not how,
    at the things I've heard.

BDELYCLEON. And just consider when you and all might revel
    in affluence, free as air,
How these same demagogues wheel you round, and cabin
    and coop you, I know not where.
And you, the lord of such countless towns, from Pontus to
    Sardo, nought obtain
Save this poor pittance you earn, and this they dole you
    in driblets, grain by grain,
As though they were dropping oil from wool, as much for-
    sooth as will life sustain.
They *mean* you all to be poor and gaunt, and I'll tell you,
    father, the reason why.
They want you to know your keeper's hand; and then if
    he hiss you on to fly
At some helpless foe, away you go, with eager vehemence
    ready and rough,
Since if they wished to maintain you well, the way to do
    it were plain enough.
A thousand cities our rule obey, a thousand cities their
    tribute pay,
Allot them twenty Athenians each, to feed and nourish
    from day to day,
And twice ten thousand citizens there, are living immersed
    in dishes of hare,
With creams and beestings and sumptuous fare, and gar-
    lands and coronals everywhere,
Enjoying a fate that is worthy the State, and worthy the
    trophy on Marathon plain.
Whilst now like gleaners ye all are fain to follow along in
    the paymaster's train.

PHILOCLEON. O what can this strange sensation mean, this
    numbness that over my hand is stealing?

My arm no longer can hold the sword: I yield, unmanned,
  to a womanish feeling.

BDELYCLEON. Let a panic possess them, they're ready to give
  Euboea at once for the State to divide,

And engage to supply for every man full fifty bushels of
  wheat beside.

But five poor bushels of barley each is all that you ever
  obtained in fact,

And that doled out by the quart, while first they worry
  you under the Alien Act.

And therefore it was that I locked you away
To keep you in ease; unwilling that these
With empty mouthings your age should bilk.
And now I offer you here to-day
Without any reserve whatever you please,
Save only a draught of—Treasurer's milk.

CHORUS. 'Twas a very acute and intelligent man, whoever it
  was, that happened to say,

Don't make up your mind till you've heard both sides, for
  now I protest you have gained the fray.

Our staves of justice, our angry mood, for ever and ever
  aside we lay,

And we turn to talk to our old compeer, our choir-com-
  panion of many a day.

Don't be a fool: give in, give in,
Nor too perverse and stubborn be;
I would to Heaven my kith and kin
Would show the like regard for me.
Some deity, 'tis plain, befriends
Your happy lot, believe, believe it;
With open arms his aid he sends,
Do you with open arms receive it.

BDELYCLEON. I'll give him whatever his years require,
A basin of gruel, and soft attire,
And a good warm rug, and a handmaid fair,
To chafe and cherish his limbs with care.
—But I can't like this, that he stands so mute,
And speaks not a word nor regards my suit.

CHORUS. 'Tis that his soberer thoughts review

The frenzy he indulged so long,
And (what he would not yield to you)
He feels his former life was wrong.
Perchance he'll now amend his plan,
Unbend his age to mirth and laughter,
A better and a wiser man
By your advice he'll live hereafter.

PHILOCLEON. O misery! O misery!

BDELYCLEON. O father, why that dolorous cry?

PHILOCLEON. Talk not of things like these to me!
Those are my pleasures, *there* would I be
Where the Usher cries
Who has not voted? let him arise.
And O that the last of the voting band
By the verdict-box I could take my stand.
On, on, my soul! why, where is she gone?[34]
Hah! by your leave, my shadowy one!
Zounds, if I catch when in Court I'm sitting
Cleon again a theft committing!

BDELYCLEON. O father, father, by the Gods comply.

PHILOCLEON. Comply with what? name any wish, save one.

BDELYCLEON. Save what, I prithee?

PHILOCLEON.   Not to judge, but that
Hades shall settle ere my soul comply.

BDELYCLEON. Well but if these are really your delights,
Yet why go *There?* why not remain at home
And sit and judge among your household here?

PHILOCLEON. Folly! judge what?

BDELYCLEON.   The same as There you do.
Suppose you catch your housemaid on the sly
Opening the door: fine her for that, one drachma.
That's what you did at every sitting There.
And very aptly, if the morning's fine,
You'll fine your culprits, sitting in the sun.
In snow, enter your judgements by the fire
While it rains on: and—though you sleep till midday,
No archon here will close the door against you.

PHILOCLEON. Hah! I like that.

BDELYCLEON. And then, however long
An orator proses on, no need to fast,
Worrying yourself (ay, and the prisoner too).

PHILOCLEON. But do you really think that I can judge
As well as now, whilst eating and digesting?

BDELYCLEON. As well? much better. When there's reckless
swearing,
Don't people say, what time and thought and trouble
It took the judges to digest the case?

PHILOCLEON. I'm giving in. But you've not told me yet
How I'm to get my pay.

BDELYCLEON. I'll pay you.

PHILOCLEON. Good,
Then I shall have mine to myself, alone;
For once Lysistratus, the funny fool,
Played me the scurviest trick. We'd got one drachma
Betwixt us two: he changed it at the fish-stall;
Then laid me down three mullet scales: and I,
I thought them obols, popped them in my mouth;
O the vile smell! O la! I spat them out
And collared him.

BDELYCLEON. And what said he?

PHILOCLEON. The rascal!
He said I'd got the stomach of a cock.
You soon digest hard coin, he says, says he.

BDELYCLEON. Then there again you'll get a great advantage.

PHILOCLEON. Ay ay, that's something: let's begin at once.

BDELYCLEON. Then stop a moment whilst I fetch the traps.

(BDELYCLEON *goes into the house.*)

PHILOCLEON. See here now, how the oracles come true.
Oft have I heard it said that the Athenians
One day would try their lawsuits in their homes,
That each would have a little Court-let built
For his own use, in his own porch, before
His entrance, like a shrine of Hecate.

BDELYCLEON (*bustles in with a quantity of judicial properties*).
Now then I hope you're satisfied: I've brought

All that I promised, and a lot besides.
See here I'll hang this vessel on a peg,
In case you want it as the suit proceeds.

PHILOCLEON. Now that I call extremely kind and thoughtful,
And wondrous handy for an old man's needs.

BDELYCLEON. And here's a fire, and gruel set beside it,
All ready when you want it.

PHILOCLEON.   Good again.
Now if I'm feverish I shan't lose my pay,
For here I'll sit, and sip my gruel too.
But why in the world have ye brought me out the cock?

BDELYCLEON. To wake you, father, crowing over head
In case you're dozing whilst a prisoner pleads.

PHILOCLEON. One thing I miss, and only one.

BDELYCLEON.   What's that?

PHILOCLEON. If you could somehow fetch the shrine of Lycus!

BDELYCLEON. Here then it is, and here's the king in person.

PHILOCLEON. O hero lord, how stern you are to see!

BDELYCLEON. Almost, methinks, like our—Cleonymus.

XANTHIAS. Ay, and 'tis true the hero has no shield!

BDELYCLEON. If you got seated sooner, I should sooner
Call a suit on.

PHILOCLEON.   Call on, I've sat for ages.

BDELYCLEON. Let's see: what matter shall I bring on first?
Who's been at mischief of the household here?
That careless Thratta now, she charred the pitcher.

PHILOCLEON. O stop, for goodness sake! you've all but killed
me.
What! call a suit on with no railing here,
Always the first of all our sacred things?

BDELYCLEON. No more there is, by Zeus.

PHILOCLEON.   I'll run myself
And forage out whatever comes to hand.

(PHILOCLEON *goes into the house.*)

BDELYCLEON. Heyday! where now? The strange infatuation!

XANTHIAS. Psha! rot the dog! To keep a cur like this!

BDELYCLEON. What's happened now?

XANTHIAS.   Why, has not Labes here
  Got to the kitchen safe, and grabbed a cheese,
  A rich Sicilian cheese, and bolted it?[35]

BDELYCLEON. Then that's the first indictment we'll bring on
  Before my father: you shall prosecute.

XANTHIAS. Thank you, not I. This other Cur declares
  If there's a charge, he'll prosecute with pleasure.

BDELYCLEON. Bring them both here.

XANTHIAS.   Yes, yes, sir, so I will.

(*Enter* PHILOCLEON, *bearing a little fence.*)

BDELYCLEON (*to* PHILOCLEON). Hallo, what's this?

PHILOCLEON.   Pigrailings from the hearth.

BDELYCLEON. Sacrilege, eh?

PHILOCLEON.   No, but I'd trounce some fellow
  (As the phrase goes) even from the very hearth.[36]
  So call away: I'm keen for passing sentence.

BDELYCLEON. Then now I'll fetch the cause-lists and the
  pleadings.

PHILOCLEON. O these delays! You weary and wear me out.
  I've long been dying to commence my furrows.

BDELYCLEON. Now then!

PHILOCLEON.   Call on.

BDELYCLEON.   Yes certainly.

PHILOCLEON.   And who
  Is first in order?

BDELYCLEON.   Dash it, what a bother!
  I quite forgot to bring the voting urns.

PHILOCLEON. Goodness! where now?

BDELYCLEON.   After the urns.

PHILOCLEON.   Don't trouble,
  I'd thought of that. I've got these ladling bowls.

BDELYCLEON. That's capital: then now methinks we have
  All that we want. No, there's no waterpiece.

PHILOCLEON. Waterpiece, quotha! pray what call you this?

BDELYCLEON. Well thought on, father: and with shrewd home
    wit.
  Ho, there within! some person bring me out
  A pan of coals, and frankincense, and myrtle,
  That so our business may commence with prayer.

CHORUS. We too, as ye offer the prayer and wine,
    We too will call on the Powers Divine
      To prosper the work begun;
      For the battle is over and done,
    And out of the fray and the strife to-day
      Fair peace ye have nobly won.

BDELYCLEON. Now hush all idle words and sounds profane.

CHORUS. O Pythian Phoebus, bright Apollo, deign
      To speed this youth's design
      Wrought here, these gates before,
      And give us from our wandering rest
      And peace for evermore.

(The shout of "Io Paean" is raised.)

BDELYCLEON. Aguieus! my neighbour and hero and lord! who
    dwellest in front of my vestibule gate,[37]
  I pray thee be graciously pleased to accept the rite that
    we new for my father create.
  O bend to a pliant and flexible mood the stubborn and
    resolute oak of his will,
  And into his heart, so crusty and tart, a trifle of honey for
    syrup instil.
    Endue him with sympathies wide,
      A sweet and humane disposition,
    Which leans to the side of the wretch that is tried,
      And weeps at a culprit's petition.
    From harshness and anger to turn,
      May it now be his constant endeavour,
    And out of his temper the stern
      Sharp sting of the nettle to sever.

CHORUS. We in thy prayers combine, and quite give in
    To the new rule, for the aforesaid reasons.
      Our heart has stood your friend
      And loved you, since we knew

        That you affect the people more
        Than other young men do.

BDELYCLEON. Is any Justice out there? let him enter.
    We shan't admit him when they've once begun.

PHILOCLEON. Where is the prisoner fellow? won't he catch it!

BDELYCLEON. O yes! attention! (*Reads the indictment.*) *Cur*
        of Cydathon
    Hereby accuses Labes of Aexone,
    For that, embezzling a Sicilian cheese,
    Alone he ate it. Fine, one fig-tree collar.

PHILOCLEON. Nay, but a dog's death, an' he's once convicted.

BDELYCLEON. Here stands, to meet the charge, the prisoner
        Labes.

PHILOCLEON. O the vile wretch! O what a thievish look!
    See how he grins, and thinks to take me in.
    Where's the Accuser, Cur of Cydathon?

CUR. Bow!

BDELYCLEON. Here he stands.

XANTHIAS.   Another Labes this,
    Good dog to yelp and lick the platters clean.

BDELYCLEON. St! take your seat. (*To* CUR.) Go up and prose-
        cute.

PHILOCLEON. Meanwhile I'll ladle out and sip my gruel.

XANTHIAS. Ye have heard the charge, most honourable judges,
    I bring against him. Scandalous the trick
    He played us all, me and the Sailor-laddies.
    Alone, in a corner, in the dark, he gorged,
    And munched, and crunched, and Siliced the cheese!

PHILOCLEON. Pheugh! the thing's evident: the brute this in-
        stant
    Breathed in my face the filthiest whiff of cheese.
    O the foul skunk!

XANTHIAS.   And would not give me any,
    Not though I asked. Yet can *he* be your friend
    Who won't throw anything to Me, the dog?

PHILOCLEON. Not give you any! No, nor Me, the state.
    The man's a regular scorcher (*burns his mouth*) like this
        gruel.

BDELYCLEON. Come, don't decide against us, pray don't,
    father,
  Before you've heard both sides.

PHILOCLEON.   But, my dear boy,
  The thing's self-evident, speaks for itself.

XANTHIAS. Don't let him off; upon my life he is
  The most lone-eatingest dog that ever was.
  The brute went coasting round and round the mortar,
  And snapped up all the rind off all the cities.

PHILOCLEON. And I've no mortar even to mend my pitcher!

XANTHIAS. So then be sure you punish him. For why?
  One bush, they say, can never keep two thieves.
  Lest I should bark, and bark, and yet get nothing.
  And if I do I'll never bark again.

PHILOCLEON. Soh! soh!
  Here's a nice string of accusations truly!
  A rare thief of a man! You think so too,
  Old gamecock? Ay, he winks his eye, he thinks so.
  Archon! Hi, fellow, hand me down the vessel.

BDELYCLEON. Reach it yourself; I'll call my witnesses.
  The witnesses for Labes, please stand forward!
  Pot, pestle, grater, brazier, water-jug,
  And all the other scarred and charred utensils.
    (*To* PHILOCLEON.) Good heavens, sir, finish there, and
      take your seat!

PHILOCLEON. I guess I'll finish *him* before I've done.

BDELYCLEON. What! always hard and pitiless, and that
  To the poor prisoners, always keen to bite!
    (*To* LABES.) Up, plead your cause: what, quite dumb-
      foundered? speak.

PHILOCLEON. Seems he's got nothing in the world to say.

BDELYCLEON. Nay, 'tis a sudden seizure, such as once
  Attacked Thucydides when brought to trial.[38]
  'Tis tongue-paralysis that stops his jaws.
    (*To* LABES.) Out of the way! I'll plead your cause myself.
    O sirs, 'tis hard to argue for a dog
  Assailed by slander: nevertheless, I'll try.
  'Tis a good dog, and drives away the wolves.

PHILOCLEON. A thief I call him, and *conspirator*.

BDELYCLEON. Nay, he's the best and worthiest dog alive,
Fit to take charge of any number o' sheep.

PHILOCLEON. What use in that, if he eat up the cheese?

BDELYCLEON. Use! why, he fights your battles, guards your
door;
The best dog altogether. If he filched,
Yet O forgive: he never learnt the lyre.

PHILOCLEON. I would to heaven he had never learned his
letters,
Then he'd not given us all this tiresome speech.

BDELYCLEON. Nay, nay, sir; hear my witnesses, I beg.
Grater, get in the box, and speak well out.
You kept the mess; I ask you, answer plainly,
Did you not grate the spoil between the soldiers?
He says he did.

PHILOCLEON.   Ay, but I vow he's lying.

BDELYCLEON. O sir, have pity upon poor toiling souls.
Our Labes here, he lives on odds and ends,
Bones, gristle: and is always on the go.
That other Cur is a mere stay-at-home,
Sits by the hearth, and when one brings aught in
Asks for a share: if he gets none, he bites.

PHILOCLEON. O me, what ails me that I grow so soft!
Some ill's afoot: I'm nearly giving in.

BDELYCLEON. O, I beseech you, father, show some pity,
Don't crush him quite. Where are his little cubs?
Up, little wretches, up; and whimpering there
Plead for your father: weep, implore, beseech.

PHILOCLEON (*deeply affected*). Get down, get down, get
down, get down.

BDELYCLEON.   I will.
Yet that "get down," I know, has taken in
A many men. However I'll get down.

PHILOCLEON. Dash it! this guzzling ain't the thing at all.
Here was I shedding tears, and seems to me
Only because I have gorged myself with gruel.

BDELYCLEON. Then will he not get off?

PHILOCLEON.   'Tis hard to know.

BDELYCLEON. O take, dear father, take the kindlier turn.
Here, hold this vote: then with shut eyes dash by
To the Far Urn. O father, do acquit him.[39]

PHILOCLEON. No, no, my boy. I never learnt the lyre.

BDELYCLEON. Here, let me lead you round the handiest way.

PHILOCLEON. Is this the Nearer?

BDELYCLEON.   This is.

PHILOCLEON.   In she goes.

BDELYCLEON (*aside*). Duped, as I live! acquits him by mis-
    take!
   (*Aloud*). I'll do the counting.

PHILOCLEON.   Well, how went the battle?

BDELYCLEON. We shall soon see. O Labes, you're acquitted!
Why, how now, father?

PHILOCLEON (*faintly*).   Water, give me water!

BDELYCLEON. Hold up, sir, do.

PHILOCLEON.   Just tell me only this,
Is he *indeed* acquitted?

BDELYCLEON.   Yes.

PHILOCLEON.   I'm done for.

BDELYCLEON. Don't take it so to heart: stand up, sir, pray.

PHILOCLEON. How shall I bear this sin upon my soul?
A man acquitted! What awaits me now?
Yet, O great gods! I pray you pardon me.
Unwilled I did it, not from natural bent.

BDELYCLEON. And don't begrudge it; for I'll tend you well,
And take you, father, everywhere with me,
To feasts, to suppers, to the public games.
Henceforth in pleasure you shall spend your days,
And no Hyperbolus delude and mock you.
But go we in.

PHILOCLEON.   Yes, if you wish it, now.

(*The Actors go into the house. The* CHORUS *turn to the
audience and deliver the Parabasis.*)

CHORUS. Yea, go rejoicing your own good way,
    Wherever your path may be;
But you, ye numberless myriads, stay
    And listen the while to me.
Beware lest the truths I am going to say,
    Unheeded to earth shall fall;
For that were the part of a fool to play,
    And not your part at all.

Now *all* ye people attend and hear, if ye love a simple and
    genuine strain,
For now our poet, with right good will, of you, spectators,
    must needs complain.
Ye have wronged him much, he protests, a bard who had
    served you often and well before;
Partly, indeed, himself unseen, assisting others to please
    you more;
With the art of a Eurycles, weird and wild, he loved to
    dive in a stranger's breast,[40]
And pour from thence through a stranger's lips full many
    a sparkling comical jest.
And partly at length in his own true form, as he chal-
    lenged his fate by himself alone,
And the Muses whose bridled mouths he drave, were
    never another's, were all his own.
And thus he came to a height of fame which none had
    ever achieved before,
Yet waxed not high in his own conceit, nor ever an arro-
    gant mind he bore.
He never was found in the exercise-ground, corrupting
    the boys: he never complied
With the suit of some dissolute knave, who loathed that
    the vigilant lash of the bard should chide
His vile effeminate boylove. No! he kept to his purpose
    pure and high,
That never the Muse, whom he loved to use, the villainous
    trade of a bawd should ply.
When first he began to exhibit plays, no paltry *men* for
    his mark he chose,
He came in the mood of a Heracles forth to grapple at
    once with the mightiest foes.

In the very front of his bold career with the jag-toothed
    Monster he closed in fight,[41]
Though out of its fierce eyes flashed and flamed the glare
    of Cynna's detestable light,
And a hundred horrible sycophants' tongues were twining
    and flickering over its head,
And a voice it had like the roar of a stream which has just
    brought forth destruction and dread,
And a Lamia's groin, and a camel's loin, and foul as the
    smell of a seal it smelt.
But He, when the monstrous form he saw, no bribe he
    took and no fear he felt,
For you he fought, and for you he fights: and then last
    year with adventurous hand
He grappled besides with the Spectral Shapes, the Agues
    and Fevers that plagued our land;[42]
That loved in the darksome hours of night to throttle
    fathers, and grandsires choke,
That laid them down on their restless beds, and against
    your quiet and peaceable folk
Kept welding together proofs and writs and oath against
    oath, till many a man
Sprang up, distracted with wild affright, and off in haste
    to the Polemarch ran.
Yet although such a champion as this ye had found, to
    purge your land from sorrow and shame,
Ye played him false when to reap, last year, the fruit of
    his novel designs he came,
Which, failing to see in their own true light, ye caused to
    fade and wither away.[43]
And yet with many a deep libation, invoking Bacchus,
    he swears this day
That never a man, since the world began, has witnessed
    a cleverer comedy.
Yours is the shame that ye lacked the wit its infinite merit
    at first to see.
But none the less with the wise and skilled the bard his
    accustomed praise will get,
Though when he had distanced all his foes, his noble Play
    was at last upset.

But O for the future, my Masters, pray
Show more regard for a genuine Bard
Who is ever inventing amusements new
And fresh discoveries, all for you.
Make much of his play, and store it away,
 And into your wardrobes throw it
With the citrons sweet: and if this you do,
Your clothes will be fragrant, the whole year through,
 With the volatile wit of the Poet.

O of old renowned and strong, in the choral dance and
  song,
  In the deadly battle throng,
And in this, our one distinction, manliest we, mankind
  among!
  Ah, but that was long ago:
  Those are days for ever past:
  Now my hairs are whitening fast,
  Whiter than the swan they grow.
Yet in these our embers low still some youthful fires must
  glow.
  Better far our old-world fashion,
   Better far our ancient truth,
  Than the curls and dissipation
   Of your modern youth.

Do you wonder, O spectators, thus to see me spliced and
  braced,
Like a wasp in form and figure, tapering inwards at the
  waist?
Why I am so, what's the meaning of this sharp and
  pointed sting,
Easily I now will teach you, though you "knew not anything."
We on whom this stern-appendage, this portentous tail is
  found,
Are the genuine old Autochthons, native children of the
  ground;
We the only true-born Attics, of the staunch heroic breed,
Many a time have fought for Athens, guarding her in
  hours of need;

When with smoke and fire and rapine forth the fierce
 Barbarian came,
Eager to destroy our wasps-nests, smothering all the town
 in flame,
Out at once we rushed to meet him: on with shield and
 spear we went,
Fought the memorable battle, primed with fiery hardi-
 ment;
Man to man we stood, and, grimly, gnawed for rage our
 under lips.
Hah! their arrows hail so densely, all the sun is in eclipse!
Yet we drove their ranks before us, ere the fall of even-
 tide:
As we closed, an owl flew o'er us, and the *Gods* were on
 our side!
Stung in jaw, and cheek, and eyebrow, fearfully they took
 to flight,
We behind them, we harpooning at their slops with all
 our might:
So that in barbarian countries, even now the people call
Attic wasps the best, and bravest, yea, the manliest tribe
 of all!

Mine was then a life of glory, never craven fear came
 o'er me,
  Every foeman quailed before me
As across the merry waters, fast the eager galleys bore me.
  'Twas not then our manhood's test,
  Who can make a fine oration?
  Who is shrewd in litigation?
  It was, *who can row the best?*
Therefore did we batter down many a hostile Median
 town.
  And 'twas we who for the nation
   Gathered in the tribute pay,
  Which the younger generation
   Merely steal away.

You will find us very wasplike, if you scan us through and
 through,

In our general mode of living, and in all our habits too
First, if any rash assailant dare provoke us, can there be
Any creature more vindictive, more irascible than we?
Then we manage all our business in a waspish sort of way.
Swarming in the Courts of Justice, gathering in from day
    to day,
Many where the Eleven invite us, many where the Archon
    calls,[44]
Many to the great Odeum, many to the city walls.
There we lay our heads together, densely packed, and
    stooping low,
Like the grubs within their cells, with movement tremu-
    lous and slow.
And for ways and means in general we're superlatively
    good,
Stinging every man about us, culling thence a livelihood.
Yet we've stingless drones amongst us, idle knaves who
    sit them still,
Shrink from work, and toil, and labour, stop at home, and
    eat their fill,
Eat the golden tribute-honey our industrious care has
    wrought.
This is what extremely grieves us, that a man who never
    fought
Should contrive our fees to pilfer, one who for his native
    land
Never to this day had oar, or lance, or blister in his hand.
Therefore let us for the future pass a little short decree,
Whoso wears no sting shall never carry off the obols three.

(*The father and son now re-enter, the son endeavouring
to persuade his father to exchange his shabby dicastic garments for more fashionable clothing.*)

PHILOCLEON. No! No! I'll never put this off alive.
    With this I was arrayed, and found my safety,
    In the invasion of the great north wind.

BDELYCLEON. You seem unwilling to accept a good.

PHILOCLEON. 'Tis not expedient: no by Zeus it is not.
    'Tis but the other day I gorged on sprats
    And had to pay three obols to the fuller.

DELYCLEON. Try it at all events: since once for all
Into my hands you have placed yourself for good.

HILOCLEON. What would you have me do?

DELYCLEON. Put off that cloak,
And wear this mantle in a cloak-like way.

HILOCLEON. Should we beget and bring up children then,
When here my son is bent on smothering me?

DELYCLEON. Come, take and put it on, and don't keep chattering.

HILOCLEON. Good heavens! and what's this misery of a thing?

DELYCLEON. Some call it Persian, others Caunacès.[45]

HILOCLEON. There! and I thought it a Thymaetian rug.

DELYCLEON. No wonder: for you've never been to Sardis,
Else you'd have known it: now you don't.

HILOCLEON. Who? I?
No more I do by Zeus: it seemed to me
Most like an overwrap of Morychus.

DELYCLEON. Nay, in Ecbatana they weave this stuff.

HILOCLEON. What! have they wool-guts in Ecbatana?

DELYCLEON. Tut, man: they weave it in their foreign looms
At wondrous cost: this very article
Absorbed with ease a talent's weight of wool.

HILOCLEON. Why, then, *wool-gatherer* were its proper name
Instead of Caunacès.

DELYCLEON. Come, take it, take it,
Stand still and put it on.

HILOCLEON. O dear, O dear,
O what a sultry puff the brute breathed o'er me!

DELYCLEON. Quick, wrap it round you.

HILOCLEON. No, I won't, that's flat.
You had better wrap me in a stove at once.

DELYCLEON. Come then, I'll throw it round you. (*To the
cloak.*) You, begone.

HILOCLEON. Do keep a flesh-hook near.

DELYCLEON. A flesh-hook! why?

HILOCLEON. To pull me out before I melt away.

BDELYCLEON. Now off at once with those confounded shoes,
And on with these Laconians, instantly.

PHILOCLEON. What I, my boy! I bring myself to wear
The hated foe's insufferable—cloutings!

BDELYCLEON. Come, sir, insert your foot, and step out firmly
In this Laconian.

PHILOCLEON.   'Tis too bad, it is,
To make a man set foot on hostile—leather.

BDELYCLEON. Now for the other.

PHILOCLEON.   O no, pray not that,
I've a toe there, a regular Lacon-hater.

BDELYCLEON. There is no way but this.

PHILOCLEON.   O luckless I,
Why I shan't have, to bless my age, one—chilblain.

BDELYCLEON. Quick, father, get them on; and then move forward
Thus; in an opulent swaggering sort of way.

PHILOCLEON. Look then! observe my attitudes: think which
Of all your opulent friends I walk most like.

BDELYCLEON. Most like a pimple bandaged round with garlic.

PHILOCLEON. Ay, ay, I warrant I've a mind for wriggling.

BDELYCLEON. Come, if you get with clever well-read men
Could you tell tales, good gentlemanly tales?

PHILOCLEON. Ay, that I could.

BDELYCLEON.   What sort of tales?

PHILOCLEON.   Why, lots,
As, first, how Lamia spluttered when they caught her,
And, next, Cardopion, how he swinged his mother.

BDELYCLEON. Pooh, pooh, no legends: give us something
human,
Some what we call domestic incident.

PHILOCLEON. O, ay, I know a rare domestic tale,
How *once upon a time a cat and mouse*—

BDELYCLEON. *O fool and clown,* Theogenes replied[46]
Rating the scavenger, what! would you tell
Tales of a cat and mouse, in company!

PHILOCLEON. What, then?

DELYCLEON.   Some stylish thing, as how you went
  With Androcles and Cleisthenes, surveying.

HILOCLEON. Why, bless the boy, I never went surveying,
  Save once to Paros, at two obols a day.

DELYCLEON. Still you must tell how splendidly, for instance,
  Ephudion fought the pancratiastic fight
  With young Ascondas: how the game old man
  Though grey, had ample sides, strong hands, firm flanks,
  An iron chest.

HILOCLEON.   What humbug! could a man
  Fight the pancratium with an iron chest!

DELYCLEON. This is the way our clever fellows talk,
  But try another tack: suppose you sat
  Drinking with strangers, what's the pluckiest feat,
  Of all your young adventures, you could tell them?

HILOCLEON. My pluckiest feat? O much my pluckiest, much,
  Was when I stole away Ergasion's vine-poles.

DELYCLEON. Tcha! poles indeed! Tell how you slew the boar,
  Or coursed the hare, or ran the torch-race, tell
  Your gayest, youthfullest act.

HILOCLEON.   My youthfullest action?
  'Twas that I had, when quite a hobbledehoy,
  With fleet Phayllus: and I caught him too:[47]
  Won by two—votes. 'Twas for abuse, that action.

DELYCLEON. No more of that: but lie down there, and learn
  To be convivial and companionable.

PHILOCLEON. Yes; how lie down?

DELYCLEON.   In an elegant, graceful way.

PHILOCLEON. Like this, do you mean?

DELYCLEON.   No, not in the least like that.

PHILOCLEON. How then?

DELYCLEON.   Extend your knees, and let yourself
  With practised ease subside along the cushions;
  Then praise some piece of plate: inspect the ceiling;
  Admire the woven hangings of the hall.
  Ho! water for our hands! bring in the tables!
  Dinner! the after-wash! now the libation.

PHILOCLEON. Good heavens! then is it in a dream we are
    feasting?

BDELYCLEON. The flute girl has performed! our fellow-guest
    Are Phanus, Aeschines, Theorus, Cleon,
    Another stranger at Acestor's head.
    Could you with these cap verses properly?[48]

PHILOCLEON. Could I? Ay, truly; no Diacrian better.

BDELYCLEON. I'll put you to the proof. Suppose I'm Cleon.
    I'll start the catch Harmodius. You're to cap it.
        (Singing) "Truly Athens never knew"

PHILOCLEON (singing).   "Such a rascally thief as you."

BDELYCLEON. Will you do that? You'll perish in your noise.
    He'll swear he'll fell you, quell you, and expel you
    Out of this realm.

PHILOCLEON.   Ay, truly, will he so?
    And if he threaten, I've another strain.
        "Mon, lustin' for power supreme, ye'll mak'
        The city capseeze; she's noo on the shak'."

BDELYCLEON. What if Theorus, lying at his feet,
    Should grasp the hand of Cleon, and begin,
        "From the story of Admetus learn, my friend, to love the
            good."
    How will you take that on?

PHILOCLEON.   I, very neatly,
        "It is not good the fox to play,
        Nor to side with both in a false friend's way."

BDELYCLEON. Next comes that son of Sellus, Aeschines,
    Clever, accomplished fellow, and he'll sing
        "O the money, O the might,
        How Cleitagora and I,
        With the men of Thessaly"—

PHILOCLEON. "How we boasted, you and I."

BDELYCLEON. Well, that will do: you're fairly up to that:
    So come along: we'll dine at Philoctemon's.
    Boy! Chrysus! pack our dinner up; and now
    For a rare drinking-bout at last.

PHILOCLEON.   No, no,
    Drinking ain't good: I know what comes of drinking,

Breaking of doors, assault, and battery,
And then, a headache and a fine to pay.

BDELYCLEON. Not if you drink with gentlemen, you know.
They'll go to the injured man, and beg you off,
Or you yourself will tell some merry tale,
A jest from Sybaris, or one of Aesop's,
Learned at the feast. And so the matter turns
Into a joke, and off he goes contented.

PHILOCLEON. O I'll learn plenty of those tales, if so
I can get off, whatever wrong I do.
Come, go we in: let nothing stop us now.

(*They go out.*)

CHORUS. Often have I deemed myself exceeding bright, acute,
            and clever,
        Dull, obtuse, and awkward never
That is what Amynias is, of Curling-borough, Sellus'
        son;[49]
Him who now upon an apple and pomegranate dines, I
        saw
        At Leogoras's table
        Eat as hard as he was able,
        Goodness, what a hungry maw!
        Pinched and keen as Antiphon.
Once to Pharsalus he travelled, our ambassador to be,
        There a solitary guest, he
        Stayed with only the Penestae,
Coming from the tribe himself, the kindred tribe, of
        Penury.

        Fortunate Automenes, we envy your felicity;
        Every son of yours is of an infinite dexterity:
        First the Harper, known to all, and loved of all exces-
            sively,
        Grace and wit attend his steps, and elegant festivity:
        Next the Actor, shrewd of wit beyond all credibility:
        Last of all Ariphrades, that soul of ingenuity,
        He who of his native wit, with rare originality,
        Hit upon an undiscovered trick of bestiality:
All alone, the father tells us, striking out a novel line.

Some there are who said that I was reconciled in amity
When upon me Cleon pressed, and made me smart with
injury,
Currying and tanning me: then as the stripes fell heavily
Th' outsiders laughed to see the sport, and hear me
squalling lustily,
Caring not a whit for me, but only looking merrily,
To know if squeezed and pressed I chanced to drop
some small buffoonery.
Seeing this, I played the ape a little bit undoubtedly.
So then, after all, the Vine-pole proved unfaithful to the
Vine.[50]

(XANTHIAS *comes hastily in.*)

XANTHIAS. O lucky tortoises, to have such skins,
Thrice lucky for the case upon your ribs:
How well and cunningly your backs are roofed
With tiling strong enough to keep out blows:
Whilst I, I'm cudgelled and tattooed to death.

CHORUS. How now, my boy? for though a man be old,
Still, if he's beaten, we may call him boy.

XANTHIAS. Was not the old man the most outrageous nuisance
Much the most drunk and riotous of all?
And yet we'd Lycon, Antiphon, Hippyllus,
Lysistratus, Theophrastus, Phrynichus;
But he was far the noisiest of the lot.
Soon as he'd gorged his fill of the good cheer,
He skipped, he leapt, and laughed, and frisked, and
whinnied,
Just like a donkey on a feed of corn:
And slapped me youthfully, calling *Boy! Boy!*
So then Lysistratus compared him thus:
Old man, says he, *you're like new wine fermenting,*
Or like a sompnour, scampering to its bran.
But he shrieked back, *And you, you're like a locust*
That has just shed the lappets of its cloak,
Or Sthenelus, shorn of his goods and chattels.
At this all clapped, save Theophrast; but he
Made a wry face, being forsooth a wit.
And pray, the old man asked him, *what makes* YOU

Give yourself airs, and think yourself so grand,
You grinning flatterer of the well-to-do?
Thus he kept bantering every guest in turn,
Making rude jokes, and telling idle tales,
In clownish fashion, relevant to nothing.
At last, well drunk, homeward he turns once more,
Aiming a blow at every one he meets.
Ah! here he's coming; stumbling, staggering on.
Methinks I'll vanish ere I'm slapped again.   *(Exit.)*

(PHILOCLEON *comes in, tipsy and mischievous, with a torch in his hand. He has with him* DARDANIS, *a flute-girl, and is followed by some of the guests whose party he has broken up.*)

PHILOCLEON. Up ahoy! out ahoy!
        Some of you that follow me
        Shall ere long be crying.
    If they don't shog off, I swear
    I'll frizzle 'em all with the torch I bear,
        I'll set the rogues a-frying.

GUEST. Zounds! we'll all make you pay for this to-morrow,
    You vile old rake, however young you are!
    We'll come and cite and summon you all together.

PHILOCLEON. Yah! hah! summon and cite!
        The obsolete notion! don't you know
        I'm sick of the names of your suits and claims?
            Faugh! Faugh! Pheugh!
            Here's my delight!
        Away with the verdict-box! Won't he go?
        Where's the Heliast? out of my sight![51]
My little golden chafer, come up here,
Hold by this rope, a rotten one perchance,
But strong enough for you. Mount up, my dear
See now, how cleverly I filched you off,
A wanton hussy, flirting with the guests.
You owe me, child, some gratitude for that.
But you're not one to pay your debts, I know.
O no! you'll laugh and chaff and slip away,
That's what you always do. But listen now,
Be a good girl, and don't be disobliging,

And when my son is dead, I'll ransom you,
And make you an honest woman. For indeed
I'm not yet master of my own affairs.
I am so young, and kept so very strict.
My son's my guardian, such a cross-grained man,
A cummin-splitting, mustard-scraping fellow.
He's so afraid that I should turn out badly,
For I'm in truth his only father now.
But here he runs. Belike he's after us.
Quick, little lady, hold these links an instant;
And won't I quizz him boyishly and well,
As he did me before the initiation.

(*Enter* BDELYCLEON.)

BDELYCLEON. You there! you there! you old lascivious dotard!
Enamoured, eh? ay, of a fine ripe coffin.
Oh, by Apollo, you shall smart for this!

PHILOCLEON. Dear, dear, how keen to taste a suit in pickle!

BDELYCLEON. No quizzing, sir, when you have filched away
The flute-girl from our party.

PHILOCLEON.   Eh? what? flute-girl?
You're out of your mind, or out of your grave, or something.

BDELYCLEON. Why, bless the fool, here's Dardanis beside you!

PHILOCLEON. What, this? why, this is a torch in the market-place!

BDELYCLEON. A torch, man?

PHILOCLEON.   Clearly; pray observe the punctures.

BDELYCLEON. Then what's this black here, on the top of her head?

PHILOCLEON. Oh, that's the rosin, oozing while it burns.

BDELYCLEON. Then this of course is not a woman's arm?

PHILOCLEON. Of course not; that's a sprouting of the pine.

BDELYCLEON. Sprouting be hanged. (*To* DARDANIS.) You come along with me.

PHILOCLEON. Hi! hi! what are you at?

BDELYCLEON. Marching her off
Out of your reach; a rotten, as I think,
And impotent old man.

PHILOCLEON. Now look ye here:
Once, when surveying at the Olympian games,
I saw how splendidly Ephudion fought
With young Ascondas: saw the game old man
Up with his fist, and knock the youngster down.
So mind your eye, or you'll be pummelled too.

BDELYCLEON. Troth, you have learned Olympia to some purpose.

BAKING GIRL. Oh, there he is! Oh, pray stand by me now!
There's the old rascal who misused me so,
Banged with his torch, and toppled down from here
Bread worth ten obols, and four loaves to boot.

BDELYCLEON. There now, you see; troubles and suits once
more
Your wine will bring us.

PHILOCLEON. Troubles? Not at all.
A merry tale or two sets these things right.
I'll soon set matters right with this young woman.

BAKING GIRL. No, by the Twain! you shan't escape scot-free,
Doing such damage to the goods of Myrtia,
Sostrata's daughter, and Anchylion's, sir!

PHILOCLEON. Listen, good woman: I am going to tell you
A pleasant tale.

BAKING GIRL. Not me, by Zeus, sir, no!

PHILOCLEON. At Aesop, as he walked one eve from supper,
There yapped an impudent and drunken bitch.
Then Aesop answered, *O you bitch! you bitch!*
If in the stead of that ungodly tongue
You'd buy some wheat, methinks you'd have more sense.

BAKING GIRL. Insult me too? I summon you before
The Market Court for damage done my goods,
And for my sompnour have this Chaerephon.

PHILOCLEON. Nay, nay, but listen if I speak not fair.
Simonides and Lasus once were rivals.
Then Lasus says, *Pish, I don't care,* says he.

BAKING GIRL. You will, sir, will you?

PHILOCLEON.   And you, Chaerephon,
  Are you her sompnour, you, like fear-blanched Ino
  Pendent before Euripides's feet?[52]

(*The* BAKING GIRL *goes out but another* COMPLAINANT *im‑
mediately makes his appearance.*)

BDELYCLEON. See, here's another coming, as I live,
  To summon you: at least he has got his sompnour.

COMPLAINANT. O dear! O dear! Old man, I summon you
  For outrage.

BDELYCLEON.   Outrage? no, by the Gods, pray don't.
  I'll make amends for everything he has done,
  (Ask what you will) and thank you kindly too.

PHILOCLEON. Nay, I'll make friends myself without compul‑
      sion.
  I quite admit the assault and battery.
  So tell me which you'll do; leave it to me
  To name the compensation I must pay
  To make us friends, or will you fix the sum?

COMPLAINANT. Name it yourself: I want no suits nor troubles.

PHILOCLEON. There was a man of Sybaris, do you know,
  Thrown from his carriage, and he cracked his skull,
  Quite badly too. Fact was, he could not drive.
  There was a friend of his stood by, and said,
  Let each man exercise the art he knows.
  So you, run off to Doctor Pittalus.

BDELYCLEON. Ay, this is like the rest of your behaviour.

COMPLAINANT (*to* BDELYCLEON). You, sir, yourself, remem‑
      ber what he says.

PHILOCLEON. Stop, listen. Once in Sybaris a girl
  Fractured a jug.

COMPLAINANT.   I call you, friend, to witness.

PHILOCLEON. Just so the jug: *it* called a friend to witness.
  Then said the girl of Sybaris, *By'r Lady,*
  If you would leave off calling friends to witness,
  And buy a rivet, you would show more brains.

COMPLAINANT. Jeer, till the Magistrate call on my case.

BDELYCLEON. No, by Demeter, but you shan't stop here,
    I'll take and carry you—

PHILOCLEON.   What now!

BDELYCLEON.   What now?
    Carry you in: or soon there won't be sompnours
    Enough for all your summoning complainants.

PHILOCLEON. The Delphians once charged Aesop—[53]

BDELYCLEON.   I don't care.

PHILOCLEON. With having filched a vessel of their God.
    But Aesop up and told them that a beetle—

BDELYCLEON. Zounds! but I'll finish you, beetles and all.

    (PHILOCLEON *is carried off by* BDELYCLEON.)

CHORUS. I envy much his fortune
        As he changes from his dry
    Ungenial life and manners,
        Another path to try.
    Now all to soft indulgence
        His eager soul will take,
    And yet perchance it will not,
        For, ah! 'tis hard to break
    From all your life-long habits;
        Yet some the change have made.
    With other minds consorting,
        By other counsels swayed.
    With us and all good people
        Great praise Philocleon's son
    For filial love and genius
        In this affair has won.
    Such sweet and gracious manners
        I never saw before,
    Nor ever with such fondness
        My doting heart gushed o'er.
    Where proved he not the victor
        In all this wordy strife,
    Seeking to raise his father
        To higher paths of life?

(XANTHIAS *runs in.*)

XANTHIAS. O Dionysus! here's a pretty mess
Into our house some power has whirligigged.
Soon as the old man heard the pipe, and drank
The long untasted wine, he grew so merry
He won't stop dancing all the whole night through
Those strange old dances such as Thespis taught;
And your new bards he'll prove old fools, he says,
Dancing against them in the lists directly.

(XANTHIAS *has barely concluded when a voice is heard
within clamouring for more space and freedom: the doors
are thrown open, and in another instant* PHILOCLEON
*bounds upon the stage in the style and attitude of a
tragedy-dancer challenging the world to a trial of skill.*)

PHILOCLEON. Who sits, who waits at the entrance gates?

XANTHIAS. More and more is this evil advancing!

PHILOCLEON. Be the bolts undone, we have just begun;
This, this is the first evolution of dancing.

XANTHIAS. First evolution of madness, I think.

PHILOCLEON. With the strong contortion the ribs twist round,
And the nostril snorts, and the joints resound,
And the tendons crack.

XANTHIAS.   O, hellebore drink!

PHILOCLEON. Cocklike, Phrynichus crouches and cowers,[54]

XANTHIAS. You'll strike by and by.

PHILOCLEON. Then he kicks his leg to the wondering sky,

XANTHIAS. O look to yourself, look out, look out.

PHILOCLEON. For now in these sinewy joints of ours
The cup-like socket is twirled about.

BDELYCLEON. 'Twon't do, by Zeus: 'twon't do: 'tis downright
madness.

PHILOCLEON. Come on, I challenge all the world to dance.
Now what tragedian thinks he dances well,
Let him come in and dance a match with me.
Well, is there one, or none?

BDELYCLEON.   Here's only one.

PHILOCLEON. Who's he, poor devil?

BDELYCLEON.   'Tis the midmost son
  Of poet Carcinus, the Crabbe.[55]

PHILOCLEON.   I'll eat him.
  'Sdeath! I'll destroy him with a knuckle-dance.
  He's a born fool at rhythm.

BDELYCLEON.   Nay, but look here!
  Here comes a brother crab, another son
  Of Carcinus.

PHILOCLEON.   'Faith, I've got crab enough.

BDELYCLEON. Nothing but crabs! 'fore Zeus, nothing but crabs!
  Here creeps a third of Carcinus's brood.

PHILOCLEON. Heyday! what's this? a vinaigrette, or spider?

BDELYCLEON. This is the Pinnoteer, of all the tribe
  The tiniest crab: a tragic poet too!

PHILOCLEON. O Carcinus! O proud and happy father!
  Here's a fine troop of wrynecks settling down.
  Well, I must gird me to the fight: and you,
  Mix pickle for these crabs, in case I beat them.

CHORUS. Come draw we aside, and leave them a wide, a roomy
        and peaceable exercise-ground,
  That before us therein like tops they may spin, revolving
        and whirling and twirling around.
    O lofty-titled sons of the ocean-roving sire,
    Ye brethren of the shrimps, come and leap
  On the sand and on the strand of the salt and barren deep.
  Whisk nimble feet around you; kick out, till all admire,
      The Phrynichean kick to the sky;
  That the audience may applaud, as they view your leg on
      high.
  On, on, in mazy circles; hit your stomach with your heel;
  Fling legs aloft to heaven, as like spinning-tops you wheel.
  Your Sire is creeping onward, the Ruler of the Sea,
  He gazes with delight at his hobby-dancers three.
  Come, dancing as you are, if you like it, lead away,
  For never yet, I warrant, has an actor till to-day
  Led out a chorus, dancing, at the ending of the Play.

1. *Sabazius.* The Phrygian Bacchus.
2. *Cleonymus.* Noted for his enormous bulk and his enormous voracity, and constantly ridiculed for his cowardice in fleeing from the battlefield and flinging away his shield to escape more rapidly.
3. *With little cloaks and staves.* That is to say, in the ordinary attire of Athenian citizens assembled in the Pnyx.
4. *An all-receptive grampus.* The omnivorous grampus with the high-pitched voice is Cleon the leather merchant, the leading demagogue of the day, and the notion that he meant to cut the city up in bits apparently refers to some scheme which he seems to have entertained of separating the various districts of the city by internal fortifications.
5. *A cwaven's head.* It should be a *flatterer's head,* Theorus being one of Cleon's recognized hangers-on.
6. *Going to the crows.* Going "to the dogs."
7. *The water-clock.* The official water-clock, wherewith the speeches of the advocates were timed and limited.
8. *Asclepius' temple.* Sick persons spent the night in Asclepius' temple, to be cured of their disease.
9. *Philocleon and Bdelycleon.* "Cleon-lover" and "Cleon-hater."
10. *Scione.* Scione, on the peninsula of Pallene, was at the time besieged by a large Athenian force.
11. *Sidono-Phrynichéan.* "Charming old songs from the 'Phoenissae' of Phrynichus." Phrynichus was a tragedian of the earlier age, whose tragedies were of a lyrical character.
12. *Byzantium's wall.* The military reminiscences of the Chorus go back to the heroic times of about a half century before.

13. *Laches.* The Athenian general, who had been sent some years previously to Sicily with twenty ships on a roving expedition which produced no adequate result. It is believed that on his return he was accused by Cleon of having received bribes from some of the Sicilian states. The impeachment, later in this play, of Labes by Cur represents the impeachment of Laches by Cleon.

14. *The Samian rebellion.* See Thucydides, i, 115–17.

15. *The son of Sellus.* Aeschines. He and Proxenides were mere empty blusterers, nothing more than smoke.

16. *Captured Naxos town.* Thucydides, i, 98.

17. *Dictynna.* Artemis.

18. *The Twain.* Demeter and Persephone. The Chorus threaten to charge Bdelycleon with profanation of the mysteries of Eleusis.

19. *Diopeithes.* A well-known soothsayer of the day, ridiculed for his fanatical frenzy.

20. *Lycus.* In some sense the patron hero of all the Athenian dicasteries.

21. *Gorgias.* The celebrated orator of Leontini. Philip was either his son or his pupil. There is no certain information about him.

22. *Cecrops.* Mythical founder of Athens. According to a legend, he sprang from a dragon's teeth; and he was popularly represented as a dragon or serpent from his waist downwards.

23. *The songs of Philocles.* The Chorus had been nurtured on the sweet melodies of Phrynichus. They would have shown more fight, Bdelycleon means, had they fed on the acrid bitter strains of Philocles. Philocles, the nephew of Aeschylus, was an ill-tempered tragic poet.

24. *Woolly-fringed Clothes.* Bdelycleon is arraigned as a monarchical conspirator, associated with Brasidas, and betraying his Spartan sympathies by the fashion of his dress and beard.

25. *On the parsley and the rue.* On the border of the garden: that is, at the beginning of your troubles.

26. *Hippias' Tyranny*. Hippias was the last tyrant of Athens.

27. *Morychus*. An epicure.

28. *Oeagrus*. A popular actor of the day. Both Aeschylus and Sophocles wrote a play called *Niobe*.

29. *Evathlus and Cowardonymus*. "Cowardonymus" is of course Cleonymus. He, Evathlus, Theorus (and possibly Euphemius also) were all minor demagogues, the satellites of Cleon.

30. *An old Ass*. A wine-flagon shaped like an ass's head. Many cups of this character are preserved in the museums.

31. *One hundred and fifty talents a year*. The pay of 6,000 dicasts would be 18,000 obols, or 3,000 drachmae, or 30 minae, or exactly half a talent a day. Exclusive of holidays on which the courts would not sit, there were 300 working days in the year; and the aggregate yearly pay of the dicasts would therefore amount to 150 talents.

32. *Connas' vote*. The expression was evidently used as a synonym for anything absolutely valueless. Connas appears to be a dissolute musician.

33. *Chaereas*. Otherwise unknown.

34. *On, on, my soul!* The term "my soul" is addressed by Philocleon, not to his soul, but to his vote. He pictures himself over the verdict-box and about to deposit his vote, as reluctant to part with it. First he exhorts it to make haste, as the usher is about to close the voting; then he pretends to lose it, and fumbles for it; finally he throws it in, with resolute energy. The words, "where is she gone?" imply that the action of Philocleon is arrested by his momentary inability to find the object required: the epithet "shadowy," as applied to the vote, means that it is lost in some obscure place.

35. *A rich Sicilian cheese*. As Laches was accused by Cleon of embezzling Sicilian spoils, so Labes is to be accused of devouring a Sicilian cheese, the special production of the island.

36. *From the very hearth*. That is to say, beginning at the very beginning, so as to do the job thoroughly, omitting nothing. The phrase had its origin in the circumstance that

in solemn festivities the first libation was poured, the first-lings of the sacrifice were offered, to Hestia, the Hearth-goddess.

37. *Aguieus.* That is, Apollo, whose obelisk stood in front of an Athenian house.

38. *Attacked Thucydides.* He means Thucydides, the son of Melesias and rival of Pericles, who, when attacked by some young orator, was so dumbfounded by the nimble-ness and versatility of his adversary's tongue that he lost not only his presence of mind but his very power of speech.

39. *The Far Urn.* There were two Voting Urns: the Nearer was the Urn of Condemnation, the Further, the Urn of Acquittal. Each dicast had one vote; if he thought the prisoner guilty he dropped it into the Nearer Urn, if innocent, into the Further.

40. *Eurycles.* A ventriloquist. Aristophanes' early comedies were produced in the name of Callistratus.

41. *With the jag-toothed Monster.* I.e., with Cleon in *The Knights. Cynna* was an Athenian prostitute.

42. *With the Spectral Shapes.* I.e., with the Sophists in *The Clouds.*

43. A reference to the failure of *The Clouds* to win the prize in the year 423 B.C.

44. *The Eleven.* These officers were at the head of the police arrangements at Athens. Each of the dicasteries had for its president one of the nine *Archons.*

45. *Caunacès.* A soft warm Persian robe of wool. Of Thy-maetian rugs nothing is known.

46. *Theogenes.* Theogenes, a man of known swinishness, must be supposed to be reproving the low-bred scavenger for saying or doing before good company things which The-ogenes himself was noted for saying or doing under other circumstances.

47. *Phayllus.* A famous runner of the day.

48. *Cap verses.* In capping verses the singer who led off took in his hand a lyre, a sprig of myrtle or of laurel, or other

badge of minstrelsy, sang his scolium, and then passed on the badge to any guest he might choose. The guest so selected had to cap the first scolium; that is to say, he had to sing a second scolium which he could link on to the first by some catchword, similarity of thought, aptness of repartee, or the like. Then he handed on the badge to a third, who in like manner was bound to produce a scolium which would fit on to the second; and so on, so that ultimately the whole series of scolia was strung together on some principle of continuity. In such a scene as the present, the connecting links would for obvious reasons be less complete; but even here they are not altogether imperceptible. In the first pair of scolia the exact adaptation to Cleon of the repartee dispenses with the necessity of any further link; but in the second couple the link is the word "good," and in the third the words "and I."

The reference to *Diacrians,* inhabitants of Attica, is unclear.

49. *Amynias.* An effeminate Athenian fop, noted for his long hair. He evidently lost all his wealth somehow; having been as rich as Leogoras, now he is as poor as Antiphon. The following references to Automenes and his sons are self-explanatory.

50. *The Vine-pole proved unfaithful to the Vine.* A proverb used in reference to persons who find the support, whereon they trusted, giving way in the hour of need. It seems probable that Aristophanes means to represent *himself* as the Vine, deceived by the faithless Vine-pole; that is, by the Athenian people. The popular sympathy, to which he had trusted for support against the machinations of Cleon, had played him false when the actual danger came.

51. *Where's the Heliast?* He means the "Guest" who has just threatened him with a lawsuit.

52. *Ino pendent before Euripides' feet.* The story of Ino, daughter of Cadmus and wife of Athamas, who, to escape her domestic miseries, threw herself, with her child, into the sea, formed one of the most moving tragedies of Euripides. And the line before us no doubt refers to some scene in that play where Ino in her desolation and misery

throws herself at the feet of some God or man. The name of Euripides seems to be substituted out of sheer mischief for the purpose of connecting the solemn philosopher-poet with a ridiculous travesty.

53. *The Delphians once charged Aesop.* It is said that the Delphians, enraged at the sarcasms of Aesop, concealed a sacred cup amongst his baggage as he was leaving Delphi. They then pursued and overtook him; and the cup being found in his possession, he was condemned to death on the charge of theft and sacrilege. It was as he was being led out to execution that he told them the fable of the Eagle and the Beetle; seeking to warn his enemies that though he might be mean as the beetle, and they exalted as the eagle, yet his blood might ascend to heaven and cry for vengeance upon his murderers. And it is for the like purpose—viz., as a protest by the weak against the strong—that Philocleon would fain employ it here as he is borne out, powerless, in the arms of his son.

54. *Cocklike, Phrynichus crouches.* Like a cock about to strike.

55. *Carcinus.* The three deformed and stunted sons of Carcinus are constant butts of Aristophanes for their preposterous dances.

LYSISTRATA

Lysistrata was written in the year 412 B.C. at the very darkest period of the Peloponnesian War, the darkest, that is to say, before the ultimate disaster of Aegospotami, and the consequent fall of Athens. It was produced at the commencement of the year 411 B.C., but whether at the Lenaea or at the Great Dionysia, and with what success, the scanty record which has come down to us contains nothing to show.

It was in the autumn of the year 413 that the news of the overwhelming catastrophe in Sicily reached the Athenian people. It was so totally unexpected that at first they refused to believe it. They were still dreaming of an ever-brightening future—anticipating daily the surrender of Syracuse, to be followed by the immediate extension of their power over the entire island, and later by the inclusion of the whole Hellenic race within the triumphant Athenian Empire—when the fatal blow fell.

Thucydides, in the first chapter of his Eighth Book, paints with a few vigorous strokes the alarm and utter hopelessness which prevailed in the city: nevertheless, he says, they determined that they would do all in their power, collecting timber and money from whatever source they could, to build a new navy in the place of the fleets they had lost. Amongst the various measures which they adopted to meet the emergency, the most important, or at all events the most interesting to a reader of the *Lysistrata*, was the creation of a Board of Ten Probuli, a sort of Committee of Public Safety.

The whole action of the comedy is concerned with the Acropolis. The scene is, throughout, the open space before its entrance. Its seizure by the women and the manner in which they hold it against the men constitute the central events around which are grouped all the various incidents of the play.

Characters of the Drama

LYSISTRATA,
CALONICE, ⎫ *Athenian Women*
MYRRHINA, ⎭
LAMPITO, *a Spartan Woman*
CHORUS OF WOMEN
STRATYLLIS, *leader of the Chorus of Women*
   A Boeotian Woman (ISMENIA), *a Corinthian Woman, a Scythian Archeress, and several Athenian Women. Also* RECONCILIATION, *the Handmaiden of* LYSISTRATA

AN ATHENIAN MAGISTRATE
CINESIAS, *the husband of* MYRRHINA
LACONIAN HERALD
LACONIAN AMBASSADORS
ATHENIAN AMBASSADORS
IDLERS
A PORTER
CHORUS OF MEN
   Scythian Archers, and several Athenians and Laconians. Also MYRRHINA'S *child*

LYSISTRATA

It is daybreak at Athens; and LYSISTRATA, *a young and beautiful woman, is standing alone, with marks of evident anxiety in her countenance and demeanour. The scene represents the sloping hill which rises from the Lower to the Upper City. In the background are the Propylaea, the splendid portals of the Athenian Acropolis.* LYSISTRATA *is on the look-out for persons who do not come, and after exhibiting various symptoms of impatience, she suddenly begins to speak with abrupt and indignant emphasis.*

LYSISTRATA. Now were they summoned to some shrine of
         Bacchus,
Pan, Colias, Genetyllis, there had been[1]
No room to stir, so thick the crowd of timbrels.
And *now!*—there's not one woman to be seen.
Stay, here comes one, my neighbour Calonice.
Good morning, friend.

CALONICE.   Good morning, Lysistrata.
Why what's the matter? Don't look gloomy, child.
It doesn't become you to knit-knot your eyebrows.

LYSISTRATA. My heart is hot within me, Calonice,
And sore I grieve for sake of womankind,
Because the men account us all to be
Sly, shifty rogues,

CALONICE.   And so, by Zeus, we are.

LYSISTRATA. Yet though I told them to be here betimes,
To talk on weighty business, they don't come,
They're fast asleep.

CALONICE.   They'll come, dear heart, they'll come.
'Tis hard, you know, for women to get out.
One has to mind her husband: one, to rouse

Her servant: one, to put the child to sleep:
One, has to wash him: one, to give him pap.

LYSISTRATA. Ah! but they've other duties still more pressing
Than such as these.

CALONICE.   Well but, Lysistrata,
Why have you, dear, convoked us? Is the matter
A weighty subject?

LYSISTRATA.   Weighty? yes.

CALONICE.   And pregnant?

LYSISTRATA. Pregnant, by Zeus.

CALONICE.   Why ever don't we come, then?

LYSISTRATA. No, it's not that: we'd have come fast enough
For such-like nonsense. 'Tis a scheme I've hit on,
Tossing it over many a sleepless night.

CALONICE. Tossing it over? then 'tis light, I fancy.

LYSISTRATA. Light? ay, so light, my dear, that all the hopes
Of all the States are anchored on us women.

CALONICE. Anchored on us! a slender stay to lean on.

LYSISTRATA. Ay, all depends on us: whether as well the
Peloponnesians all shall cease to be—

CALONICE. Sure and 'tis better they should cease to be.

LYSISTRATA. And all the dwellers in Boeotia perish—

CALONICE. Except the eels; do pray except the eels.[2]

LYSISTRATA. But about Athens, mark you, I won't utter
Such words as these: you must supply my meaning.
But if the women will but meet here now,
Boeotian girls, Peloponnesian girls,
And we ourselves, we'll save the States between us.

CALONICE. What can we women do? What brilliant scheme
Can we, poor souls, accomplish? we who sit
Trimmed and bedizened in our saffron silks,
Our cambric robes, and little finical shoes.

LYSISTRATA. Why, they're the very things I hope will save us,
Your saffron dresses, and your finical shoes,
Your paints, and perfumes, and your robes of gauze.

CALONICE. How mean you, save us?

LYSISTRATA. So that nevermore
Men in our day shall lift the hostile spear—

CALONICE. O, by the Twain, I'll use the saffron dye.[3]

LYSISTRATA. Or grasp the shield—

CALONICE. I'll don the cambric robe.

LYSISTRATA. Or draw the sword.

CALONICE. I'll wear the finical shoes.

LYSISTRATA. Should not the women, then, have come betimes?

CALONICE. Come? no, by Zeus; they should have flown with
wings.

LYSISTRATA. Ah, friend, you'll find them Attic to the core:
Always too late in everything they do.
Not even one woman from the coast has come,
Not one from Salamis.

CALONICE. O they, no doubt,
Will cross this morning, early, in their boats.

LYSISTRATA. And those I counted sure to come the first,
My staunch Acharnian damsels, they're not here—
Not they.

CALONICE. And yet Theagenes' wife[4]
Consulted Hecate, as if to come.

(*Several women enter, headed by* MYRRHINA, *from the village of Anagyrus. Others soon follow.*)

Hi! but they're coming now: here they all are:
First one, and then another. Hoity toity!
Whence come all these?

LYSISTRATA. From Anagyre.

CALONICE. Aha!
We've stirred up Anagyre at all events.[5]

MYRRHINA. Are we too late, Lysistrata? Well? What?
Why don't you speak?

LYSISTRATA. I'm sorry, Myrrhina.
That you should come so late on such a business.

MYRRHINA. I scarce could find my girdle in the dark.
But if the thing's so pressing, tell us now.

LYSISTRATA. No, no, let's wait a little, till the women
    Of Peloponnesus and Boeotia come
    To join our congress.

MYRRHINA.   O yes, better so.
    And here, good chance, is Lampito approaching.

(LAMPITO, *a Spartan woman, enters, accompanied by her
friends.*)

LYSISTRATA. O welcome, welcome, Lampito, my love.
    O the sweet girl! how hale and bright she looks!
    Here's nerve! here's muscle! here's an arm could fairly
    Throttle a bull!

LAMPITO.   Weel, by the Twa, I think sae.[6]
    An' I can loup an' fling an' kick my hurdies.

LYSISTRATA. See here's a neck and breast; how firm and lusty!

LAMPITO. Wow, but ye pradd me like a fatted calf.

LYSISTRATA. And who's this other damsel? whence comes she?

LAMPITO. Ane deputation frae Boeoty, comin'
    To sit amang you.

LYSISTRATA.   Ah, from fair Boeotia,
    The land of plains!

CALONICE.   A very lovely land,
    Well cropped, and trimmed, and spruce with penny-royal.

LYSISTRATA. And who's the next?

LAMPITO.   A bonnie burdie she,
    She's a Corinthian lassie.

LYSISTRATA.   Ay, by Zeus,
    And so she is. A bonnie lass, indeed.

LAMPITO. But wha ha' ca'ed thegither a' thae thrangs
    O' wenches?

LYSISTRATA.   I did.

LAMPITO.   Did ye noo? then tell us
    What 'tis a' for.

LYSISTRATA.   O yes, my dear, I will.

MYRRHINA. Ay, surely: tell us all this urgent business.

LYSISTRATA. O yes, I'll tell you now; but first I'd ask you
    One simple question.

MYRRHINA. Ask it, dear, and welcome.

LYSISTRATA. Do ye not miss the fathers of your babes,
    Always on service? well I wot ye all
    Have got a husband absent at the wars.

CALONICE. Ay, mine, worse luck, has been five months away
    In Thracian quarters, watching Eucrates.[7]

MYRRHINA. And mine's been stationed seven whole months at
    Pylus.

LAMPITO. An' my gude mon nae suner comes frae war
    Than he straps targe an' gangs awa' again.

LYSISTRATA. No husbands now, no sparks, no anything.
    For ever since Miletus played us false,[8]
    We've had no joy, no solace, none at all.
    So will you, will you, if I find a way,
    Help me to end the war?

MYRRHINA. Ay, that we will.
    I will, be sure, though I'd to fling me down
    This mantling shawl, and have a bout of—drinking.[9]

CALONICE. And I would cleave my very self in twain
    Like a cleft turbot, and give half for Peace.[10]

LAMPITO. An' I, to glint at Peace again, wad speel
    Up to the tap rig o' Taygety.

LYSISTRATA. I'll tell you now: 'tis meet ye all should know.
    O ladies! sisters! if we really mean
    To make the men make Peace, there's but one way,
    We must abstain—

MYRRHINA. Well! tell us.

LYSISTRATA. Will ye do it?

MYRRHINA. Do it? ay, surely, though it cost our lives.

LYSISTRATA. We must abstain—each—from the joys of Love.
    How! what! why turn away? where are ye going?
    What makes you pout your lips, and shake your heads?
    What brings this falling tear, that changing colour?
    Will ye, or will ye not? What mean ye, eh?

MYRRHINA. I'll never do it. Let the war go on.

CALONICE. Zeus! nor I either. Let the war go on.

LYSISTRATA. You, too, Miss Turbot? you who said just now
    You'd cleave, for Peace, your very self in twain?

CALONICE. Ask anything but this. Why, if needs be,
    I'd walk through fire: only, not give up Love.
    There's nothing like it, dear Lysistrata.

LYSISTRATA. And what say you?

MYRRHINA.   I'd liefer walk through fire.

LYSISTRATA. O women! women! O our frail, frail sex!
    No wonder tragedies are made from us.
    Always the same: nothing but loves and cradles.
    O friend! O Lampito! if you and I
    Are of one mind, we yet may pull things through;
    Won't *you* vote with me, dear?

LAMPITO.   Haith, by the Twa',
    'Tis sair to bide your lane, withouten men.
    Still it maun be: we maun hae Peace, at a' risks.

LYSISTRATA. O dearest friend; my one true friend of all.

CALONICE. Well, but suppose we do the things you say,
    Pray Heaven avert it, but put case we do,
    Shall we be nearer Peace?

LYSISTRATA.   Much, much, much nearer.
    For if we women will but sit at home,
    Powdered and trimmed, clad in our daintiest lawn,
    Employing all our charms, and all our arts
    To win men's love, and when we've won it, then
    Repel them, firmly, till they end the war,
    We'll soon get Peace again, be sure of that.

LAMPITO. Sae Menelaus, when he glowered, I ween,[11]
    At Helen's breastie, coost his glaive awa'.

CALONICE. Eh, but suppose they leave us altogether?

LYSISTRATA. O, faddle! then we'll find some substitute.

CALONICE. If they try force?

LYSISTRATA.   They'll soon get tired of that
    If we keep firm. Scant joy a husband gets
    Who finds himself at discord with his wife.

CALONICE. Well, then, if so you wish it, so we'll have it.

LAMPITO. An' our gude folk we'se easily persuade
    To keep the Peace wi' never a thocht o' guile:
    But your Athanian hairumscairum callants
    Wha sall persuade *them* no to play the fule?

LYSISTRATA. O we'll persuade our people, never fear.

LAMPITO. Not while you've gat thae gallies rigged sae trim,
An' a' that rowth o' siller nigh the Goddess.[12]

LYSISTRATA. O but, my dear, we've taken thought for that:
This very morn we seize the Acropolis.
Now, whilst we're planning and conspiring here,
The elder women have the task assigned them,
Under pretence of sacrifice, to seize it.

LAMPITO. A' will gae finely, an' ye talk like that.

LYSISTRATA. Then why not, Lampito, at once combine
All in one oath, and clench the plot securely?

LAMPITO. Weel, you propound the aith, an' we'se a' tak' it.

LYSISTRATA. Good; now then, Scythianess, don't stand there
gaping.[13]
Quick, set a great black shield here, hollow upwards,
And bring the sacrificial bits.

CALONICE. And how
Are we to swear, Lysistrata?

LYSISTRATA. We'll slay
(Like those Seven Chiefs in Aeschylus) a lamb[14]
Over a shield.

CALONICE. Nay, when our object's Peace,
Don't use a shield, Lysistrata, my dear.

LYSISTRATA. Then what shall be the oath?

CALONICE. Could we not somehow
Get a grey mare, and cut her up to bits?

LYSISTRATA. Grey mare, indeed!

CALONICE. Well, what's the oath will suit
Us women best?

MYRRHINA. I'll tell you what I think.
Let's set a great black *cup* here, hollow upwards:
Then for a lamb we'll slay a Thasian wine-jar,
And firmly swear to—pour no water in.

LAMPITO. Hech, the braw aith! my certie, hoo I like it.

LYSISTRATA. O yes, bring out the wine-jar and the cup.

(A SERVANT *brings out a jar of wine and an immense cup.*)

CALONICE. La! here's a splendid piece of ware, my dears.
    Now that's a cup 'twill cheer one's heart to take.

LYSISTRATA (*to the* SERVANT). Set down the cup, and take
        the victim boar.[15]

    O Queen Persuasion, and O Loving Cup,
    Accept our offerings, and maintain our cause!

    (*The* SERVANT *pours the wine into the cup, the women all
    pressing round to see.*)

CALONICE. 'Tis jolly coloured blood, and spirts out bravely

LAMPITO. Ay, an' by Castor, vera fragrant too!

MYRRHINA. Let *me* swear first, my sisters?

CALONICE.   Yes, if *you*
    Draw the first lot; not else, by Aphrodite.[16]

LYSISTRATA. All place your hands upon the wine-cup: so.
    One, speak the words, repeating after me.
    Then all the rest confirm it. Now begin.

    I will abstain from Love and Love's delights.[17]

CALONICE. *I will abstain from Love and Love's delights.*

LYSISTRATA. And take no pleasure though my lord invites.

CALONICE. *And take no pleasure though my lord invites.*

LYSISTRATA. And sleep a vestal all alone at nights.

CALONICE. *And sleep a vestal all alone at nights.*

LYSISTRATA. And live a stranger to all nuptial rites.

CALONICE. *And live a stranger to all nuptial rites.*
    I don't half like it though, Lysistrata.

LYSISTRATA. I will abjure the very name of Love.

CALONICE. *I will abjure the very name of Love.*

LYSISTRATA. So help me Zeus, and all the Powers above.

CALONICE. *So help me Zeus, and all the Powers above.*

LYSISTRATA. If I do this, my cup be filled with wine.

CALONICE. *If I do this, my cup be filled with wine.*

LYSISTRATA. But if I fail, a water draught be mine.

CALONICE. *But if I fail, a water draught be mine.*

LYSISTRATA. You all swear this?

MYRRHINA.   O yes, my dear, we do.

(LYSISTRATA *takes the wine-cup in her hand.*)

LYSISTRATA. I'll now consume these fragments.

CALONICE.   Shares, my friend,
  Now at first starting let us show we're friends.

(*A sound of persons cheering is heard in the distance.*)

LAMPITO. Hark! what's yon skirlin'?

LYSISTRATA.   That's the thing I said.
  They've seized the Acropolis, Athene's castle,
  Our comrades have. Now, Lampito, be off:
  You, go to Sparta, and arrange things there,
  Leaving us here these girls as hostages.
  And we will pass inside the castle walls,
  And help the women there to close the bars.

CALONICE. But don't you think that very soon the Men
  Will come, in arms, against us?

LYSISTRATA.   Let them come!
  They will not bring or threats or fire enough
  To awe our woman hearts, and make us open
  These gates again, save on the terms we mentioned.

CALONICE. By Aphrodite, no! else 'twere for nought
  That people call us bold, resistless jades.

(*The crowd now disperses:* LAMPITO *leaving for her homeward journey, and the others disappearing through the
gates of the Propylaea. After a pause the* CHORUS OF MEN
*are seen slowly approaching from the Lower City. They are
carrying heavy logs of firewood, and a jar of lighted cinders; and as they move, they sing their entrance song.*)

CHORUS OF MEN. On, sure and slow, my Draces, go: though
        that great log you're bringing
  Of olive green, is sore, I ween, your poor old shoulder
      wringing.
  O dear, how many things in life bely one's expectations!
  Since who'd have thought, my Strymodore, that these
      abominations,
      Who would have thought that sluts like these,
      Our household pests, would have waxed so bold,

As the Holy Image by fraud to seize,[18]
As the City Castle by force to hold,
With block and bolt and barrier vast,
Making the Propylaea fast.

Press on, Philurgus, towards the heights; we'll pile a great
    amazing

Array of logs around the walls, and set them all a-blazing:

And as for these conspirators, a bonfire huge we'll make
    them,

One vote shall doom the whole to death, one funeral pyre
    shall take them,

And thus we'll burn the brood accurst, but Lycon's wife
    we'll burn the first.[19]

No, never, never, whilst I live, shall woman-folk deride
    me:

Not scatheless went Cleomenes, when he like this defied
    me,[20]

And dared my castle to seize: yet He,
A Spartan breathing contempt and pride,
Full soon surrendered his arms to me,
And a scanty coat round his loins he tied,
And with unwashed limbs, and with unkempt head,
And with six years' dirt, the intruder fled;

So strict and stern a watch around my mates and I were
    keeping,

In seventeen rows of serried shields before the fortress
    sleeping.

And *these*, whom both Euripides and all the Powers on
    high

Alike detest, shall these, shall these, my manly rage defy?

Then never be my Trophy shown, on those red plains of
    Marathon!

But over this snubby protruding steep
Ere we reach our goal at the Castle keep,
We've still, with our burdensome load, to creep.
And how to manage that blunt incline
Without a donkey, I can't divine.

Dear, how these two great firelogs make my wearied
    shoulders toil and ache.

But still right onward we needs must go,
And still the cinders we needs must blow,
Else we'll find the fire extinguished, ere we reach our
      journey's end.
      Puff! Puff! Puff!
      O the smoke! the smoke!

O royal Heracles! what a lot
Of fire came raging out of the pot,
And flew, like a dog, at my eyes, red hot.
      'Twas a jet from the Lemnian mines, I ween,
      It came so fierce, and it bit so keen,
And worried, with persistence sore, my two poor eyes,
      inflamed before.
      On, Laches, on! to the castle press,
      And aid the God in her dire distress;
Surely, if we e'er would help her, now's the very time, my
      friend.
      Puff! Puff! Puff!
      O the smoke! the smoke!

Thank heaven the fire is still alight, and burning beauti-
      fully bright.
So here we'll lay our burdens down, with eager hearts
      delighted,
And dip the vine-torch in the pot, and get it there ignited.
Then all together at the gates like battering rams we'll
      butt.
And if our summons they reject, and keep the barriers
      shut,
We'll burn the very doors with fire, and them with smoke
      we'll smother.
So lay the burdens down. Pheugh! Pheugh! O how this
      smoke does bother!
What general from the Samian lines an active hand will
      lend us?[21]
Well, well, I'm glad my back is freed from all that weight
      tremendous.
O pot, 'tis now your turn to help: O send a livelier jet
Of flame this way, that I to-day the earliest light may get.

O Victory, immortal Queen, assist us Thou in rearing[22]
A trophy o'er these woman-hosts, so bold and domineer-
    ing.

(*During the last few lines the* MEN *have been completing
their preparations, and the air above them is now growing
lurid with the smoke and the flame of their torches. As the*
MEN *relapse into silence, the voices of* WOMEN *are heard
in the distance. They come sweeping round from the north
side of the Acropolis, carrying their pitchers of water, and
singing, in turn, their entrance song. The two Choruses
are for the present concealed from each other by the
northwestern angle of the Acropolis.*)

CHORUS OF WOMEN. Redly up in the sky the flames are begin-
    ning to flicker,
Smoke and vapour of fire! come quicker, my friends, come
    quicker.

    Fly, Nicodice, fly,
    Else will Calyce burn,
    Else Critylla will die,
    Slain by the laws so stern,
    Slain by the old men's hate.
Ah, but I fear! I fear! can it chance that I come too late?
Trouble it was, forsooth, before my jug I could fill,
All in the dusk of the morn, at the spring by the side of
    the hill,
    What with the clatter of pitchers,
    The noise and press of the throng,
    Jostling with knaves and slaves,
    Till at last I snatched it along,
  Abundance of water supplying
  To friends who are burning and dying.

    Yea, for hither, they state,
    Dotards are dragging, to burn us,
    Logs of enormous weight,
    Fit for a bath-room furnace,
    Vowing to roast and to slay
Sternly the reprobate women. O Lady, O Goddess, I pray,

Ne'er may I see them in flames! I hope to behold them
    with gladness,
Hellas and Athens redeeming from battle and murder and
    madness.
    This is the cause why they venture,
    Lady, thy mansions to hold,
    Tritogeneia, Eternal
    Champion with helmet of gold!
    And O, if with fire men invade them,
    O help us with water to aid them.

(*At this juncture the* WOMEN *wheel round the corner of
the Acropolis, and the two Choruses suddenly meet face
to face.*)

Stop! easy all! what have we here? (*To the* MEN.) You
    vile, abandoned crew,
No good and virtuous men, I'm sure, would act in the
    way you do.

CHORUS OF MEN. Hey, here's an unexpected sight! hey, here's
    a demonstration!
A swarm of women issuing out with warlike preparation!

CHORUS OF WOMEN. Hallo, you seem a little moved! does this
    one troop affright you?
You see not yet the myriadth part of those prepared to
    fight you.

CHORUS OF MEN. Now, really, Phaedrias, shall we stop to hear
    such odious treason?
Let's break our sticks about their backs, let's beat the
    jades to reason.

CHORUS OF WOMEN. Hi, sisters, set the pitchers down, and
    then they won't embarrass
Our nimble fingers, if the rogues attempt our ranks to
    harass.

CHORUS OF MEN. I warrant, now, if twice or thrice we slap
    their faces neatly,
That they will learn, like Bupalus, to hold their tongues
    discreetly.[23]

CHORUS OF WOMEN. Well, here's my face: I won't draw back:
    now slap it if you dare,
And I won't leave one ounce of you for other dogs to tear.

CHORUS OF MEN. Keep still, or else your musty Age to very
shreds I'll batter.

CHORUS OF WOMEN. Now only touch Stratyllis, sir; just lift one
finger at her!

CHORUS OF MEN. And what if with these fists, my love, I pound
the wench to shivers?

CHORUS OF WOMEN. By Heaven, we'll gnaw your entrails out,
and rip away your livers.

CHORUS OF MEN. There is not than Euripides a bard more wise
and knowing,

For women *are* a shameless set, the vilest creatures going.

CHORUS OF WOMEN. Pick up again, Rhodippe dear, your jug
with water brimming.

CHORUS OF MEN. What made you bring that water here, you
God-detested women?

CHORUS OF WOMEN. What made you bring that light, old
Tomb? to set *yourselves* afire?

CHORUS OF MEN. No, but to kindle for your friends a mighty
funeral pyre.

CHORUS OF WOMEN. Well, then, we brought this water here to
put your bonfire out, sirs.

CHORUS OF MEN. *You* put our bonfire out, indeed!

CHORUS OF WOMEN.   You'll see, beyond a doubt, sirs.

CHORUS OF MEN. I swear that with this torch, offhand, I've
half a mind to fry you.

CHORUS OF WOMEN. Got any soap, my lad? If so, a bath I'll
soon supply you.

CHORUS OF MEN. A bath for *me*, you mouldy hag!

CHORUS OF WOMEN.   And that a bride-bath, too.

CHORUS OF MEN. Zounds, did you hear her impudence?

CHORUS OF WOMEN.   Ain't I freeborn as you?

CHORUS OF MEN. I'll quickly put a stop to this.

CHORUS OF WOMEN.   You'll judge no more, I vow!

CHORUS OF MEN. Hi! set the vixen's hair on fire.

CHORUS OF WOMEN.   Now, Achelous, now![24]

CHORUS OF MEN. Good gracious!

CHORUS OF WOMEN.   What! you find it hot?

CHORUS OF MEN. Hot? murder! stop! be quiet!

CHORUS OF WOMEN. I'm watering you, to make you grow.

CHORUS OF MEN. I wither up from shivering so.

CHORUS OF WOMEN. I tell you what: a fire you've got,
    So warm your members by it.

(*At this crisis the tumult is stayed for an instant by the
appearance on the stage of a venerable official personage,
one of the Magistrates who, after the Sicilian catastrophe,
were appointed, under the name of Probuli, to form a
Directory or Committee of Public Safety. He is attended
by four* SCYTHIAN ARCHERS, *part of the ordinary police of
the Athenian Republic. The* WOMEN *retire into the background.*)

MAGISTRATE. Has then the women's wantonness blazed out,
    Their constant timbrels and Sabaziuses,
    And that Adonis-dirge upon the roof[25]
    Which once I heard in full Assembly-time.
    'Twas when Demostratus (beshrew him) moved
    To sail to Sicily: and from the roof
    A woman, dancing, shrieked *Woe, woe, Adonis!*
    And *he* proposed to enrol Zacynthian hoplites;
    And *she* upon the roof, the maudlin woman,
    Cried *Wail Adonis!* yet he forced it through,
    That God-detested, vile Ill-temprian.
    Such are the wanton follies of the sex.

CHORUS OF MEN. What if you heard their insolence to-day,
    Their vile, outrageous goings on? And look,
    See how they've drenched and soused us from their
           pitchers,
    Till we can wring out water from our clothes.

MAGISTRATE. Ay, by Poseidon, and it serves us right.
    'Tis all our fault: they'll never know their place,
    These pampered women, whilst we spoil them so.
    Hear how we talk in every workman's shop.
    Goldsmith, says one, *this necklace that you made,
    My gay young wife was dancing yester-eve,
    And lost, sweet soul, the fastening of the clasp;*

> *Do please reset it, Goldsmith.* Or, again,
> *O Shoemaker, my wife's new sandal pinches*
> *Her little toe, the tender, delicate child,*
> *Make it fit easier, please.*—Hence all this nonsense!
> Yea, things have reached a pretty pass, indeed,
> When I, the State's Director, wanting money
> To purchase oar-blades, find the Treasury gates
> Shut in my face by these preposterous women.
> Nay, but no dallying now: bring up the crowbars,
> And I'll soon stop *your* insolence, my dears.

(*He turns to the* SCYTHIANS, *who, instead of setting to work, are looking idly around them.*)

> What! gaping, fool? and *you,* can *you* do nothing
> But stare about with tavern-squinting eye?
> Push in the crowbars underneath the gates,
> You, stand that side and heave them: I'll stop here
> And heave them here.

(*The gates are thrown open, and* LYSISTRATA *comes out.*)

LYSISTRATA.   O let your crowbars be.
  Lo, I come out unfetched! What need of crowbars?
  'Tis wits, not crowbars, that ye need to-day.

MAGISTRATE. Ay, truly, traitress, say you so? Here, Archer!
  Arrest her, tie her hands behind her back.

LYSISTRATA. And if he touch me with his finger-tip,
  The public scum! 'fore Artemis, he'll rue it.

MAGISTRATE. What, man, afeared? why, catch her round the
            waist.
  And *you* go with him, quick, and bind her fast.

CALONICE (*coming out*). And if you do but lay one hand
            upon her,
  'Fore Pandrosus, I'll stamp your vitals out.[26]

MAGISTRATE. Vitals, ye hag? Another Archer, ho!
  Seize this one first, because she chatters so.

MYRRHINA (*coming out*). And if you touch her with your
            finger-tip,
  'Fore Phosphorus, you'll need a cupping shortly.

MAGISTRATE. Tcha! what's all this? lay hold of this one,
    Archer!
  I'll stop this sallying out, depend upon it.

STRATYLLIS. And if he touch her, 'fore the Queen of Tauris,[27]
  I'll pull his squealing hairs out, one by one.

MAGISTRATE. O dear! all's up! I've never an archer left.
  Nay, but I swear we won't be done by women.
  Come, Scythians, close your ranks, and all together
  Charge!

LYSISTRATA.   Charge away, my hearties, and you'll soon
  Know that we've here, impatient for the fight,
  Four woman-squadrons, armed from top to toe.

MAGISTRATE. Attack them, Scythians, twist their hands behind
    them.

LYSISTRATA. Forth to the fray, dear sisters, bold allies!
  O egg-and-seed-and-potherb-market-girls,
  O garlic-selling-barmaid-baking-girls,
  Charge to the rescue, smack and whack, and thwack
    them,
  Slang them, I say: show them what jades ye be.

(*The* WOMEN *come forward. After a short struggle the*
ARCHERS *are routed.*)

  Fall back! retire! forbear to strip the slain.

MAGISTRATE. Hillo! my archers got the worst of that.

LYSISTRATA. What did the fool expect? Was it to fight
  With *slaves* you came? Think you we Women feel
  No thirst for glory?

MAGISTRATE.   Thirst enough, I trow;
  No doubt of that, when there's a tavern handy.

CHORUS OF MEN. O thou who wastest many words, Director of
    this nation,
  Why wilt thou with such brutes as these thus hold nego-
    tiation?
  Dost thou not see the bath wherewith the sluts have dared
    to lave me,
  Whilst all my clothes were on, and ne'er a bit of soap they
    gave me?

CHORUS OF WOMEN. For 'tis not right, nor yet polite, to strik
      a harmless neighbour,
And if you do, 'tis needful too that she your eyes belabour
Full fain would I, a maiden shy, in maiden peace b
      resting,
Not making here the slightest stir, nor any soul molesting
Unless indeed some rogue should strive to rifle and despo
      my hive.[28]

(*The field is now open for a suspension of hostilities, an
a parley takes place between the leaders of the two con
tending factions.*)

CHORUS OF MEN. O how shall we treat, Lord Zeus, such crea
      tures as these?
Let us ask the cause for which they have dared to seize
To seize this fortress of ancient and high renown,
This shrine where never a foot profane hath trod,
The lofty-rocked, inaccessible Cranaan town,[29]
      The holy Temple of God.

Now to examine them closely and narrowly,
      probing them here and sounding them there,
Shame if we fail to completely unravel the
      intricate web of this tangled affair.

MAGISTRATE. Foremost and first I would wish to inquire o
      them,
    what is this silly disturbance about?
Why have ye ventured to seize the Acropolis,
    locking the gates and barring us out?

LYSISTRATA. Keeping the silver securely in custody,
    lest for its sake ye continue the war.

MAGISTRATE. What, is the war for the sake of the silver, then

LYSISTRATA. Yes; and all other disputes that there are.
Why is Peisander for ever embroiling us,[30]
      why do the rest of our officers feel
Always a pleasure in strife and disturbances?
      Simply to gain an occasion to steal.
Act as they please for the future, the treasury
      never a penny shall yield them, I vow.

MAGISTRATE. How, may I ask, will you hinder their getting it?

LYSISTRATA. We will ourselves be the Treasurers now.

MAGISTRATE. You, woman, you be the treasurers?

LYSISTRATA.   Certainly.
      Ah, you esteem us unable, perchance!
   Are we not skilled in domestic economy,
         do we not manage the household finance?

MAGISTRATE. O, that is different.

LYSISTRATA.   Why is it different?

MAGISTRATE. This is required for the fighting, my dear.

LYSISTRATA. Well, but the fighting itself isn't requisite.

MAGISTRATE. Only, without it, we're ruined, I fear.

LYSISTRATA. *We* will deliver you.

MAGISTRATE.   You will deliver us!

LYSISTRATA. Truly we will.

MAGISTRATE.   What a capital notion!

LYSISTRATA. Whether you like it or not, we'll deliver you.

MAGISTRATE. Impudent hussy!

LYSISTRATA.   You seem in commotion.
      Nevertheless we will do as we promise you.

MAGISTRATE. That were a terrible shame, by Demeter.

LYSISTRATA. Friend, we must save you.

MAGISTRATE.   But how if I wish it not?

LYSISTRATA. That will but make our resolve the completer.

MAGISTRATE. Fools! what on earth can possess you to meddle
         with
      matters of war, and matters of peace?

LYSISTRATA. Well, I will tell you the reason.

MAGISTRATE.   And speedily,
         else you will rue it.

LYSISTRATA.   Then listen, and cease
      Clutching and clenching your fingers so angrily;
         keep yourself peaceable.

MAGISTRATE.   Hanged if I can;
      Such is the rage that I feel at your impudence.

STRATYLLIS. Then it is *you* that will rue it, my man.

MAGISTRATE. Croak your own fate, you ill-omened antiquity
   (*To* LYSISTRATA.) *You* be the spokeswoman, lady.

LYSISTRATA.   I will.
   Think of our old moderation and gentleness,
         think how we bore with your pranks, and were still
   All through the days of your former pugnacity,
         all through the war that is over and spent:
   Not that (be sure) we approved of your policy;
         never our griefs you allowed us to vent.
   Well we perceived your mistakes and mismanagement.
         Often at home on our housekeeping cares,
   Often we heard of some foolish proposal you
         made for conducting the public affairs.
   Then would we question you mildly and pleasantly,
         inwardly grieving, but outwardly gay;
   Husband, how goes it abroad? we would ask of him;
         what have ye done in Assembly to-day?
   What would ye write on the side of the Treaty stone?[31]
         Husband says angrily, *What's that to you?*
   You, hold your tongue! And I held it accordingly.

STRATYLLIS. That is a thing which I *never* would do!

MAGISTRATE. Ma'am, if you hadn't, you'd soon have repented
   it.

LYSISTRATA. Therefore I held it, and spake not a word.
   Soon of another tremendous absurdity,
         wilder and worse than the former we heard.
   Husband, I say, with a tender solicitude,
         Why have ye passed such a foolish decree?
   Vicious, moodily, glaring askance at me,
         Stick to your spinning, my mistress, says he,
   Else you will speedily find it the worse for you,
         War is the care and the business of men![32]

MAGISTRATE. Zeus! 'twas a worthy reply, and an excellent!

LYSISTRATA. What! you unfortunate, shall we not then,
   Then, when we see you perplexed and incompetent,
         shall we not tender advice to the State?
   So when aloud in the streets and the thoroughfares
         sadly we heard you bewailing of late,

Is there a Man to defend and deliver us?
        No, says another, *there's none in the land;*
Then by the Women assembled in conference
        jointly a great Revolution was planned,
Hellas to save from her grief and perplexity.
        Where is the use of a longer delay?
Shift for the future our parts and our characters;
        you, as the women, in silence obey;
We, as the men, will harangue and provide for you;
        then shall the State be triumphant again,
Then shall we do what is best for the citizens.

MAGISTRATE. Women to do what is best for the men!
    That were a shameful reproach and unbearable!

LYSISTRATA. Silence, old gentleman.³³

MAGISTRATE.   Silence for *you?*
    Stop for a wench with a wimple enfolding her?
        No, by the Powers, may I *die* if I do!

LYSISTRATA. Do not, my pretty one, do not, I pray,
    Suffer my wimple to stand in the way.
    Here, take it, and wear it, and gracefully tie it,
    Enfolding it over your head, and be quiet.
        Now to your task.

CALONICE. Here is an excellent spindle to pull.

MYRRHINA. Here is a basket for carding the wool.

LYSISTRATA. Now to your task.
    Haricots chawing up, petticoats drawing up,³⁴
    Off to your carding, your combing, your trimming,
    War is the care and the business of women.

(*During the foregoing lines the* WOMEN *have been array-ing the* MAGISTRATE *in the garb and with the apparatus of a spinning-woman: just as below, they bedeck him in the habiliments of a corpse.*)

CHORUS OF WOMEN. Up, up, and leave the pitchers there,
        and on, resolved and eager,
    Our own allotted part to bear
        in this illustrious leaguer.

    I will dance with resolute, tireless feet all day;
    My limbs shall never grow faint, my strength give way;

I will march all lengths with the noble hearts and the
 true,
For theirs is the ready wit and the patriot hand,
And womanly grace, and courage to dare and do,
  And Love of our own bright land.

Children of stiff and intractable grandmothers,
  heirs of the stinging viragoes that bore you,
On, with an eager, unyielding tenacity,
  wind in your sails, and the haven before you.

LYSISTRATA. Only let Love, the entrancing, the fanciful,
  only let Queen Aphrodite to-day
Breathe on our persons a charm and a tenderness,
  lend us their own irresistible sway,
Drawing the men to admire us and long for us;
  then shall the war everlastingly cease,
Then shall the people revere us and honour us,
  givers of Joy, and givers of Peace.

MAGISTRATE. Tell us the mode and the means of your doing
 it.

LYSISTRATA. First we will stop the disorderly crew,
Soldiers in arms promenading and marketing.

STRATYLLIS. Yea, by divine Aphrodite, 'tis true.

LYSISTRATA. Now in the market you see them like Corybants,[35]
  jangling about with their armour of mail.
Fiercely they stalk in the midst of the crockery,
  sternly parade by the cabbage and kale.

MAGISTRATE. Right, for a soldier should always be soldierly!

LYSISTRATA. Troth, 'tis a mighty ridiculous jest,
Watching them haggle for shrimps in the market-place,
  grimly accoutred with shield and with crest.

STRATYLLIS. Lately I witnessed a captain of cavalry,
  proudly the while on his charger he sat,
Witnessed him, soldierly, buying an omelet,
  stowing it all in his cavalry hat.
Comes, like a Tereus, a Thracian irregular,[36]
  shaking his dart and his target to boot;
Off runs a shop-girl, appalled at the sight of him,
  down he sits soldierly, gobbles her fruit.

MAGISTRATE. You, I presume, could adroitly and gingerly
    settle this intricate, tangled concern:
You in a trice could relieve our perplexities.

LYSISTRATA. Certainly.

MAGISTRATE.   How? permit me to learn.

LYSISTRATA. Just as a woman, with nimble dexterity,
    thus with her hands disentangles a skein,
Hither and thither her spindles unravel it,
    drawing it out, and pulling it plain.
So would this weary Hellenic entanglement
    soon be resolved by our womanly care,
So would our embassies neatly unravel it,
    drawing it here and pulling it there.

MAGISTRATE. Wonderful, marvellous feats, not a doubt of it,
    you with your skeins and your spindles can show;
Fools! do you really expect to unravel a
    terrible war like a bundle of tow?

LYSISTRATA. Ah, if you only could manage your politics
    just in the way that we deal with a fleece!

MAGISTRATE. Tell us the recipe.

LYSISTRATA.   First, in the washing-tub
    plunge it, and scour it, and cleanse it from grease,
Purging away all the filth and the nastiness;
    then on the table expand it and lay,
Beating out all that is worthless and mischievous,
    picking the burrs and the thistles away.
Next, for the clubs, the cabals, and the coteries,
    banding unrighteously, office to win,
Treat them as clots in the wool, and dissever them,
    lopping the heads that are forming therein.
Then you should card it, and comb it, and mingle it,
    all in one basket of love and of unity,
Citizens, visitors, strangers, and sojourners,
    all the entire, undivided community.
Know you a fellow in debt to the Treasury?
    Mingle him merrily in with the rest.
Also remember the cities, our colonies,
    outlying states in the east and the west,

Scattered about to a distance surrounding us,
       these are our shreds and our fragments of wool;
These to one mighty political aggregate
       tenderly, carefully, gather and pull,
Twining them all in one thread of good fellowship;
       thence a magnificent bobbin to spin,
Weaving a garment of comfort and dignity,
       worthily wrapping the People therein.

MAGISTRATE. Heard any ever the like of their impudence,
       these who have nothing to do with the war,
Preaching of bobbins, and beatings, and washing-tubs?

LYSISTRATA. Nothing to do with it, wretch that you are!
We are the people who feel it the keenliest,
       doubly on us the affliction is cast;
Where are the sons that we sent to your battle-fields?

MAGISTRATE. Silence! a truce to the ills that are past.

LYSISTRATA. Then in the glory and grace of our womanhood,
       all in the May and the morning of life,
Lo, we are sitting forlorn and disconsolate,
       what has a soldier to do with a wife?
We might endure it, but ah! for the younger ones,
       still in their maiden apartments they stay,
Waiting the husband that never approaches them,
       watching the years that are gliding away.

MAGISTRATE. Men, I suppose, have their youth everlastingly.

LYSISTRATA. Nay, but it isn't the same with a man:
Grey though he be when he comes from the battle-field,
       still if he wishes to marry, he can.
Brief is the spring and the flower of our womanhood,
       once let it slip, and it comes not again;
Sit as we may with our spells and our auguries,
       never a husband will marry us then.

MAGISTRATE. Truly whoever is able to wed—[37]

LYSISTRATA. Truly, old fellow, 'tis time you were dead.
   So a pig shall be sought, and an urn shall be bought,
   And I'll bake you and make you a funeral cake.[38]
       Take it and go.[39]

CALONICE. Here are the fillets all ready to wear.

MYRRHINA. Here is the chaplet to bind in your hair.

LYSISTRATA. Take it and go.
>   What are you prating for? What are you waiting for?
>   Charon is staying, delaying his crew,
>   Charon is calling and bawling for you.

MAGISTRATE. See, here's an outrage! here's a scandalous shame!
>   I'll run and show my fellow magistrates
>   The woeful, horrid, dismal plight I'm in.

LYSISTRATA. Grumbling because we have not laid you out?
>   Wait for three days, and then with dawn will come,
>   All in good time, the third-day funeral rites.[40]

(*The* MAGISTRATE *runs off in his grave-clothes to complain
of and exhibit the treatment he has received.* LYSISTRATA
and her friends withdraw into the Acropolis. The two
CHORUSES *remain without, and relieve the tedium of the
siege with a little banter.*)

CHORUS OF MEN. This is not a time for slumber;
>   now let all the bold and free,
> Strip to meet the great occasion,
>   vindicate our right with me.
> I can smell a deep, surprising
> Tide of Revolution rising,
> Odour as of folk devising
>   Hippias's tyranny.[41]
> And I feel a dire misgiving,
> Lest some false Laconians, meeting
>   in the house of Cleisthenes,[42]
> Have inspired these wretched women
>   all our wealth and pay to seize,
> Pay from whence I get my living.
> Gods! to hear these shallow wenches
>   taking citizens to task,
> Prattling of a brassy buckler,
>   jabbering of a martial casque!
> Gods! to think that they have ventured
>   with Laconian men to deal,
> Men of just the faith and honour
>   that a ravening wolf might feel!

Plots they're hatching, plots contriving,
    plots of rampant Tyranny;
But o'er *us* they shan't be Tyrants,
    no, for on my guard I'll be,
And I'll dress my sword in myrtle,
    and with firm and dauntless hand,
Here beside Aristogeiton[43]
    resolutely take my stand,
Marketing in arms beside him.
    This the time and this the place
When my patriot arm must deal a
    —blow upon that woman's face.

CHORUS OF WOMEN. Ah, your mother shall not know you,
    impudent! when home you go.
Strip, my sisters, strip for action,
    on the ground your garments throw.
Right it is that I my slender
Tribute to the state should render,
I, who to her thoughtful tender
    care my happiest memories owe;[44]
Bore, at seven, the mystic casket;
Was, at ten, our Lady's miller;
    then the yellow Brauron bear;
Next (a maiden tall and stately
    with a string of figs to wear)
Bore in pomp the holy Basket.
Well may such a gracious City
    all my filial duty claim.
What though I was born a woman,
    comrades, count it not for blame
If I bring the wiser counsels;
    I an equal share confer
Towards the common stock of Athens,
    I contribute men to her.
But the noble contribution,
    but the olden tribute-pay,
Which your fathers' fathers left you,
    relic of the Median fray,
Dotards, ye have lost and wasted!
    nothing in its stead ye bring,

Nay ourselves ye're like to ruin,
    spend and waste by blundering.
Murmuring are ye? Let me hear you,
    only let me hear you speak,
And from this unpolished slipper
    comes a—slap upon your cheek!

CHORUS OF MEN. Is not this an outrage sore?
    And methinks it blows not o'er,
    But increases more and more.
Come, my comrades, hale and hearty,
    on the ground your mantles throw,
In the odour of their manhood
    men to meet the fight should go,
Not in these ungodly wrappers
    swaddled up from top to toe.

On, then on, my white-foot veterans, ye who thronged
    Leipsydrium's height[45]
In the days when we were Men!
Shake this chill old Age from off you,
Spread the wings of youth again.

O these women! give them once a
    handle howsoever small,
And they'll soon be nought behind us
    in the manliest feats of all.
Yea, they'll build them fleets and navies
    and they'll come across the sea,
Come like Carian Artemisia,[46]
    fighting in their ships with me.
Or they'll turn their first attention,
    haply, to equestrian fights,
If they do, I know the issue,
    there's an end of all the knights!
Well a woman sticks on horseback:
    look around you, see, behold,
Where on Micon's living frescoes
    fight the Amazons of old!
Shall we let these wilful women,
    O my brothers, do the same?

Rather first their necks we'll rivet
tightly in the pillory frame.

CHORUS OF WOMEN. If our smouldering fires ye wake,
Soon our wildbeast wrath will break
Out against you, and we'll make,
Make you howl to all your neighbours,
currycombed, poor soul, and tanned.
Throw aside your mantles, sisters,
come, a firm determined band,
In the odour of your wrathful
snappish womanhood to stand.

Who'll come forth and fight me? garlic, nevermore, no
beans for him.
Nay, if one sour word ye say,
I'll be like the midwife beetle,
Following till the eagle lay.[47]

Yea, for you and yours I reck not
whilst my Lampito survives,
And my noble, dear Ismenia,
loveliest of the Theban wives.
Keep decreeing seven times over,
not a bit of good you'll do,
Wretch abhorred of all the people
and of all our neighbours too.
So that when in Hecate's honour
yesterday I sent to get
From our neighbours in Boeotia
such a dainty darling pet,
Just a lovely, graceful, slender,
white-fleshed eel divinely tender,
Thanks to your decrees, confound them,
one and all refused to send her.
And you'll never stop from making
these absurd decrees I know,
Till I catch your leg and toss you
—Zeus-ha'-mercy, there you go!

(*An interval of several days must here be supposed to
elapse. The separation of the sexes has now become insup-*

*portable to both parties, and the only question is which
side will hold out the longest. The* CHORUS OF WOMEN *are
alarmed at seeing* LYSISTRATA *come on the stage, and walk
up and down with an anxious and troubled air. The first
twelve lines of the dialogue which ensues are borrowed and
burlesqued from Euripides.)*

CHORUS OF WOMEN. Illustrious leader of this bold emprize,
    What brings thee forth, with trouble in thine eyes?

LYSISTRATA. Vile women's works: the feminine hearts they
        show:
    These make me pace, dejected, to and fro.

CHORUS OF WOMEN. O what! and O what!

LYSISTRATA. 'Tis true! 'tis true!

CHORUS OF WOMEN. O to your friends, great queen, the tale
    unfold.

LYSISTRATA. 'Tis sad to tell, and sore to leave untold.

CHORUS OF WOMEN. What, what has happened? tell us, tell us
    quick.

LYSISTRATA. Aye, in one word. The girls are—husband-sick.

CHORUS OF WOMEN. O Zeus! Zeus! O!

LYSISTRATA. Why call on Zeus? the fact is surely so.
    I can no longer keep the minxes in.
    They slip out everywhere. One I discovered
    Down by Pan's grotto, burrowing through the loophole:
    Another, wriggling down by crane and pulley:
    A third deserts outright: a fourth I dragged
    Back by the hair, yestreen, just as she started
    On sparrow's back, straight for Orsilochus's:[48]
    They make all sorts of shifts to get away.

(A woman is seen attempting to cross the stage.)

    Ha! here comes one, deserting. Hi there, Hi!
    Where are you off to?

FIRST WOMAN *(hurriedly)*. I must just run home.
    I left some fine Milesian wools about,
    I'm sure the moths are at them.

LYSISTRATA.   Moths indeed!
    Get back.

FIRST WOMAN. But really I'll return directly,
 I only want to spread them on the couch.

LYSISTRATA. No spreadings out, no running home to-day.

FIRST WOMAN. What! leave my wools to perish?

LYSISTRATA.   If need be.

(*A second woman now attempts to cross the stage.*)

SECOND WOMAN. O goodness gracious! O that lovely flax
 I left at home unhackled!

LYSISTRATA.   Here's another!
 She's stealing off to hackle flax forsooth.
 (*To the second woman.*)
 Come, come, get back.

SECOND WOMAN.   O yes, and so I will,
 I'll comb it out and come again directly.

LYSISTRATA. Nay, nay, no combing: once begin with that
 And other girls are sure to want the same.

(*Several women enter one after the other.*)

THIRD WOMAN. O holy Eileithyia, stay my labour[49]
 Till I can reach some lawful travail-place.

LYSISTRATA. How now!

THIRD WOMAN.   My pains are come.

LYSISTRATA.   Why yesterday
 You were not pregnant.

THIRD WOMAN.   But to-day I am.
 Quick, let me pass, Lysistrata, at once
 To find a midwife.

LYSISTRATA.   What's it all about?
 What's this hard lump?

THIRD WOMAN.   That's a male child.

LYSISTRATA.   Not it.
 It's something made of brass, and hollow too.
 Come, come, out with it. O you silly woman,
 What! cuddling up the sacred helmet there[50]
 And say you're pregnant?

THIRD WOMAN.   Well, and so I am.

LYSISTRATA. What's this for then?

THIRD WOMAN.   Why, if my pains o'ertake me
In the Acropolis, I'd creep inside
And sit and hatch there as the pigeons do.

LYSISTRATA. Nonsense and stuff: the thing's as plain as can be.
Stay and keep here the name-day of your—helmet.

FOURTH WOMAN. But I can't sleep a single wink up here,
So scared I was to see the holy serpent.[51]

FIFTH WOMAN. And I shall die for lack of rest, I know,
With this perpetual hooting of the owls.

LYSISTRATA. O ladies, ladies, cease these tricks, I pray.
Ye want your husbands. And do you suppose
They don't want *us*? Full wearisome, I know,
Their nights without us. O bear up, dear friends,
Be firm, be patient, yet one little while,
For I've an oracle (here 'tis) which says
We're sure to conquer if we hold together.

WOMEN. O read us what it says.

LYSISTRATA.   Then all keep silence.

(LYSISTRATA *reads out the oracle.*)

*Soon as the swallows are seen collecting and crouching
    together,*
*Shunning the hoopoes' flight and keeping aloof from the
    Love-birds,*[52]
*Cometh a rest from ill, and Zeus the Lord of the Thunder
Changeth the upper to under.*

WOMEN.   Preserve us, shall *we* be the upper?

LYSISTRATA. *Nay, but if once they wrangle, and flutter away
    in dissension*
*Out of the Temple of God, then all shall see and ac-
    knowledge,*
Never a bird of the air so perjured and frail as the swallow.

WOMEN. Wow, but that's plain enough! O all ye Gods,
Let us not falter in our efforts now.
Come along in. O friends, O dearest friends,
'Twere sin and shame to fail the oracle.

(The WOMEN, *with* LYSISTRATA, *re-enter the Acropolis. The two* CHORUSES *again indulge in an interchange of banter. The* MEN *begin.)*

CHORUS OF MEN. Now to tell a little story
    Fain, fain I grow,
  One I heard when quite an urchin
    Long, long ago.
    How that once
  All to shun the nuptial bed
  From his home Melanion fled,[53]
  To the hills and deserts sped,
    Kept his dog,
    Wove his snares,
    Set his nets,
    Trapped his hares;
  Home he nevermore would go,
  He detested women so.
  We are of Melanion's mind,
  We detest the womankind.

MAN. May I, mother, kiss your cheek?

WOMAN. Then you won't require a leek.[54]

MAN. Hoist my leg, and kick you, so?

WOMAN. Fie! what stalwart legs you show!

MAN. Just such stalwart legs and strong,
    Just such stalwart legs as these,
  To the noble chiefs belong,
    Phormio and Myronides.[55]

(It is now the WOMEN's *turn.)*

CHORUS OF WOMEN. Now to tell a little story
    Fain, fain am I,
  To your tale about Melanion
    Take this reply.
    How that once
  Savage Timon, all forlorn,
  Dwelt amongst the prickly thorn
  Visage-shrouded, Fury-born.
    Dwelt alone,
    Far away,

> Cursing men
> Day by day;
> Never saw his home again,
> Kept aloof from haunts of men:
> Hating men of evil mind,
> Dear to all the womankind.

WOMAN. Shall I give your cheek a blow?

MAN. No, I thank you, no, no, no!

WOMAN. Hoist my foot and kick you too?

MAN. Fie! what vulgar feet I view.

WOMAN. Vulgar feet! absurd, absurd,
> Don't such foolish things repeat;
> Never were, upon my word,
> Tinier, tidier little feet.

(The two CHORUSES *now retire into the background: and there is again a short pause. Suddenly the voice of* LYSISTRATA *is heard calling eagerly to her friends.)*

LYSISTRATA. Ho, ladies! ladies! quick, this way, this way!

WOMAN. O what's the matter and what means that cry?

LYSISTRATA. A man! a man! I see a man approaching
> Wild with desire, beside himself with love.
> O lady of Cyprus, Paphos, and Cythera,
> Keep on, straight on, the way you are going now!

WOMAN. But where's the man?

LYSISTRATA *(pointing).* Down there, by Chloe's chapel.[56]

WOMAN. O so he is: whoever can he be!

LYSISTRATA. Know you him, any one?

MYRRHINA. O yes, my dear,
> I know him. That's Cinesias, my husband.

LYSISTRATA. O then 'tis yours to roast and bother him well;
> Coaxing, yet coy: enticing, fooling him,
> Going all lengths, save what our Oath forbids.

MYRRHINA. Ay, ay, trust *me.*

LYSISTRATA. And I'll assist you, dear;
> I'll take my station here, and help befool
> And roast our victim. All the rest, retire.

(The others withdraw, leaving LYSISTRATA *alone upon the wall.* CINESIAS *approaches underneath.)*

CINESIAS. O me! these pangs and paroxysms of love,
   Riving my heart, keen as a torturer's wheel!

LYSISTRATA. Who's this within the line of sentries?

CINESIAS.   I.

LYSISTRATA. A man?

CINESIAS.   A man, no doubt.

LYSISTRATA.   Then get you gone.

CINESIAS. Who bids me go?

LYSISTRATA.   I, guard on outpost duty.

CINESIAS. O call me out, I pray you, Myrrhina.

LYSISTRATA. Call you out Myrrhina! And who are you?

CINESIAS. Why I'm her husband, I'm Cinesias.

LYSISTRATA. O welcome, welcome, dearest man; your name
   Is not unknown nor yet unhonoured here.
   Your wife for ever has it on her lips.
   She eats no egg, no apple, but she says
   This to Cinesias!

CINESIAS.   O, good heaven! good heaven!

LYSISTRATA. She does, indeed: and if we ever chance
   To talk of men, she vows that all the rest
   Are veriest trash beside Cinesias.

CINESIAS. Ah! call her out.

LYSISTRATA.   And will you give me aught?

CINESIAS. O yes, I'll give you anything I've got.

LYSISTRATA. Then I'll go down and call her.

(Exit LYSISTRATA.*)*

CINESIAS.   Pray be quick.
   I have no joy, no happiness in life,
   Since she, my darling left me. When I enter
   My vacant home I weep; and all the world
   Seems desolate and bare: my very meals
   Give me no joy, now Myrrhina is gone.

MYRRHINA *(within)*. Ay, ay, I love, I love him, but he won't
   Be loved by me: call me not out to him.

CINESIAS. What mean you, Myrrhina, my sweet, sweet love?
Do, do come down.

MYRRHINA.   No, no, sir, not to you.

CINESIAS. What, won't you when I call you, Myrrhina?

MYRRHINA. Why, though you call me, yet you want me not.

CINESIAS. Not want you, Myrrhina! I'm dying for you.

MYRRHINA. Good-bye.

CINESIAS.   Nay, nay, but listen to the child
At all events: speak to Mama, my child.

CHILD. Mama! Mama! Mama!

CINESIAS. Have you no feeling, mother, for your child,
Six days unwashed, unsuckled?

MYRRHINA.   Ay, 'tis I
That feel for baby, 'tis Papa neglects him.

CINESIAS. Come down and take him, then?

MYRRHINA.   O what it is
To be a mother! I must needs go down.

(*She descends from the wall, and four lines below reappears through the gate. While she is gone* CINESIAS *speaks.*)

CINESIAS. She looks, methinks, more youthful than she did,
More gentle-loving, and more sweet by far.
Her very airs, her petulant, saucy ways,
They do but make me love her, love her more.

MYRRHINA. O my sweet child, a naughty father's child,
Mama's own darling, let me kiss you, pet.

CINESIAS. Why treat me thus, you baggage, letting others
Lead you astray: making me miserable
And yourself too?

MYRRHINA.   Hands off! don't touch me, sir.

CINESIAS. And all our household treasures, yours and mine,
Are gone to wrack and ruin.

MYRRHINA.   I don't care.

CINESIAS. Not care, although the fowls are in the house
Pulling your threads to pieces?

MYRRHINA.   Not a bit.

CINESIAS. Nor though the sacred rites of wedded love
    Have been so long neglected? Won't you come?

MYRRHINA. No, no, I won't unless you stop the war,
    And all make friends.

CINESIAS.   Well, then, if such your will,
    We'll e'en do this.

MYRRHINA.   Well, then, if such your will,
    I'll e'en come home; but now I've sworn I won't.[57]

CINESIAS. Come to my arms, do, after all this time!

MYRRHINA. No, no—and yet I won't say I don't love you.

CINESIAS. You love me? Then come to my arms, my dearie!

MYRRHINA. You silly fellow, and the baby here?

CINESIAS. O, not at all—(to slave) here, take the baby home.
    There now, the baby's gone out of the way.
    Come to my arms.

MYRRHINA.   Good heavens, where, I ask you!

CINESIAS. Pan's grotto will do nicely.[58]

MYRRHINA.   Oh, indeed!
    How shall I make me pure to ascend the Mount?

CINESIAS. Easy enough: bathe in the Clepsydra.

MYRRHINA. I've sworn an oath, and shall I break it, man?

CINESIAS. On my head be it; never mind the oath.

MYRRHINA. Well, let me bring a pallet.

CINESIAS.   Not at all;
    The ground will do.

MYRRHINA.   What—one so much to me?
    I swear I'll never let us lie o' the ground.

(Exit MYRRHINA.)

CINESIAS. The woman loves me, plain enough, you see.

(Enter MYRRHINA with pallet.)

MYRRHINA. There, lie down, do make haste; I'll take my
        things off
    But wait a minute, I must find a mattress.

CINESIAS. Bother the mattress, not for me.

MYRRHINA. Why yes,
It's nasty on the cords.

CINESIAS. Give me a kiss.

MYRRHINA. There then.

CINESIAS. Smack, smack. Come back, look sharp about it.

(*Exit* MYRRHINA *and returns with mattress.*)

MYRRHINA. There now, lie down, see, I take off my things—
But wait a minute—what about a pillow?

CINESIAS. But I don't want a pillow.

MYRRHINA. I do, though.

(*Exit* MYRRHINA.)

CINESIAS. A veritable feast of Barmecides.[59]

(MYRRHINA *returns with pillow.*)

MYRRHINA. Up with your head, hop up!

CINESIAS. I've all I want.

MYRRHINA. What, *all?*

CINESIAS. Yes, all but you; come here, my precious!

MYRRHINA. There goes the girdle. But remember now,
You must not play me false about the peace.

CINESIAS. God damn me if I do!

MYRRHINA. You have no rug.

CINESIAS. I want no rug, I want you in my arms.

MYRRHINA. Oh, all right, you shall have me, I'll be quick.

(*Exit* MYRRHINA.)

CINESIAS. She'll be the death of me with all these bedclothes!

(*Enter* MYRRHINA *with rug.*)

MYRRHINA. Up now!

CINESIAS. I'm up enough, be sure of that.

MYRRHINA. Some nice sweet ointment?

CINESIAS. By Apollo, no!

MYRRHINA. By Aphrodite, yes! Say what you like.

(*Exit* MYRRHINA.)

CINESIAS. Lord Zeus, I pray the ointment may be spilt!

(*Enter* MYRRHINA *with ointment.*)

MYRRHINA. Put out your hand, take some, anoint yourself.

CINESIAS. I swear this stuff is anything but sweet,
The brand is Wait-and-see, no marriage smell!

MYRRHINA. How stupid! Here I've brought the Rhodian kind.

CINESIAS. It's good enough, my dear.

MYRRHINA.   Rubbish, good man!

(*Exit* MYRRHINA.)

CINESIAS. Perdition take the man that first made ointment!

(*Enter* MYRRHINA *with a flask.*)

MYRRHINA. Here, take this flask.

CINESIAS.   I've all the flask I want.
Come to my arms, you wretched creature you!
No more things, please!

MYRRHINA.   I will, by Artemis.
There go my shoes, at least. Now don't forget,
You'll vote for peace, my dearest.

CINESIAS.   Oh, I'll see.

(*Exit* MYRRHINA *into Acropolis.*)

The creature's done for me, bamboozled me,
Gone off and left me in this wretched state.
    What will become of me? Whom shall I fondle
        Robbed of the fairest fair?
    Who will be ready this orphan to dandle?
        Where's Cynalopex? Where?[60]
            Find me a nurse!

CHORUS OF MEN. She's left you a curse.
        Oh I'm sorry, O I grieve for ye.
            Tis more than a man can bear;
    Not a soul, not a loin, not a heart, not a groin,
        Can endure such pangs of despair.

CINESIAS. O Zeus, what pangs and throes I bear!

CHORUS OF MEN. All this woe she has wrought you, she only,
the
Utterly hateful, the utterly vile.

CHORUS OF WOMEN. Not so; but the darling, the utterly sweet.

CHORUS OF MEN. Sweet, sweet, do you call her? Vile, vile, I
repeat.
Zeus, send me a storm and a whirlwind, I pray,
To whisk her away, like a bundle of hay,
Up, up, to the infinite spaces,
And toss her and swirl her, and twist her, and twirl her,
Till, tattered and torn, to the earth she is borne,
To be crushed—in my ardent embraces.

(*Enter* LACONIAN HERALD.)

HERALD. Whaur sall a body fin' the Athanian senate,
Or the gran' lairds? Ha' gotten news to tell.

MAGISTRATE. News have you, friend? And what in the world
are you?

HERALD. A heralt, billie! Jist a Spartan heralt,
Come, by the Twa, anent a Peace, ye ken.[61]

MAGISTRATE. And so you come with a spear beneath your arm-
pit!

HERALD. Na, na, not I.

MAGISTRATE.   Why do you turn away?
Why cast your cloak before you? Is your groin
A trifle swollen from the march?

HERALD.   By Castor
This loon's a rogue.

MAGISTRATE.   Look at yourself, you brute!

HERALD. There's naught amiss wi' me, don't play the fule.

MAGISTRATE. Why then, what's this?

HERALD.   A Spartan letter-staff.

MAGISTRATE (*pointing to himself*). Yes, if *this* is a Spartan
letter-staff!
Well, and how fare the Spartans? Tell me that;
And tell me truly, for I know the fact.

HERALD. They're bad eneugh, they canna weel be waur;
They're sair bested, Spartans, allies, an' a'.

MAGISTRATE. And how and whence arose this trouble first?
  From Pan?[62]

HERALD.   Na, na, 'twer' Lampito, I ween,
  First set it gangin'; then our hizzies, a'
  Risin' like rinners at ane signal word,
  Loupit, an' jibbed, an' dang the men awa'.

MAGISTRATE. How like ye that?

HERALD.   Och, we're in waefu' case.
  They stan' abeigh, the lassies do, an' vow
  They'll no be couthie wi' the laddies mair
  Till a' mak' Peace, and throughly en' the War.

MAGISTRATE. This is a plot they have everywhere been hatch-
      ing,
  These villanous women: now I see it all.
  Run home, my man, and bid your people send
  Envoys with absolute powers to treat for peace,
  And I will off with all the speed I can,
  And get our Council here to do the same.

HERALD. Nebbut, I'se fly, ye rede me weel, I'm thinkin'.

  (*The* HERALD *leaves for Sparta; the* MAGISTRATE *returns to
  the Senate; and the two* CHORUSES *now advance for a final
  skirmish.*)

CHORUS OF MEN. There is nothing so resistless as a woman in
      her ire,
  She is wilder than a leopard, she is fiercer than a fire.

CHORUS OF WOMEN. And yet you're so daft as with women to
      contend,
  When 'tis in your power to win me and have me as a
      friend.

CHORUS OF MEN. I'll never, never cease all women to detest.

CHORUS OF WOMEN. That's as you please hereafter: meanwhile
      you're all undressed.
  I really can't allow it, you are getting quite a joke;
  Permit me to approach you and to put you on this cloak.

CHORUS OF MEN. Now that's not so bad or unfriendly I declare;
  It was only from bad temper that I stripped myself so bare.

CHORUS OF WOMEN. There, now you look a man: and none will
      joke and jeer you:

And if you weren't so spiteful that no one can come near
you,
I'd have pulled out the insect that is sticking in your eye.

CHORUS OF MEN. Ay, that is what's consuming me, that little
biter-fly.
Yes, scoop it out and show me, when you've got him safe
away:
The plaguy little brute, he's been biting me all day.

CHORUS OF WOMEN. I'll do it, sir, I'll do it: but you're a cross
one, you.
O Zeus! here's a monster I am pulling forth to view.
Just look! don't you think 'tis a Tricorysian gnat?[63]

CHORUS OF MEN. And he's been dig, dig, digging (so I thank
you much for that)
Till the water, now he's gone, keeps running from my eye.

CHORUS OF WOMEN. But although you've been so naughty, I'll
come and wipe it dry,
And I'll kiss you.

CHORUS OF MEN.   No, not kiss me!

CHORUS OF WOMEN.   Will you, nill you, it must be.

CHORUS OF MEN. Get along, a murrain on you. Tcha! what
coaxing rogues are ye!
That was quite a true opinion which a wise man gave
about you,
We can't live with such tormentors, no, by Zeus, nor yet
without you.
Now we'll make a faithful treaty, and for evermore agree,
I will do no harm to women, they shall do no harm to me.
Join our forces, come along: one and all commence the
song.

JOINT CHORUS. Not to objurgate and scold you,
    Not unpleasant truths to say,
    But with words and deeds of bounty
        Come we here to-day.
    Ah, enough of idle quarrels,
        Now attend, I pray.
    Now whoever wants some money,
    Minas two or minas three,

Let them say so, man and woman,
  Let them come with me.
Many purses, large and—empty,
  In my house they'll see.
Only you must strictly promise,
Only you indeed must say
That whenever Peace re-greet us,
  You will—not repay.
Some Carystian friends are coming,
Pleasant gentlemen, to dine;
And I've made some soup, and slaughtered
  Such a lovely swine;
Luscious meat ye'll have and tender
  At this feast of mine.
Come along, yourselves and children,
Come to grace my board to-day;
Take an early bath, and deck you
  In your best array;
Then walk in and ask no questions,
  Take the readiest way.
Come along, like men of mettle;
Come as though 'twere all for you:
Come, you'll find my only entrance
  Locked and bolted too.

(*The* LACONIAN AMBASSADORS *are seen approaching.*)

CHORUS. Lo here from Sparta the envoys come: in a pitiful
        plight they are hobbling in.
  Heavily hangs each reverend beard; heavily droops and
        trails from the chin.
  Laconian envoys! first I bid you welcome,
  And next I ask how goes the world with *you?*

LACONIAN. I needna mony words to answer that!
  'Tis unco plain hoo the warld gangs wi' us.

CHORUS. Dear, dear, this trouble grows from bad to worse.

LACONIAN. 'Tis awfu' bad: 'tis nae gude talkin', cummer.
  We maun hae peace whatever gaet we gang till't.

CHORUS. And here, good faith, I see our own Autochthons
  Bustling along. They seem in trouble too.

(*The* ATHENIAN AMBASSADORS *enter.*)

ATHENIAN. Can some good soul inform me where to find
  Lysistrata? Our men are (*shrugging his shoulders*)
  as you see.[64]

(*He perceives the* LACONIAN AMBASSADORS.)

CHORUS. Sure, we are smitten with the same complaint.
  Say, don't you get a fit i' the early morning?

ATHENIAN. Why, we are all worn out with doing this;
  So Cleisthenes will have to serve our turn
  Unless we can procure a speedy peace.

CHORUS. If you are wise, wrap up, unless you wish
  One of those Hermes-choppers to catch sight o' you.[65]

ATHENIAN. Prudent advice, by Zeus.

LACONIAN.   Aye, by the Twa;
  Give us the clout to cover up oorsels.

ATHENIAN. Aha, Laconians! a bad business this.

LACONIAN. 'Deed it is, lovey; though it grow nae waur,
  Gin they see us too all agog like this.[66]

ATHENIAN. Well, well, Laconians, come to facts at once.
  What brings you here?

LACONIAN.   We're envoys sent to claver
  Anent a Peace.

ATHENIAN.   Ah, just the same as we.
  Then let's call out Lysistrata at once,
  There's none but she can make us friends again.

LACONIAN. Ay, by the Twa', ca' oot Lysistrata.

CHORUS. Nay, here she is! no need, it seems, to call.
  She heard your voices, and she comes uncalled.

(LYSISTRATA *comes forward attended by her handmaid*
RECONCILIATION.)

O Lady, noblest and best of all! arise, arise, and thyself
      reveal,
Gentle, severe, attractive, harsh, well skilled with all our
      complaints to deal,
The first and foremost of Hellas come, they are caught by
      the charm of thy spell-drawn wheel,
They come to Thee to adjust their claims, disputes to
      settle, and strifes to heal.

LYSISTRATA. And no such mighty matter, if you take them
    In Love's first passion, still unsatisfied.
    I'll try them now. Go, Reconciliation,
    Bring those Laconians hither, not with rude
    Ungenial harshness hurrying them along,
    Not in the awkward style our husbands used,
    But with all tact, as only women can.
    So; so: now bring me those Athenians too.[67]
    Now then, Laconians, stand beside me here,
    And you stand there, and listen to my words.
    I am a woman, but I don't lack sense;
    I'm of myself not badly off for brains,
    And often listening to my father's words
    And old men's talk, I've not been badly schooled.
    And now, dear friends, I wish to chide you both,
    That ye, all of one blood, all brethren sprinkling
    The selfsame altars from the selfsame laver,
    At Pylae, Pytho, and Olympia, ay[68]
    And many others which 'twere long to name,
    That ye, Hellenes—with barbarian foes
    Armed, looking on—fight and destroy Hellenes!
    So far one reprimand includes you both.

ATHENIAN. And I, I'm dying all for love, sweetheart.

LYSISTRATA. And ye, Laconians, for I'll turn to you,
    Do ye not mind how Pericleidas came,[69]
    (His coat was scarlet but his cheeks were white),
    And sat a suppliant at Athenian altars
    And begged for help? 'Twas when Messene pressed
    Weighing you down, and God's great earthquake too.
    And Cimon went, Athenian Cimon went
    With his four thousand men, and saved your State.
    And ye, whom Athens aided, now in turn
    Ravage the land which erst befriended you.

ATHENIAN. 'Fore Zeus they're wrong, they're wrong, Lysis-
    trata.

LACONIAN. O ay, we're wrang, but she's a braw ane, she.

LYSISTRATA. And you, Athenians, think ye that I mean
    To let You off? Do *ye* not mind, when ye
    Wore skirts of hide, how these Laconians came[70]

And stood beside you in the fight alone,
And slew full many a stout Thessalian trooper,
Full many of Hippias's friends and helpers,
And freed the State, and gave your people back
The civic mantle for the servile skirt?

LACONIAN. Danged, an' there ever waur a bonnier lassie!

ATHENIAN. Hanged if I ever saw so sweet a creature!

LYSISTRATA. Such friends aforetime, helping each the other,
What is it makes you fight and bicker now?
Why can't ye come to terms? Why can't ye, hey?

LACONIAN. Troth an' we're willin', gin they gie us back
Yon girdled neuk.[71]

ATHENIAN.   What's that?

LACONIAN.   Pylus, ye ninny,
Whilk we've been aye langin' an' graipin' for.

ATHENIAN. No, by Poseidon, but you won't get that.

LYSISTRATA. O let them have it, man.

ATHENIAN.   How can we stir
Without it?

LYSISTRATA.   Ask for something else instead.

ATHENIAN. Hum! haw! let's see; suppose they give us back
Echinus first, then the full-bosomed gulf
Of Melis, then the straight Megaric limbs.

LACONIAN. Eh, mon, ye're daft; ye'll no hae everything.

LYSISTRATA. O let it be: don't wrangle about the limbs.

ATHENIAN. I'fecks, I'd like to strip, and plough my field.

LACONIAN. An' I to bring the midden, by the Twa'.

LYSISTRATA. All this ye'll do, when once ye come to terms.
So if ye would, go and consult together
And talk it over, each with your allies.

ATHENIAN. Allies, says she! Now my good soul consider:
What *do* they want, what *can* they want, but this,
Their wives again?

LACONIAN.   The fient anither wiss
Ha' mine, I ween.

ATHENIAN.   Nor my Carystians either.[72]

LYSISTRATA. O that is well: so purify yourselves;
  And in the Acropolis we'll feast you all
  On what our cupboards still retain in store.
  There, each to other, plight your oath and troth,
  Then every man receive his wife again,
  And hie off homeward.

ATHENIAN.   That we will, and quickly.

LACONIAN. Gae on: we'se follow.

ATHENIAN.   Ay, as quick as quick.

(LYSISTRATA *and the* AMBASSADORS *go in.*)

CHORUS. Gorgeous robes and golden trinkets,
      Shawls and mantles rich and rare,
    I will lend to all who need them,
        Lend for youths to wear,
      Or if any comrade's daughter
        Would the Basket bear.[73]
    One and all I here invite you,
    Freely of my goods partake,
    Nought is sealed so well, but boldly
        Ye the seals may break,
    And of all that lurks behind them,
        Quick partition make.
    Only, if you find the treasures,
    Only, if the stores you spy,
    You must have, I tell you plainly,
        Keener sight than I.
    Is *there* any man among you,
    With a lot of children small,
    With a crowd of hungry servants,
        Starving in his hall?
    I have wheat to spare in plenty,
        I will feed them all.
    Loaves, a quart apiece, I'll give them,
    Come along, whoever will,
    Bring your bags, and bring your wallets
        For my slave to fill;
    Manes, he's the boy to pack them
        Tight and tighter still.

Only you must keep your distance,
Only you must needs take care,
Only—don't approach my doorway,
    Ware the watch-dog, ware!

(*Some* IDLERS *come in from the market-place, and attempt
to enter the house in which the* AMBASSADORS *are feasting.*)

IDLER. Open the door there, ho!

PORTER.   Be off, you rascal!

IDLER. What, won't you stir? I've half a mind to roast you
    All with this torch. No, that's a vulgar trick.
    I won't do that. Still if the audience wish it,
    To please their tastes we'll undertake the task.

SECOND IDLER. And we, with you, will undertake the task.

PORTER. Hang you, be off! what are you at? you'll catch it.
    Come, come, begone; that these Laconians here,
    The banquet ended, may depart in peace.

(*The* BANQUETEERS *begin to come out.*)

FIRST ATHENIAN. Well, if I ever saw a feast like this!
    What cheery fellows those Laconians were,
    And we were wondrous witty in our cups.

SECOND ATHENIAN. Ay, ay, 'tis when we're sober, we're so daft.
    Now if the State would take a friend's advice,
    'Twould make its envoys always all get drunk.
    When we go dry to Sparta, all our aim
    Is just to see what mischief we can do.
    We don't hear aught they say; and we infer
    A heap of things they never said at all.
    Then we bring home all sorts of differing tales.
    Now everything gives pleasure: if a man,
    When he should sing Cleitagora, strike up
    With Telamon's song, we'd clap him on the back,[74]
    And say 'twas excellent; ay, and swear it too.

(*The* IDLERS *again approach.*)

PORTER. Why, bless the fellows, here they come again,
    Crowding along. Be off, you scoundrels, will you?

IDLER. By Zeus, we must: the guests are coming out.

(*The* AMBASSADORS *come out from the banquet.*)

LACONIAN. O lovey mine, tak' up the pipes an' blaw.
    An' I'se jist dance an' sing a canty sang
    Anent the Athanians an' our ainsells too.

ATHENIAN. Ay, by the Powers, take up the pipes and blow.
    Eh, but I dearly love to see you dance.

LACONIAN. Stir, Memory, stir the chiels
      Wi' that auld sang o' thine,
      Whilk kens what we an' Attics did
      In the gran' fechts lang syne.

      At Artemisium They
      A' resolute an' strang
      Rushed daurly to the fray,
      Hurtlin' like Gudes amang
    The timmered ships, an' put the Medes to rout.
      An' Us Leonidas led out
      Like gruesome boars, I ween,
      Whettin' our tuskies keen.
Muckle around the chaps was the white freath gleamin',
Muckle adoon the legs was the white freath streamin',
      For a' unnumbered as the sands
      Were they, thae Persian bands.

      O Artemis, the pure, the chaste,
      The virgin Queller o' the beasties,
      O come wi' power an' come wi' haste,
      An' come to join our friendly feasties.
        Come wi' thy stoutest tether,
        To knit our sauls tegither,
        An' gie us Peace in store,
        An' Luve for evermore.
        Far hence, far hence depart
        The tod's deceitfu' heart!
      O virgin huntress, pure an' chaste,
      O come wi' power, an' come wi' haste.

LYSISTRATA. There, all is settled, all arranged at last.
    Now, take your ladies; you, Laconians, those,
    And you, take these; then standing side by side,

Each by his partner, lead your dances out
In grateful honour to the Gods, and O
Be sure you nevermore offend again.

CHORUS. Now for the Chorus, the Graces, the minstrelsy.
Call upon Artemis, queen of the glade;
Call on her brother, the Lord of festivity,
Holy and gentle one, mighty to aid.
Call upon Bacchus, afire with his Maenades;
Call upon Zeus, in the lightning arrayed;
Call on his queen, ever blessed, adorable;
Call on the holy, infallible Witnesses,[75]
Call them to witness the peace and the harmony,
This which divine Aphrodite has made.
Allala! Lallala! Lallala, Lallala!
Whoop for victory, Lallalalae!
Evoi! Evoi! Lallala, Lallala!
Evae! Evae! Lallalalae.

Our excellent new song is done;
Do you, Laconian, give us one.

LACONIAN. Leave Taygety, an' quickly
Hither, Muse Laconian, come.
Hymn the Gude o' braw Amyclae,
Hymn Athana, Brassin-dome.
Hymn the Tyndarids, for ever
Sportin' by Eurotas river.
Noo then, noo the step begin,
Twirlin' licht the fleecy skin;
Sae we'se join our blithesome voices,
Praisin' Sparta, loud an' lang,
Sparta wha of auld rejoices
In the Choral dance an' sang.
O to watch her bonnie dochters
Sport alang Eurotas' waters!
Winsome feet for ever plyin',
Fleet as fillies, wild an' gay,
Winsome tresses tossin', flyin',
As o' Bacchanals at play.
Leda's dochter, on before us,
Pure an' sprety, guides the Chorus.

Onward go,
Whilst your eager hand represses
A' the glory o' your tresses;
Whilst your eager foot is springin'
  Like the roe;
Whilst your eager voice is singin'
Praise to Her in might excellin'
Goddess o' the Brassin Dwellin'.

1. *Pan, Colias, Genetyllis.* All Gods of Wine and Love, the chief pleasures, according to Aristophanes, of the Athenian women.

2. *The eels.* The Copaic eel, from Boeotia, was the darling of the Athenian epicure.

3. *By the Twain.* Demeter and Persephone.

4. *Theagenes' wife.* Theagenes' notorious superstition in never leaving home without consulting the shrine of Hecate at his house door is here transferred to his wife.

5. *Anagyre.* To stir up Anagyre (meaning the nauseous-smelling shrub of that name) was a proverb, used of persons who brought some unpleasantness on themselves.

6. *By the Twa.* The "Twain" in the mouth of a Spartan meant Castor and Polydeuces.

7. *Eucrates.* We know nothing of the circumstances to which the speaker alludes.

8. *Miletus.* Miletus had fallen away from Athens during the preceding summer. (Thucydides, viii, 17.)

9. *A bout of—drinking.* "Fighting" was the word expected; but Aristophanes is, throughout this scene, playing upon the alleged bibulous propensities of Athenian women.

10. *A cleft turbot.* Calonice is alluding to the popular notion that two flat fishes are in reality but one fish cut in halves.

11. *Menelaus.* The legend is that, after the fall of Troy, Menelaus, when about to slay his faithless wife, was so softened by her beauty that he cast his sword away.

12. *A' that rowth o' siller nigh the Goddess.* Lampito is referring to the 1,000 silver talents which Pericles had set apart at the commencement of the war (Thucydides, ii, 24) to be used only on the most pressing emergency.

13. *Scythianess.* Scythian archers were employed to keep order in the Athenian Assemblies.

14. *Seven Chiefs in Aeschylus.* In the *Seven against Thebes.*

15. *The victim boar.* She means the *Wine-jar*, but she speaks of it as a victim whose blood is about to be shed.

16. *The first lot.* Much of the humour underlying this dialogue has passed unnoticed because annotators have failed to observe that, in the peculiar form of oath which Lysistrata is about to administer, *to swear* has much the same meaning as *to drink.*

17. The substance of the oath is translated by Rogers, but not all its literal details.

18. *The Holy Image.* The sacrosanct image of Athene Polias.

19. *Lycon's wife.* Rhodia, a woman of infamous life.

20. *Cleomenes.* The story of Cleomenes, King of Sparta, is told in the fifth and sixth books of the History of Herodotus. Cleomenes seized the Acropolis, but was forced to capitulate.

21. *Samian lines.* During all this period of the war, Samos was the permanent headquarters of the Athenian armaments.

22. *O Victory.* As they are (supposed to be) approaching the Acropolis, they have full in view the Temple of Wingless Victory, otherwise Athene Nike.

23. *Bupalus.* If we smite them on the cheek, as Hipponax the poet threatened in his lampoons to smite his unhappy antagonist, Bupalus.

24. *Achelous.* The largest Hellenic river. The name Achelous was used to denote water generally. The Women are deluging their opponents.

25. *Adonis-dirge.* Plutarch, in his *Life of Nicias* (chapter 13), describes these and similar omens of ill which preceded the Athenian expedition to Sicily. And he also (chapter 12) tells us that the orator Demostratus took a leading part in recommending that fatal measure.

26. *Pandrosus.* Since in every other speech throughout this short altercation the Women invoke Artemis in one or

other of her characters, I cannot but believe that in this invocation also the name of Pandrosus, the All-bedewer, is intended to apply to Artemis as identical with Hecate or the Moon.

27. *Queen of Tauris.* Artemis.

28. *Hive.* The Women speak of a wasps' or hornets' nest, not a very desirable place to rifle for honey; and I suspect that Aristophanes is mocking the line of Sophocles about taking honey from a wasps' nest; while the Women may be wishing to let their opponents know that, if they try to rifle their sweets, they will bring a swarm of hornets about their ears.

29. *Cranaan.* In the time of the Pelasgians, Herodotus tells us, the Athenians went by the name of Cranaans.

30. *Peisander.* A turbulent and restless intriguer, he was at this moment one of the chief promoters of the scheme for subverting the democracy and establishing the rule of the Four Hundred in its place.

31. *The Treaty stone.* Treaties were inscribed on pillars. In the present passage we are dealing with the pillar containing the Peace of Nicias. Some three years later Alcibiades persuaded the Athenians to write on this pillar, underneath the Treaty, that the Lacedaemonians had failed to abide by their oaths. This is no doubt the transaction to which Lysistrata is alluding.

32. *War is the care and the business of men!* From the speech of Hector to Andromache, in the sixth book of the *Iliad.*

33. *Silence, old gentleman.* Lysistrata is putting her system into immediate practice, and therefore addresses the same language and assigns the same duties to the Magistrate, as the Men had been accustomed aforetime to address and assign to the Women.

34. *Haricots chawing up.* Women were in the habit of chewing some eatable as they wove or spun.

35. *Corybants.* Ever since the occupation of Deceleia by the Spartans the whole population of Athens had been under arms. It is no wonder, therefore, that men were seen marketing in full armour, "like Corybants," for the Cory-

bants, the Phrygian priests of Cybele, wore a complete set of armour.

36. *A Thracian irregular.* This is one of the Thracians who were engaged to serve as auxiliaries to the Athenian armies. He comes in as if he were Tereus, the famous Thracian king.

37. *Truly whoever is able to wed—* Apparently he was about to add "will soon find a wife," but Lysistrata interrupts him, and she and her companions dress him up like a corpse.

38. *A funeral cake.* A honey-cake was placed in the hand of the dead to serve as a sop for Cerberus.

39. *Take it and go.* She is giving him the small change required to pay Charon's fare.

40. *The third-day funeral rites.* A banquet in honour of the dead, after three days of fasting.

41. *Hippias' tyranny.* They accuse their adversaries of conspiring to reintroduce the tyranny of Hippias, the last tyrant of Athens.

42. *Cleisthenes.* Cleisthenes, the perpetual butt of the comic poets for his gross effeminacy, is selected as a fitting intermediary between the Athenian *women* and the Laconian *men,* as partaking of the nature of both.

43. *Aristogeiton.* He is probably assuming the very attitude in which Aristogeiton was represented in the sculpture delivering the blow "which slew the tyrant."

44. We have here an enumeration of the distinctions which a young Athenian girl might hope to attain.

45. *White-foot.* A play on *lykopodes,* the name given to the outlawed Alcmaeonids when they returned to Attica and established themselves on Leipsydrium, in their first fruitless attempt to overthrow the tyranny of Hippias.

46. *Carian Artemisia.* Artemisia led her ships across the Aegean to fight on the side of the Persian invaders against the Hellenic fleet at Salamis.

47. *The Eagle and the Beetle.* Aesop's well-known fable about the Eagle and the Beetle. The fable told how the insig-

nificant beetle, when injured by the mighty eagle, contrived to break its adversary's eggs no matter where they were laid, even when they were laid in the bosom of Zeus.

8. *On sparrow's back.* A bird which was harnessed to Aphrodite's car might well serve as a steed for a lovesick woman. *Orsilochus* was a brothel-keeper.

9. *Eileithyia.* The goddess invoked by women at childbirth. It was unlawful to bear children on the Acropolis, since it was holy ground.

0. *The sacred helmet.* Lysistrata means, in my judgement, the great bronze helmet of Athene Promachos.

1. *The holy serpent.* This is the famous serpent which dwelt in the Erechtheium.

2. *The Love-birds.* The women are represented by the swallows, and the men by the hoopoes; in accordance with the old Attic legend in which the swallow was Procne (or Philomela), pursued by her husband, Tereus the hoopoe. In the name *phales* (the phallus personified) there is an allusion to another bird, our *coot.*

3. *Melanion.* The suitor who won Atalanta by dropping three golden apples in the course of a race. Atalanta was a hater of men; the Chorus of Men have changed the story, making Melanion a hater of women.

4. *A leek.* To produce artificial tears: you shall shed real ones.

5. *Phormio* and *Myronides.* National heroes. Myronides' remarkable victories over the Corinthians and the Boeotians, 459–456 B.C., extended the Athenian supremacy by land to the utmost limits it ever attained—and Phormio's brilliant achievements in the Corinthian gulf at the commencement of the Peloponnesian War established the Athenian supremacy by sea.

6. *Chloe's chapel.* By the chapel of Demeter Chloe, which was very near the Propylaea.

7. The remainder of the scene between Myrrhina and Cinesias (the following 75 lines in the original) was omitted by Rogers and is supplied here from the Loeb Classical Library version.

58. *Pan's grotto.* The grotto of Pan, and the Clepsydra, spring, were on the Acropolis.

59. *Feast of Barmecides.* A feast at which no food is served

60. *Cynalopex.* Cinesias must hire a "nurse" for his "child from Philostratus, a brothel-keeper who was nicknamee Cynalopex. The passage plays on obvious double mean ings.

61. The following eight lines were omitted by Rogers. The are supplied here from the Loeb Classical Library version

62. *Pan.* All sudden commotions and disturbances of th mind were attributed to Pan's influence.

63. *Tricorysian gnat.* The marshy region of Tricorythus, nea Marathon, was noted for its gnats and mosquitoes.

64. The following nine lines, omitted by Rogers, are supplies here from the Loeb Classical Library version.

65. *Hermes-choppers.* The desecrators who knocked the phall off the figures of Hermes which stood at Athenian house doors. See Thucydides, vi, 27.

66. This one line, omitted by Rogers, is supplied here from the Loeb Classical Library version.

67. Two lines in this passage are omitted by Rogers: "If he won't give his hand, *mentula prehensum duc.*" and "Take hold of whatever they offer."

68. *Pylae, Pytho, and Olympia.* The Olympian and Pythian festivals are well known. Pylae refers to the annual autum nal meeting of the Amphictyonic Council.

69. *Pericleidas.* See Plutarch, *Cimon,* chapter 16. Thucydides, i, 102; iii, 54.

70. *How these Laconians came.* See Herodotus, v, 64, 65.

71. *Yon girdled neuk.* The desire of recovering their lost pos sessions is for the moment merged in their desire for Lysistrata, and their reciprocal demands are throughout worded with reference to her dress and person. The restoration of Pylus had been for years a paramount object to the Lacedaemonians.

72. *Carystians.* From Carystus, in the south of Euboea. They

were supposed to be a remnant of one of the old pre-Hellenic populations.

73. *The Basket bear.* To bear the golden basket in the Panathenaic procession was the crowning distinction of a maiden's life.

74. *Telamon's song.* When *scolia* were sung at an Athenian symposium, as the lyre, sprig of myrtle, scolium-cup, or other badge of minstrelsy was passed on from one guest to another, the recipient was expected to *cap* the scolium sung by the previous holder, that is to say, to sing a scolium which should be linked on to the former by some catchword, similarity of thought, or the like.

75. *The holy Witnesses.* Those secondary Powers whose special business it is to witness the conclusion of a treaty and to punish its infraction.

ANCHOR BOOKS

DRAMA

4Ab

ANCHOR BOOKS

FICTION

ANCHOR BOOKS

CLASSICS AND MYTHOLOGY

ANCHOR BOOKS

LITERARY ESSAYS AND CRITICISM

10Ab